# THE AMUSEMENT PARK AT SLOAN'S LAKE

# THE AMUSEMENT PARK AT SLOAN'S LAKE

*The Lost History of Denver's Manhattan Beach*

## DAVID FORSYTH

# TWODOT®

ESSEX, CONNECTICUT
HELENA, MONTANA

**A · T W O D O T® · B O O K**

An imprint of Globe Pequot, the trade division of
The Rowman & Littlefield Publishing Group, Inc.
4501 Forbes Blvd., Ste. 200
Lanham, MD 20706
www.rowman.com

Distributed by NATIONAL BOOK NETWORK

British Library Cataloguing in Publication Information available

**Library of Congress Cataloging-in-Publication Data**
Names: Forsyth, David, 1977– author.
Title: The amusement park at Sloan's Lake : the lost history of Denver's Manhattan
Beach / David Forsyth.
Description: Essex, Connecticut : TwoDot, [2024] | Includes bibliographical references.
Identifiers: LCCN 2023049059 (print) | LCCN 2023049060 (ebook) | ISBN
9781493076970 (paperback) | ISBN 9781493076987 (epub)
Subjects: LCSH: Amusement parks—Colorado—Denver—History. | Manhattan Beach
(Denver, Colo.)—History | Denver (Colo.)—Social life and customs.
Classification: LCC GV1853.3.C62 M364 2024 (print) | LCC GV1853.3.C62 (ebook)
| DDC 791.06878883—dc23/eng/20231114
LC record available at https://lccn.loc.gov/2023049059
LC ebook record available at https://lccn.loc.gov/2023049060

♾™ The paper used in this publication meets the minimum requirements of American
National Standard for Information Sciences—Permanence of Paper for Printed Library
Materials, ANSI/NISO Z39.48-1992.

*For Robert Camron Riney*

*Robbie, love isn't a big enough word.*

# CONTENTS

Acknowledgments . . . . . . . . . . . . . . . . . . . . . . . ix

Introduction: Sloan's Leak . . . . . . . . . . . . . . . . . . .1

CHAPTER 1: Manhattan Beach, A City's Beauty Spot. . . . . 23

CHAPTER 2: Manhattan Beach and the Southern
Investment Company . . . . . . . . . . . . . . . . . . . . . 43

CHAPTER 3: A Fine Outing . . . . . . . . . . . . . . . . . . 59

CHAPTER 4: Beautiful and Genuine Novelties. . . . . . . . 79

CHAPTER 5: Manhattan Beach and the People from Detroit 113

CHAPTER 6: Luna Park, Denver's Prettiest Resort. . . . . . 147

Conclusion: Sloan's Lake Park . . . . . . . . . . . . . . . . 183

Notes. . . . . . . . . . . . . . . . . . . . . . . . . . . . . 195

Bibliography . . . . . . . . . . . . . . . . . . . . . . . . . 221

# ACKNOWLEDGMENTS

The idea for this book grew out of my book on Lakeside Amusement Park. I originally intended to write a history of what I was calling the lost amusement parks of Denver, which would have included Manhattan Beach. Life and other writing projects got in the way of that book until 2020. With much of the world brought to a halt by the curse of the virus, that summer marked the first time since 1890 that Denverites were unable to visit an amusement park with both Lakeside and Elitch Gardens closed. I finally decided it was time to write the long-delayed book as it would allow me to visit, at least in my mind, Denver's amusement parks of the past. However, I quickly decided that Manhattan Beach deserved a book devoted only to it.

When the Stephen H. Hart Library at History Colorado reopened to researchers in the summer of 2020, I became a frequent visitor, filling in the gaps in my Manhattan Beach research. I would like to especially thank Jori Johnson and Bethany Williams who helped bring out files, photographs, and newspapers for my research visits. Thyria Wilson and Jeanne Abrams at the University of Denver sent me photographs of Manhattan Beach donated by Albert Lewin's daughter Mildred Sweet, as well as a copy of the oral history she did in 1981 that told of her father's many entertainment ventures in Denver. As always, the staff at the Denver Public Library's Western History Department was enormously helpful with getting files I wanted to look at as I researched Manhattan Beach and other Denver amusement parks, and Kellen Cutsforth helped get me the photos I wanted to use in this book.

I happened to be at the Denver Public Library doing research one day when I met Anna Staver and Brandon Rittiman of Channel 9 who were working on a story about Roger the elephant, one of the star attractions at Manhattan Beach. Although I reluctantly wound up in front of a television camera that day, the two of them were quite generous in sharing their own research on Roger and what may have become of him after his time at Manhattan Beach, and they helped point me in the direction of some sources about Manhattan Beach that I had not yet found.

I talked to several members of the Bethell and Foster families, who owned Manhattan Beach for most of its existence, and although they did not have information on the park to share, they were happy to hear someone was researching it and encouraged my efforts. My friend Jerrod "J" Brito was also very encouraging, especially when, at times, it felt like I had reached a dead end. I also thank my friend Jim Prochaska for letting me once again borrow his notes for the Denver tours that he used to lead.

Sue Carter helped me to clean up my final version of the book; at TwoDot, Sarah Parke, Lauren Younker, Debra Murphy, Alden Perkins, and Jason Rossi helped guide this book through the process to the final version.

As always, I thank my family for their love and support as I continue to share all my wacky amusement park stories.

# Introduction

## *Sloan's Leak*

ON A COLD FEBRUARY DAY IN 1889, ADAM GRAFF WAS CUTTING ice at Denver's Sloan's Lake when he stopped to rest for a moment. Looking out over the ice, according to his daughter Elizabeth, he suddenly wished it were summer again, imagining the people who would be fishing or swimming in the lake or going out on rowboats. It was then, said his daughter, that a vision came to him of the lakeshore lined with pavilions, a theater, a large dock for boats, and even a hotel, reminiscent of summer playgrounds he had known in his native Germany. Graff laid down his saw and went to talk with his business partners, George Darrow and Jacob E. Sackett, about his new idea. The seed for Manhattan Beach was planted that day.[1]

Sometime in the years after it closed, Manhattan Beach became incorrectly known as either the first or the largest amusement park west of the Mississippi River with an opening date of 1881. Amusement parks as most people would know them did not exist in 1881, and neither did Manhattan Beach. What did exist at the time were a variety of amusement resorts, beer gardens, picnic grounds, and other public playgrounds. In Europe, amusement resorts and beer gardens started appearing outside of major cities in the 1600s. Offerings at these parks included zoos, athletic displays and games, shooting competitions, acrobatic shows, and animal fights. In the 1790s some of them began offering balloon

Manhattan Beach in the early 1900s with visitors enjoying rowboats on Sloan's Lake. The theater and boathouse are on the left, and the dance pavilion is the structure with the conical roof sections on the right. The steamboat dock is the domed building to the right of the center. *Source:* The Denver Public Library, Western History Collection, C Photo 466.

ascensions and parachute jumps, features that would remain standard amusement park attractions more than a century later. Elaborate illumination also became standard at these early parks, with one park boasting that its 60,000 oil lamps turned night into day.[2]

In the United States, the amusement centers that grew up around cities offered many of the same attractions as the European parks, but beer and other refreshments were common. Some of the parks offered rides such as swings or hand-powered carousels. Among the best known of these early parks was Jones's Woods in New York City, which offered a variety of amusements and hosted large gatherings. Parker's Grove outside of Cincinnati, Ohio, had a dance hall and refreshment stands, a mule-powered merry-go-round, target shooting, and swings. It later became Coney Island Amusement Park. Lake Compounce Park in Connecticut, which opened in 1846, featured bowling alleys, a revolving swing, and boating on its lake. Schuetzen Park in New Jersey, established in 1875, offered athletic games, bowling, shooting, and magic shows before being converted into an amusement park in the 1920s. Kennywood outside of Pittsburgh, Pennsylvania, was another early amusement resort that eventually became one of the best-known amusement parks in the country. In fact, many of these early amusement resorts became amusement parks after Captain Paul Boyton opened what is considered the first true amusement park, Sea Lion Park, on Coney Island in 1895.[3]

The amusement park grew out of the Midway Plaisance at the 1893 Columbian Exposition in Chicago. The grand and dignified buildings around the Court of Honor at the exposition were designed to inspire people, showing them what cities could become. But fair organizers also knew that people wanted entertainment, so they created the Midway to keep those vulgar and popular amusements, which included recreated foreign villages, theaters, restaurants, and even the Ferris wheel, away from the Court of Honor. The amusement park took the concept of the Midway and transferred it to a space enclosed by a fence with a gate that required an admission fee to enter. The admission fee was designed to keep potentially undesirable customers, who might cause trouble, out of the parks. The rides and other attractions inside the amusement parks brought people from all walks of life together as they laughed or screamed (sometimes in terror, sometimes in pleasure) on rides, struck up temporary friendships with people in lines, saw more of each other exposed than polite society allowed, and witnessed exciting spectacles. It was all acceptable inside the confines of the amusement park. Throughout the United States, backers constructed new parks and converted older amusement resorts into amusement parks, creating nearly 5,000 of the new parks between 1895 and the 1920s.[4]

The rise of the amusement park came just as Americans were beginning to have more leisure time. Labor reformers had been working hard to secure eight-hour workdays, half-day Saturdays, and free Sundays for most industrial workers, while moral authorities started to find taking part in games and other recreational activities on Sundays less objectionable. With the country transitioning from a largely rural and agricultural society to an industrialized urban society, and with more people moving to cities, there was a need for more leisure activities. Amusement parks, fantasy lands insulated from the demands and cares of everyday life, were the perfect places to spend some of that new leisure time.[5]

After growing rapidly in the second half of the nineteenth century, Denver had become a dirty, dusty city with few places for the public to enjoy rest and relaxation. As William B. Vickers wrote in his 1880 *History of Denver*, "Denver, it must be confessed, is sorely lacking in places of legitimate amusement." Saloons, gambling halls, and houses of ill repute were hardly places for respectable citizens or families to spend their leisure time. Denver purchased its first park land in 1881, when the state legislature allowed the city to buy 320 acres of school land that eventually became City Park. Twenty years later Denver had twelve parks that covered 436 acres, but other than City Park, most of them were relatively undeveloped and offered few attractions for visitors. To fill the gap, Denverites eagerly latched onto any place that allowed them to get away from the city, breathe fresh air, and enjoy themselves. When Riverside Cemetery opened north of the city in 1876, residents flocked to it on Sunday afternoons, riding in carriages or strolling through the beautifully landscaped grounds, admiring the architecture of the monuments and cemetery buildings, and eating a picnic lunch or dinner. When the even grander Fairmount Cemetery opened in 1890, the same thing happened because it was a beautiful, respectable place to enjoy leisure time. In fact, the cemetery was such a popular place to visit that when residents took attendees of the 1906 Elks' Convention to visit the cemetery, the newspapers reported that many people were upset by the "untidy appearance" of weeds growing on some of the graves.[6]

In 1882, Walter von Richtofen built San Souci, an amusement resort on Logan Street between what is now East Dakota and East Virginia Avenues. Located along the tracks of the Denver Circle Railway, San Souci was a typical German beer garden. It was also home to a concert hall and, according to the *Rocky Mountain News*, was "fitted up in a style in accordance with all that capital and good taste can provide." The newspaper described the concert hall as "highly artistic and ornamental in its general design," and said it could be rented for private dance parties. Public dancing, considered immoral, was not allowed at the park, and the *News* said "disreputable characters are to be kept off the grounds." Von Richtofen had the park filled with flowerbeds, flowering bushes, and trees, and at the end of one of the paths near the concert hall was a fountain and rockery. The *News* said San Souci filled "a place that this community has long felt the need of." San Souci opened on July 1, 1882, but it did not attract many people during its first weeks, which led von Richtofen to announce that he would set aside one night when Denver's "sporting element"—which was understood to include gamblers, pimps, prostitutes, saloon keepers, and other undesirable people—could visit the park. The night turned into a drunken free-for-all that permanently damaged San Souci's reputation. Von Richtofen reorganized the bankrupt resort late in 1882, but the following June he sold it to Mrs. Jenkins of New York for $11,000. She continued to run it as a resort, but in 1887 a sign for an Episcopal mission appeared at the park. The last mention of San Souci was in the 1894 *Denver City Directory*, after which it was sold for building lots.[7]

On July 4, 1887, John Brisben Walker opened River Front Park along the Platte River between Fifteenth and Nineteenth Streets. The park included a racetrack, boating on the Platte, a baseball diamond, and a three-story exhibition building that resembled a castle. The grand opening was less than spectacular. According to the *Colorado Daily Chieftain*, Walker had leased the park to H. Tabor Treloan, who promised free admission on the afternoon of the Fourth for the public to watch military drills by several companies. People were shocked, said the newspaper, to arrive at the park and find a sign announcing a 25-cent admission fee. While many left in disgust, those who did pay admission found "not a sign of shade" except under the porch of the exhibition building, which Treloan charged a separate quarter admission fee to enter. After somewhat overcoming its opening day problems, the park hosted a variety of events during its short existence, including bicycle and horse races, musical events, baseball games, and a Roman three-horse chariot race. In the winter, the park offered ice skating and sledding on slides constructed by the Denver Toboggan Club. Some of the slides were reportedly 1,000 feet long and sledders could reach speeds of 180 miles per hour. On September 20, 1888, the park hosted an Emancipation Day celebration for Black people from throughout Colorado (Emancipation Day celebrations would later become a tradition at Manhattan Beach). When Walker bought *Cosmopolitan Magazine* in 1889, his business interests shifted to New York and he tried to sell the park to the City of Denver for $1 million. The city rejected Walker's offer, saying that the lack of easy access to the grounds and the poor air quality in the area made it an unsuitable location for a city park. Walker eventually sold the land to the Union Pacific Railroad for $1.2 million and it became home to the railroad's yard.[8]

Adam Graff's idea for a recreational resort on the shores of Sloan's Lake in 1889 fit well with what had already been tried in Denver, and he was planning to construct it at a place that had long helped to fulfill the city's recreational needs. The history of Sloan's Lake is a curious, and probably forever incomplete, story. When Denver was first settled in 1859 the lake did not exist, and the road that connected Denver to Golden ran across what would one day be the lakebed. In a 1909 interview with the *Colorado Transcript*, George F. Turner, a stagecoach driver in the 1860s, said that when he came to Denver to keep a stage station in June 1861, the lake was not there. He also remembered driving a stage across the road that ran through the future site of the lake. When Turner returned to Denver in 1863, the road was gone and the lake was there. The most commonly accepted story about how the lake came to be is that in 1861 Thomas Sloan staked a claim on 160 acres of land for a farm. While digging a well on the property,

Sloan believed that he tapped into an underground aquifer or spring. The next morning, the story goes, he awoke to find a lake covering most of his property. (One story says that he floated out of bed the next morning, but Turner said Sloan's house stood for many years on the shore of the lake.) The new body of water received a variety of mocking names, including Sloan's Leak, but it was mostly known as Sloan's Lake. While many people doubt that version of the story, they offer no alternative. Others suggest that the lake did not form until 1866, when Sloan actually received title to the land. George Turner's story, however, clearly states that the lake was there in 1863, and he said he swam in it in 1866. Nearby Cooper Lake, which would eventually become part of Sloan's Lake, also formed from an underground spring.[9]

Thomas Sloan was born in Pennsylvania in 1801. He and his first wife, Eliza, had three children before her death in 1831: William, Clarissa, and Amanda. Sloan and his second wife, Sarah, had five children: John, Ann, Louisa, Thomas, and Sarah. The Sloans arrived in Denver in 1859. For many years they operated the Sloan House Hotel at Larimer and G (now 16th) Streets. The hotel was known as the Broadwell House when it first opened, but after the Sloans bought it, they advertised that it had been "thoroughly repaired, and every room papered, from cellar to garret, and fitted-up for a first-class hotel." From February to April of 1872, Sloan attempted to sell the land around his lake, advertising it as "the best farm in Colorado," situated on 100 acres on the road from Denver to Georgetown. Apparently, no one bought the land as Sloan platted it as Lakeville in December of 1873. Two months later, on February 14, 1874, Thomas Sloan died in Denver and the title to the land remained a point of contention for many years. In fact, the battle over his estate continued into the 1890s, reaching all the way to the United States Supreme Court. Shortly before Sloan's death, the Boulevard and Sloan Lake Steam Navigation Company got an option on the lake and land around it and announced its intention to build a steamboat to cruise on the lake.[10]

As soon as Sloan's Lake emerged, it became a favorite recreation spot for Denverites. Ice skating was popular during winter months, and the editor of Central City's *Sunday School Casket* newspaper wrote on January 1, 1868 "what a sliding, tumbling, laughing, frollicsome [sic] time a few of us enjoyed at Sloan's lake a few days ago . . . and though we had not attempted to skate for twelve or fifteen years, we did absolutely prepare ourself and *tumble* around for hours among the boys and girls, to their infinite amusement." In the summer, rowboats and sailboats were common on the lake, and it became a popular fishing spot. In 1867, a promoter staged boxing matches on the southern side of the lake. Stories also circulated that "American Indians" had once used the site of the lake for horse races and that it was a buffalo wallow. A history of neighboring Edgewater, published in 1961, states that in the 1870s a "friendly Indian tribe," looking to escape the snow in the mountains, built wigwams at the northwest side of the lake and made frequent trips to Denver for supplies.[11]

In 1872, John C. Dexter, a Denver tree farmer, under the name Captain J. C. Dexter, had a boat built that he named the *Dolly Varden*. On June 11, 1872, the *Denver Daily Times* reported that Dexter's boat was "a veritable fact" and that he intended to take a "select party" out for a cruise on the Platte River. After the trial trip, Dexter intended to make regular trips for paying customers from the Larimer Street bridge over Cherry Creek each day at 4 p.m. Dexter's plan to regularly cruise the Platte fell through, but by the end of June he was making daily trips in the *Dolly Varden* on Sloan's Lake. In his advertisement for his services, he "respectfully ask[ed] for the patronage of ladies and gentlemen," and vowed that he would do his best to deserve it. A carriage took people to and from the lake for the boat ride, with requests for transport to be left at the *Daily Times* office. Dexter's boat operated for only one summer, but he remained in Denver until his death in 1891.[12]

The brief run of the *Dolly Varden* on Sloan's Lake must have intrigued others and convinced them to try the boat business for themselves. On February 12, 1874, the *Denver Daily Times* announced that a new company planned to build a 30-foot-wide, 5-foot-deep canal from the Grand View Hotel on the Boulevard (later known as Federal Boulevard) at 17th Avenue to Sloan's Lake. The newspaper reported that "an easy and practicable route" had been surveyed by "competent persons." After joking that the canal would surely "dissolve the myth of the 'Great American Desert,'" the newspaper said that the canal would be the place for picnickers, pleasure parties, and excursions of every kind, and that the company behind it would surely make a profit.[13]

Lewis Ellsworth and his partners started construction of the $14,000 Grand View Hotel in 1873. On June 6 that year the *Rocky Mountain News* said that when completed it would be a very "neat and substantial" building and that with all of the modern comforts it would be a "very comfortable hotel." The architectural firm of Lewis and Bancroft designed the frame building, which was eighty feet by sixty feet and had two towers on it. The Halleck Brothers began construction on the hotel later in June. The two-story building was located next to a small pond fed by a spring. The hotel opened for guests on March 23, 1874, with the *Times* reporting that "large crowds visited the hotel during the day via the street cars."[14]

Just a few weeks before the hotel's opening, on March 1, Lewis Ellsworth, F. D. Hagger, J. B. Cofield, John Clough, Daniel Witter, William Anderson, Theodore W. Poole, J. Alexander Pace, Solomon Fisher, and Wellington George Sprague joined together to form the Boulevard and Sloan Lake Steam Navigation Company. The first, and as it would turn out only, board of directors of the company included William Anderson as president, F. D. Hagger as secretary and treasurer, and Lewis Ellsworth, J. B. Cofield,

The Grand View Hotel at the Boulevard (now Federal Boulevard) and 17th Avenue in the 1870s. The beginning of the steamboat canal, which ran along 17th Avenue to Sloan's Lake, is visible to the left of the hotel. *Source:* The Denver Public Library, Western History Collection, X-19293.

Theodore Poole, and John Clough as directors. The *Times* asserted that "the moneyed ability and character of these gentlemen is a guarantee that no impediment will be allowed to prevent the speedy completion and successful working of this novel project." The purpose of the company was to build a three-mile-long canal along 17th Avenue from the pond beside the Grand View Hotel to Sloan's Lake "for irrigation, mechanical and culinary purposes, and to float boats, barges and vessels for the carriage of freight and passengers." The men planned to fill the canal with water from Sloan's Lake. The canal itself would run southeast from Sloan's Lake, through nearby Cooper Lake, and then east to the hotel.[15]

To navigate the canal and lake, the company purchased a used steamboat from the Mississippi River Steamship Company. According to Alice M. Coleman's history of Edgewater, the boat was dismantled and shipped to Denver in sections to be reassembled. In late March, the *Times* reported that while it had looked doubtful for a few weeks that the project would actually happen, everything fell into place once the company purchased Cooper Lake and the adjoining land, finally securing the right-of-way for the canal. As soon as that was done, a telegraph went to Chicago placing the order for the engine for the steamboat's propeller. Construction of the boat itself, according to the newspapers, was under the supervision of C. H. Brown, who had built several boats for the Hoboken Yacht Club, including the *Eveline* and *T. B. Astor*. Charles Smith, the general contractor hired to build the canal, started work on it on March 26, 1874.[16]

William Anderson, as president of the new company, oversaw construction on the canal, and in early April the *Rocky Mountain News* reported that crews were at work on both ends of it. They were digging toward the center, which would only be removed after each crew reached a certain point. Thirty-five teams were hard at work on the thirty-foot-wide, five-foot-deep canal. The *News* stated that the soil was hard pan so it would have no trouble holding water. Large crowds gathered at the Grand View Hotel each day to watch the work, and Anderson told the *News* that he expected to have water in the canal by early May. By May 5, the canal connecting Sloan's Lake and Cooper Lake had been cut and filled (an island made of dirt from the dig is still visible on the eastern end of Sloan's Lake), and the propeller for the boat, which the *Times* reported was "a beautiful piece of workmanship," was at the lake.[17]

News of the canal inspired at least one copycat in Denver. Ed Kettle, who owned a nursery in Denver, announced that he had made arrangements to cut a canal from the "lake" in front of his shop to Cherry Creek, and that he had signed a contract to build a "beautiful steamer" that would carry "excursionists" during the summer. Nothing ever came of Kettle's plan. Historian Phil Goodstein writes that as construction on the Sloan's Lake canal proceeded, nearby farmers and residents objected to it, fearing that it would drain water from their land, and they managed to get a court order to stop the project. The company rushed to complete it before the injunction went into effect, and the level of Cooper Lake dropped by four feet when water first flowed into the canal. The *Daily Times* reported on May 16 that the canal was done despite those who "laughed or doubted."[18]

As unique as the canal was, equally unique was the boat that the company's organizers had chosen to take passengers from the hotel to Sloan's Lake and back. The parts of the secondhand steamboat arrived in Denver, by both wagon and railroad, in mid-April. The company named the boat the *City of Denver*. They initially planned to launch the boat on May 9, but the launch was postponed due to high winds because, as the *Rocky Mountain News* put it, "it was feared she would drag her anchor, slip her cable, go over Cheltenham Heights and wreck herself on Castle Rock." The boat finally went into the water on May 19, 1874, and was promptly anchored in the middle of Sloan's Lake. This, according to the *Daily Times*, was so that it could receive a thorough painting before taking on its first passengers.[19]

The canal company officially launched the *City of Denver* on May 23, 1874, and it took its first paying passengers on May 26. That afternoon the boat made five trips, each lasting a little less than hour, and carried sixty-six passengers. The following day, the *Times* reported that "the famous craft on our inland canal" was making regular trips from the Grand View to Sloan's Lake and back. With the boat operational, the canal company was at work on a dock and passenger station at Sloan's Lake and was building rowboats for those who wanted to "blister their hands in rowing about the lakes." Crews were also driving in piles along the length of the canal to keep the banks from giving way and were grading a drive around Cooper Lake. On May 27, a group of dignitaries that included Alfred Sayer, Dr. J. H. Morrison, Rev. J. M. Sturdevant, C. W. Wright, J. R. Hanna, and General H. B. Bearce were invited to inspect improvements in the northwest part of Denver. Their tour included a trip through the canal on the *City of Denver*, which the *Rocky Mountain News* reported "was a complete demonstration of the remarkable success of this enterprise."[20]

The *Rocky Mountain News* reported that, on average, 1,000 people rode the streetcars on Sundays to the Grand View Hotel and the canal. The newspaper also noted that a "great many roughs and hoodlums" also rode the streetcars to visit the dance halls and saloons in the vicinity of Sloan's Lake, particularly in neighboring Edgewater. According to the newspapers, those visiting the dance halls and saloons smoked in the cars and used "coarse and ungentlemanly language." This was an early sign of a problem that would plague more than one amusement park in Denver as less than desirable businesses opened around them. With business initially so good, despite the presence of some questionable characters, the canal company announced plans to build a second steamer of the same size. However, those plans quickly fell through.[21]

For decades after it was launched people claimed that the *City of Denver* was the first steamship in Colorado, but some rightfully took issue with that. Shortly after the boat was launched, the editor of the *Daily Central City Register* reminded readers that William B. Walling, a lumber dealer and sawmill operator in Gilpin and Boulder counties, had launched a steamboat on the lake at the head of Lake Gulch, south of Central City, in 1872, two years ahead of the *City of Denver*. John Bennett's Lake House, also called the Lake View House, at Lake Gulch was a popular dance hall and the site of an annual Fourth of July celebration in Gilpin County beginning in 1864. Walling launched his boat on the afternoon of July 4, 1872, and as it "left its moorings, its decks were thronged with passengers, the whistle reverberated from mountain to mountain, and the beach was lined with spectators." While initially popular, Walling's steamship disappeared at the end of that summer, followed by the Lake House at the end of the summer of 1873.[22]

By early August 1874, the *City of Denver* was making regular trips from the Grand View to Sloan's Lake and back every hour from 8 a.m. to 10 p.m. When the new Elysium Hall theater opened near the Grand View that month, the owners of the theater even arranged to have live music, dancing, and refreshments at the steamboat landing at the hotel along with trips on the steamboat. The boat and canal, they said, offered "mountain and city views unsurpassed by any place around Denver." A ticket to ride cost twenty-five cents, but for an additional dime, passengers could also visit Johnson's Park at Sloan's Lake once they arrived there. James M. Johnson sold wine at his store on Fifteenth Street in Denver. In the spring of 1874, he constructed a dance hall and pavilion at the head of Sloan's Lake, and also rented out boats on Sloan's Lake as part of his operation. On June 22, 1874, the *Daily Times* advertised a moonlight excursion on the *City of Denver* to the park. For thirty-five cents, customers got to ride on the steamboat and enjoy "the best of music and dining under the grand pavilion" at Johnson's Park, returning to the Grand View at 10 p.m.[23]

However, just as had happened with the boats operated by J. C. Dexter and William Walling, by the end of the summer the novelty of the *City of Denver* was wearing off, and business dropped quickly. The last advertisement for regular trips on the boat appeared in the *Rocky Mountain News* on September 3, 1874. The canal company originally planned to stop running the boat for the season after the Colorado Industrial Association's Second Annual Fair, which ran from September 22 to 26, but before that could happen disaster struck. On the afternoon of September 16, the lower end of the canal (at the Grand View) gave way and the water flooded out onto the Boulevard. The *Colorado Daily Chieftain* reported that the water did "considerable damage" to the road, while the *Rocky Mountain News* said that it amounted to about $700 worth of damage. The canal immediately closed for the season and never reopened. In early November another part of the canal washed out, and the sheriff seized the *City of Denver*. The boat was sold at auction on November 7, 1874, to help pay the company's debts, but for a few years afterward people regularly advertised in newspapers trying to sell their notes against the Boulevard and Sloan Lake Steam Navigation Company. By the time the boat was sold it had even become somewhat of a joke. Reporting on several Denver residents visiting St. Louis that November during heavy rains, the editor of the *Rocky Mountain News* wrote that the men were hoping to board the *City of Denver* to "take a pleasure excursion through some of the business streets."[24]

The canal was eventually filled in and, without the draw of the steamboat and canal, the Grand View Hotel soon closed as well. For a brief time, the hotel served as an insane asylum, but in 1881 it became the home of St. Luke's Hospital when the Episcopalians purchased it for $7,000 (they paid another $900 for the furnishings). In 1891, the church sold the building for $10,000 to help fund the hospital's move to 19th and Pearl Streets. The failure of the steamship was also bad news for Johnson's Park at Sloan's Lake. On September 12 and September 19, 1874, the *Daily Times* announced boat races at the park, with the race on the 19th including a "Champion Belt and a purse." In March of 1875, Johnson told the *Rocky Mountain News* that he planned to put in grain and market gardens on 170 acres around his park in addition to planting 2,000 cottonwood trees in the park. That was the last ever heard of Johnson's Park. James Johnson eventually moved to California, where he died in 1913.[25]

Despite the failure of the steamboat and Johnson's Park, Sloan's Lake remained a popular recreation destination for boating, fishing, and ice skating. And, with so much activity taking place on the lake, it could sometimes be deadly. The *Fort Collins Courier* reported on October 20, 1881, that a duck hunter drowned in the lake when his boat capsized, and in June of 1888 the *Silver Standard* newspaper reported that two boys drowned in Sloan's Lake. Not all who went into the water perished though. The *Colorado Daily Chieftain* reported on May 14, 1874, that four printers "took an involuntary bath" when their boat tipped over. According to the newspaper the men lost everything but "their lives and their beloved whiskey."[26]

In 1881, Henry Lee, a member of the Colorado House of Representatives, attempted to introduce a bill that called for selling the land that eventually became City Park and an equal amount of land around Sloan's Lake to the city of Denver for public parks. Although the proposal passed the House, opponents in the state Senate stalled it. Historian Jerome Smiley wrote in his 1901 *History of Denver* that many residents opposed the bill because "they neither saw nor appreciated the necessity, value nor utility of parks." When the bill finally passed the state Senate, the section that would have created Edgewater Park (the Sloan's Lake property) was stripped from it, but the land for City Park remained. As Smiley wrote, supporters "accepted the half-loaf as being far better than none." Smiley estimated that the value of the Sloan's Lake land in 1901 was about $1 million.[27]

The lake was also a popular place for ice cutters in the winter. So much ice came out of Sloan's and Cooper lakes that in 1877 one reader sarcastically asked the editors of the *Daily Times*, "Is all the ice water that we drink in the city cut on Cooper Lake and Sloan Lake?" And it was ice cutting that put Adam Graff on Sloan's Lake that day in February 1889 when he first dreamed of an amusement resort on the shore of the lake.[28]

Adam Graff was born in Germany in 1848. He came to the United States at age 18 and quickly made his way to Colorado. By 1873 he was working as a carpenter, a profession he followed for the next ten years. In 1875 he married Julia Roederer, whose grandparents were friends with General James Denver. She was born in Leavenworth, Kansas, on Christmas Eve 1859 as her parents were preparing to leave by ox train for Cherry Creek. Adam and Julia lived at 1918 Downing Street for most of their time in Denver and eventually had six children: sons Adam and Jakob and daughters Elizabeth, Katherine, Madeline, and Julia. In

1883 or 1884 Graff gave up the carpentry business to become an ice dealer. He opened a store in the 1300 block of 17th Street in Denver and cut ice in the winters on Sloan's Lake, which was then owned by the Rocky Mountain Water Company.[29]

Adam Graff, the man behind Manhattan Beach. *Source: Rocky Mountain News*, February 18, 1940.

On March 5, 1889, Graff, capitalist Theodore Schrott, and saloon owner Ernst Steinke incorporated the Sloan Lake and Park Company with a capital stock of $100,000. As stated in the incorporation papers for the company, the purpose of the new business was to "control the lake and adjoining property . . . and to make the same a place of public resort and amusement." Among the plans for the new resort were a public garden, parks, and bathing and boating facilities. Although not mentioned in the incorporation papers, Graff also planned to build a hotel at the lake. Joining Graff, Schrott, and Steinke on the board of the new corporation were Vigil M. Came and John P. Brockway.[30]

Adam Graff's new venture at Sloan's Lake received little attention from Denver area newspapers. According to a later interview with his daughter Elizabeth Graff Klien, Graff's ice company associate Jacob Sackett supervised most of the construction at the site, although Graff did put his old carpenter skills to use to help build it. Construction on the new resort appears to have taken place throughout 1889 and into early 1890. Ernst Steinke and his brother Robert, who owned the Golden Gate Saloon in neighboring Edgewater, played a major role in the park once it opened.[31]

Graff's Sloan's Park opened on July 3, 1890. In reporting on the new amusement area, the Swedish newspaper *Svensk-Amerikanska Western* said that the pavilion the men built at the lake had seats for 3,000 people and that "everything is arranged in the best way." The *Rocky Mountain News* said that "a beautiful, unobstructed view of the mountains can be obtained from the pavilion." The pavilion and hotel were located along a new canal that the men built on the north side of the lake. Both the canal and lake were fenced to keep children from falling into the water. Albert Siggel's military band provided musical entertainment for customers every day throughout the summer. No alcohol was served at the pavilion, with the owners instead relying on "drinks of a milder nature, such as lemonade," sold at the octagon-shaped lemonade

Adam Graff's original plans for Manhattan Beach were far grander than anything that was ever built. A simplified version of the hotel (the large building with multiple towers on it) was the only part of this plan ever built. *Source:* The Denver Public Library, Western History Collection, F13581.

stand, which also had an attached milk stand where visitors could get fresh milk from an Alderney cow.[32]

The park's boathouse was forty-four feet by forty feet and housed two sailboats and forty rowboats and was supervised by Captain Louis Alveburg, an "old salt-water captain." Graff and his partners had also purchased a used steamboat that had seen service on the Mississippi River as a coal boat. Like the owners of the 1874 steamship, Graff and his partners named the new boat *City of Denver.* To ensure the safety of all visitors to the park, management announced that they would have six policemen at the park at all times. The new park could also rely on Denver's streetcars to bring visitors directly to the park. The *Rocky Mountain News* reported that the Ashland Avenue (now West 29th Avenue) electric streetcar line already ran to the park, while the Agate Avenue (now West 23rd Avenue) line and the Larimer Street Cable Company would soon reach the park.[33]

Not mentioned in the *Svensk-Amerikanska* article is the hotel, but the men did indeed build it. Unfortunately, no details about it appear to have survived. In October of 1890, as the first season at the new park wound down, R.J. Spaulding of Rosita, Colorado attempted to demonstrate a "flying machine" at Sloan's Lake in front of a crowd of about 5,000 people. According to the *Colorado Daily Chieftain*, Spaulding had been working on the machine for about fifteen years, but the demonstration at Sloan's Lake was a dismal failure. The newspaper reported that the only things that flew that day were the rocks thrown by the "disgusted crowd," and Spaulding was escorted home by a sheriff's deputy. Neither the pavilion nor the hotel were mentioned in the article about the demonstration, but it seems likely that the crowd would have gathered at the pavilion to watch.[34]

Two months before Sloan's Park opened, John and Mary Elitch opened Elitch Gardens at 38th and Tennyson, one mile north of Graff's park. The couple had purchased the Chilcott Farm to supply fresh produce for their Elitch Palace Dining Car Restaurant at 1541 Arapahoe in Denver. The farm reminded them of Woodward Gardens in San Francisco, where they had spent a

The hotel at Adam Graff's Sloan's Park. The building burned down in 1891. *Source:* History Colorado, Object # 89.451.5602.

great deal of time when they were first married, and they decided to open it to the public so they could enjoy it as well. Originally a zoo and garden, the park would grow to include a theater in 1891. Mayor Wolfe Londoner spoke at the opening of Elitch's, but no such official recognition took place at Sloan's Park.[35]

The year before opening Elitch Gardens, while Adam Graff was planning Sloan's Park, John Elitch had tried to create a similar resort at Berkeley Lake, about three miles north of Sloan's Lake. Elitch built a boathouse and café at the lake and also had plans for a bathhouse, dancing pavilion, and hotel. He ordered thirty boats for the lake, which included a steam launch, pedal boat, ten sailboats, and several rowboats. When they arrived in Denver in April 1889, they were loaded onto wagons decorated with red, white and blue bunting and paraded through the streets of downtown before being taken to the lake. Elitch also dreamed of opening a zoo at Berkeley Lake. On December 12, 1889, the animals that he purchased from Adam Forepaugh of Philadelphia, including camels, lions, monkeys, cockatoos, and a "sacred cow," arrived in Denver after a two-week journey. Although the zoo and other features moved from Berkeley to Elitch Gardens, John Elitch continued to operate the boats on Berkeley Lake through 1890.[36]

The joy of Graff's new resort was regrettably short lived. On April 17, 1891, the *Denver Republican* reported that the hotel and pavilion were completely destroyed by a fire at about 3 o'clock that morning. Unlike the pavilion, the hotel did serve liquor and the newspaper said that the fire started about 2:30 a.m. with a "spontaneous explosion of a large quantity of liquors" stored in the hotel's barroom. The report of the explosion was "terrific" and the entire side of the barroom was blown out by it. The explosion immediately set fire to the west end of the hotel, then quickly spread to the rest of the structure. Louis Alveburg (the captain of the steamboat) and George Wonder were sleeping over the barroom at the time the fire broke out and only managed to escape in time because a barking dog woke them up. The newspaper estimated the loss from the fire at $10,000. While the loss of the pavilion and hotel was a blow to Graff and his new amusement resort, two weeks later, on April 30, 1891, Graff and his original ice company associates Jacob Sackett and George Darrow formed a new corporation for an even bigger and better park that would soon be known as Manhattan Beach.[37]

## CHAPTER I

# Manhattan Beach, A City's Beauty Spot

ADAM GRAFF AND HIS ASSOCIATES ALREADY HAD BIG CHANGES underway at Sloan's Park at the time that the fire destroyed the pavilion and hotel. On April 8, 1891, a reporter from the *Denver Times* met with Park Manager Jacob Sackett to look at what was in store for visitors that coming summer. Planned additions to the front and rear of the hotel as well as a rooftop garden were obviously dropped after the fire, but the rest of the changes moved forward.[1]

The main entrance gate was on the north side of the park at Emerald Street (later 25th Avenue and then Byron Place) and Sherman Street (which later became Zenobia). Visitors to the park would encounter a new building right inside the gates that housed the administrative offices for the park along with a room set aside for the press. To the right of the hotel, the men planned to build a replica of the Eiffel Tower complete with elevators and a searchlight mounted on top of it. The searchlight, according to Sackett, would turn night into day on the grounds of the park. Many amusement parks of the era also used such searchlights to help keep troublemakers under control in the park. After all, if they might literally be in the spotlight at any moment, they were less likely to misbehave.[2]

The entrance gate to Manhattan Beach at Byron Place and Zenobia Street. One of the park's concession stands is visible through the gate. *Source:* The Denver Public Library, Western History Collection, X-19530.

A new boathouse on the opposite side of the park from the entrance, and north of the bathing beach that was then under construction, replaced the park's original boathouse. The boathouse's dock was made up of small slips that were just wide enough for a single boat. This arrangement of the slips allowed for people to step into boats from either side rather than having to crawl over the seats. Several barges joined the rowboats, sailboats, and canoes already at the lake for people who wanted to take a large party out onto it. Management planned to buy one or two more steamboats to join the *City of Denver* on the lake, but those plans fell through. The *Denver Times* reported on May 13 that each boat would be "gaily painted" and that the lake would "look very pretty dotted with these little crafts."[3]

Also under construction at the northwest corner of the park was a new theater modeled after the Auditorium Theater in

Chicago. The building could seat 2,000 people and park management had arranged to present both opera and vaudeville. Sackett told the *Times* that they planned to do performances almost every night, with an hour-and-a-half each devoted to opera and vaudeville designed to "suit all tastes." Located between the theater and the boathouse, at the east end of the grounds, was the park's new zoo. A large outdoor tank housed the sea lions, while the main building for the zoo was 275 feet by 45 feet. Connected to that building were five smaller buildings. The Shetland pony track, for children who wanted to ride one of the small horses, was in front of the main zoo building. To reach the menagerie, visitors had to cross a rustic-style bridge that went over the canal created the year before. There were twenty-eight cages in the main building, while the smaller buildings were meant to house only one kind of animal each. Among the animals who would call Manhattan Beach home were monkeys, ostriches, an elephant, and two hippopotamuses. The cage for the hippos held a large tank of water for them, and the *Times* assured its readers that there was "ample room" for them. Management had hopes to breed the animals in the zoo and had ordered males and females of each species.[4]

Two other large buildings, located between the boat house and the fence around the park, housed a bowling alley and a free gym "with all the modern appliances." In front of those two buildings were the café and restaurant where, Sackett said, the "services would be first class in every respect." The men planned to scatter other amusements throughout the grounds, including a camera obscura and a Flying Jennie (carousel) copied from the one operating on the Champs-Élysées in Paris, but they would have to wait for the next year. Opening day festivities were also supposed to include fireworks and a battle between two men-of-war on the lake. To make room for all of the proposed changes, Graff and his associates spent $100,000 to buy an additional ninety acres of land at Sloan's Lake from Roger W. Woodbury on April 24, 1891.[5]

Manhattan Beach's Animal House as it looked in the early 1900s.
*Source:* The Denver Public Library, Western History Collection, X-19523.

Extensive changes were also underway at the lake. Under construction was a new grandstand to provide seating for people watching aquatic events. Plans also called for a 250-foot pier that would lead to a bandstand where the locally famous Hungarian Girls Band would replace Albert Siggel's band. (It is unclear if the pier was ever built.) Also under construction was a 20-foot-wide asphalt path that ran from the grandstand to the boathouse. Every forty feet over the path were arches with multicolored lights, creating a "magnificent, illuminated promenade three-quarters of a mile long." For swimmers, the park's owners were building a 500–square foot bathing beach, covered with two feet of sand. Sackett said the park would provide swimsuits for bathers and that they planned to name the bathing area Manhattan Beach.[6]

Sackett told the *Times* that the improvements to the park would cost over $100,000 but "the company is perfectly willing to expend that amount to make the place a resort for the better classes of Denver." To demonstrate that the owners meant to cater to what Sackett considered the better classes, he told the newspapers that they planned to continue their policy of not serving alcohol at the park, although he also said that the 25-cent admission fee and ready access to the park by streetcar would "place the pleasures of the resort within the reach of everyone." Sackett seemingly also forgot the existence of nearby Elitch's when he said there was nothing like Sloan's Park in Denver.[7]

Management originally intended to open the park for the season on June 7, 1891, but by May 7 the date had been pushed back to June 13. The park had also gone through a name change by mid-May, with the entire area taking on the Manhattan Beach name. The *Times* reported that several hundred men were at work on the park and "everything about the grounds appears to be in the wildest confusion." The theater was complete up to the balcony level and the foundations of the café, which would be an open structure with a roof supported by pillars, had been laid. The café and attached dairy were west of the main entrance to the park.[8]

—MANHATTAN BEACH STATION—WEST END ELECTRIC RAILWAY CO.

The West End Electric Streetcar Station at Manhattan Beach on the corner of Sheridan Boulevard and Byron Place. The park's theater building is visible behind the station. *Source:* History Colorado, Object # 89.451.2600.

By mid-May, when a reporter for the *Times* visited the park to check on progress, workers were beginning to install a unique fountain that would be a centerpiece of the park. The basin for the fountain was glass and fifty feet in diameter. The fountain shot four streams of water into the air. The center stream reached 100 feet high, while the others reached seventy-five feet. Underneath the basin were colored lights, which allowed the jets of water to appear in many different colors. The *Times* said the fountain was "one of the prettiest spectacles imaginable" and that the only other fountain in the world like it was in Paris. Another fountain was installed across from the main zoo building, and its basin was filled with a large variety of water lilies. The sides of the canal on the north side of the park were covered with rocks. The *Times* reported that workers planted "all sorts of pretty plants and flowers" between the rocks, making for a beautiful site. The park's owners also planned to have four streams of water running through the canal at all times to keep the lake water pure.[9]

The *Times* said that the results of the labor crew's work in the park would soon be apparent in "handsome buildings, pretty walks shaded by tropic and native shrubbery and trees and crystal fountains throwing many colored waters in the air." The newspaper said Manhattan Beach would be a unique combination of a bathing resort, zoo, and park, with a concert hall and theater thrown into the mix. (Elitch's opened its theater in 1891, but since the park lacked a bathing beach, it apparently did not come close to touching Manhattan Beach in the opinion of the *Times*.) The new resort, the *Times* said, "promises to be one of the most beautiful in the country."[10]

June 13 came and went without the park opening, as delays in getting everything ready pushed the date back once again. On June 24, 1891, the *Times* reported that workers were busy putting in plants, flowers, and shrubs, and that a number of "clever performers" and an opera company had been engaged. The animals for the zoo arrived in Denver by train on the night of

June 26. Eight wagons met the train, and the caged animals were loaded first. The *Denver Republican* reported that the "monkeys chattered and the other beasts expostulated a little against their shaking up," but the move from train to wagon was accomplished with little trouble. Next off the train was the soon-to-be star of Manhattan Beach, Roger the elephant, who was on loan from the Central Park Menagerie in New York and owned by circus owner William Washington Cole. Park employees expected to have a hard time getting him off the train, but the *Republican* said that he happily walked down the ramp, "grunted complacently" when he reached solid ground, and was anxious to begin the journey to the park, where he would quickly become the most famous and notorious inhabitant of the Manhattan Beach zoo. After Roger, the camel left the train in an "ecstasy of delight," and when he reached the ground he laid down and "rolled vigorously, over and over, a dozen times."[11]

With all of the animals except Roger and the camel loaded into the wagons, the parade of animals moved out from the freight depot at Union Station. According to the *Republican* they marched up 15th Street to Highlands Avenue, and then followed that street almost all the way to Sloan's Lake. A few people who lived along the route had heard about the "midnight parade" that would be taking place and stood outside to watch the wagons pass, followed by the elephant and camel. The procession finally reached Manhattan Beach at almost exactly midnight. Roger "surveyed his new home with a snort of curiosity" and was led to a quiet place to rest while the other animals were put into their new cages.[12]

While the animals for the zoo were in place, the rest of Manhattan Beach was far from finished, even though opening day was set for June 28. The zoo building itself, according to the *Republican*, was nowhere near complete though enough cages were ready for the animals who "most needed roomy quarters." There were 200 men at work in the park until 11 p.m. on the night of June

26, and the newspaper said that the number of lights made it seem as if it were daytime even at night. The newspaper estimated that it would take another week or so to get everything done, but all of the attractions were indeed ready for opening day. On June 25, three days before the park was set to open, one of the sea lions managed to escape, but she was captured in Golden and returned to the park on the 27th. (At the time, some people thought the escape was a publicity stunt.)[13]

Manhattan Beach officially opened to the public at 2 p.m. on June 28, 1891, and more than 10,000 people passed through the park's gates that day. An advertisement in the newspaper on June 28 proclaimed that Manhattan Beach had the only African ostrich farm, bathing beach, large menagerie, grand auditorium, family of sea lions, and electric fountain (which the newspaper promised would be in working order on opening day). The *Rocky Mountain News* reported the next day that the city's pleasure resorts could not have asked for a more perfect day, calling it a "model day for pleasure seekers." Streetcars and carriages were loaded with people traveling to Berkeley Lake, Elitch's, and Manhattan Beach. At Manhattan, the *News* reported that "perfect order was maintained." Although the boathouse was incomplete, the newspaper said that all of the boats were in use and "the beautiful lake presented a pretty picture covered with sails, together with the steamer and the row boats."[14]

While a few of the buildings were still incomplete, the *News* said that all of them were "handsome," in particular the circular theater with a stage measuring 45 feet by 70 feet. There were four proscenium boxes on each side of the stage with plaster relief figures representing music and drama above them, and there were no pillars inside the building, which meant there were no obstructed views. The electric lights above the stage could be raised and lowered as needed. The stage curtain was designed by T. U. Tschuldi. The newspaper said the theater was somewhat of a surprise because, although not large, "it was elegant in design, cool, convenient and well lighted, naturally and artificially," and that the first performance in the building on opening night "possessed unusual merit." Pietro Satriano's fourteen-piece band and the seven-piece Hungarian Girls Orchestra performed on the park grounds throughout the first summer the park was open. As promised, the park had off-duty Denver police officers patrolling the grounds, with Lieutenant Newmeyer, Captain Williams, H. Thompson, Gus Nobles, J. L Kirwin, and Thomas O'Donnell present on the first day of business. Denver's newspapers included interesting bits of information about the park, such as that the showers in the park's bath house were fed by an artesian well near the building, and that the iron bars in the zoo's cages would stretch fourteen miles if straightened. In all, the newspapers reported, Graff and his associates had spent about $150,000 on improvements at the park in the months before it opened. The *Denver Times* reported that although the park's buildings were not finished on opening day, "the visitors overlooked this and enjoyed themselves on the lake and in the menagerie and theater." At the menagerie, the park's ostriches, who had just arrived on opening day, and Roger the elephant received the most attention.[15]

As the *Republican* had predicted, it took about a week to finish the incomplete attractions at Manhattan Beach. The *Denver Times* reported that the bathing beach, boathouse, and electric fountain were finally completed just in time for the Fourth of July celebration at the park. As had been the case on opening day a week earlier, the city's streetcars were overloaded with people making their way to Elitch's or Manhattan Beach. Jacob Sackett stood at the streetcar loop in Highlands urging people to go to the Beach, where the special attraction for the day was a balloon ascension by Lady Gray, wife of H. D. Belden, who was also a well-known balloon performer. Balloon ascensions were popular attractions at amusement parks in the late 1890s and early 1900s. With flight being a true novelty then, people flocked to parks to see performers soar upward in their homemade balloons and,

Manhattan Beach's theater in the early 1900s. The theater was the most-publicized part of the park until the building burned down in 1908. *Source:* The Denver Public Library, Western History Collection, F5866.

sometimes, jump out of them or perform gymnastic stunts on ropes hanging from the baskets. In Denver, Ivy Baldwin, Wayne Abbott, and Frank Frazier, among others, became stars as they performed at the city's parks.[16]

Although her husband had made a name for himself in ballooning, Lady Gray was relatively new to the field, having made her first ascension and jump over the Platte River just two days before her scheduled performance at Manhattan Beach. Prior to that, she had mainly preformed trapeze acts and rope tricks above stages in theaters. At 11 a.m. on July 4, the crowd at the park, described as comprised of several thousand people, gathered to watch her balloon inflate. Twenty minutes later, Sackett led Lady Gray through the crowd to the balloon. The *Republican* reported that she "looked pale, but full of determination" and within a few minutes she was 3,000 feet over Sloan's Lake. She leapt from the balloon and parachuted into the lake, landing in the water near the southern shore. In the excitement of preparing for the jump no one at the park had thought to have a boat ready to retrieve her once she landed. It took several minutes for a boat to be dispatched as people in the crowd began to cry out that she would surely drown and "many ladies turned and fled from the lake." As it turned out, Lady Gray had landed in a shallow part of the lake and was in fact standing on the bottom of it as she waited for the boat. When she finally stepped ashore, "her hair, wet and bedraggled . . . and her purple tights glistened with water," the crowd cheered and clapped as she bowed to them.[17]

Sackett announced that Lady Gray would perform a second ascension and jump at 5 p.m. An even larger crowd gathered to watch, but the second jump ran into trouble after the balloon had risen only forty feet. The rope holding the parachute to the balloon broke and Lady Gray fell to the ground. "Amid cries of horror," her husband rushed to her side where he found that, fortunately, she was not injured. She made her third ascension of the day two hours later, and although the balloon did not go as high as on the first attempt, she successfully parachuted into the middle of Sloan's Lake. That time there were several boats waiting for her, and even though it took several minutes to extract her from the ropes of the parachute, it was a successful performance. She later told the *Republican* that she could not swim but her experiences that day convinced her to learn, and while she had felt uneasy at times, she was never scared. Lady Gray was back at Manhattan Beach on July 5 to perform more balloon ascensions and jumps and would, unintentionally, play a part in the tragedy that would become legendary in the history of Manhattan Beach.[18]

There were two attractions involving animals at the park that were especially popular with children. The park had an elaborate coach (in some accounts it was referred to as a Cinderella-type coach) that a team of ostriches pulled through the park, much to the delight of the children riding in it. The park also had a special seat that could be strapped to Roger the elephant, allowing a total of six children to ride on him. The usual route for Roger started at the animal house, went over the bridge that led to the animal house, and back. Boys, the *Rocky Mountain News* reported, happily accepted the opportunity to ride, but girls sometimes took a little convincing. In fact, the *News* said that one of the "pleasantest sights seen by the observer as he entered the grounds of Manhattan Beach" on July 5 "was a merry crowd of little ones" riding on Roger. Seeing Roger was a "delight of childhood," and the children loved giving him peanuts "and all manner of bon-bons."[19]

Shortly after 4 p.m. on July 5, 1891, Roger's keeper, Fred Knight, loaded Minnie and Charles Ober, Blanche and John Gremschilt, and six-year-old George Eaton onto the seat on Roger's back. Outside of the animal house, and directly in front of Roger as the children prepared for their ride, was Lady Gray's balloon, which was being inflated for another ascension. Lady Gray, dressed in pink tights with a life preserver under her arm, made her way through the crowd and strapped herself into her parachute. She gave the command "Let go!" and the balloon took off. A massive crowd of people rushed toward the fence that surrounded the lake to watch her dive, and George Eaton, according to park advertising agent Mr. Hannaford, stood up from his seat on Roger to get a better view of the balloon. The combination of the rushing wall of people and the balloon taking off startled Roger, whose trumpeting caused people to look away from the balloon. What they saw was terrifying.[20]

The frightened elephant's instinct was to get back to the safety of his corral. "He began whirling swiftly about in his frenzy," breaking Knight's nose, though whether it was a blow from his trunk or his foot that caused the injury varied in newspaper accounts. In the commotion, George Eaton fell from the seat and was trampled to death by Roger as he tried to return to his corral. As the crowd at the park first ran for safety and then returned to watch the struggle between Roger and his keeper, Knight tried to get the elephant, who still had four children on his back, under control. He sunk an iron hook into Roger's hide in an attempt to make him kneel, but that only caused Roger to whirl faster, throwing Knight to the ground. Mr. Weitseg, the assistant keeper, pulled Knight to safety through the corral fence. Knight came back with a pitchfork, which he pushed into Roger's trunk. He held Roger with the pitchfork while Weitseg and other animal house workers chained him. The remaining four children were removed from the seat "more scared than hurt," and while Knight continued to hold Roger, workers tried to remove the seat. Roger bellowed and threw the seat off his back, leading some to worry he was about to charge again. Knight forced Roger to lie down on his back, though, putting an end to his rampage.[21]

The *Rocky Mountain News* and the *Denver Times* attempted to one-up each other in their efforts to describe the shocking scene as graphically as possible. The *News* wrote of "a huge elephant, wild with the frenzy of fear, loose in a crowd of men, women, and children," and referred to Roger as an aroused beast, a frenzied

"ROGER'S" TERRIBLE CHARGE.

A drawing depicting Roger the Elephant and the death of George Eaton in 1891. This is the only image of Roger while he was at Manhattan Beach even though he was one of the park's star attractions. *Source: Rocky Mountain News*, July 5, 1891.

beast, and a maddened monster. In describing George Eaton's death, the *News* wrote "the huge foot of the animal was above the boy's head. It descended upon the white forehead! A human life was blotted out," and that "a great pool of blood poured from his head and the brains oozed out, making a horrible sight." The *Times* was far more graphic in its coverage, describing the scene as "the little fellow's head was shattered like an egg shell under the terrible weight of the monster and his brains were scattered upon the ground." After Roger was under control in his corral, the newspaper said "between the crowd and the elephant there was an open space, and in that space were strewn the brains of George Eaton." The tragedy even made national news, with stories appearing in newspapers throughout the country in the days after the incident.[22]

George Eaton was at Manhattan Beach that day with his parents, Pressley and Harriet, and a younger brother. After the accident, according to the *News*, Harriet threw herself at George's feet, refusing to believe he was dead, until being taken to the family's home at 3722 Franklin Street. Pressley Eaton remained at the park waiting for the coroner to arrive, saying "'I can't believe it. He was such a bright boy, our oldest. How we loved him and planned for his future. I don't know what to do. I can't realize what has happened. Ten thousand grounds like these couldn't pay us for his loss.'"[23]

George Eaton's body was carried first to an empty house that still stood on the park grounds and then to the coroner's office. A deputy sheriff present at the park (likely one of the off-duty police officers working as security) wanted the park to close, but George Darrow, president of the park, refused to do so. Most of the customers left on their own, however, generally expressing that it was a tragic accident and foolish to have put the balloon so close to the elephant. The park pledged to help the Eaton family in any way they could. George's official cause of death was listed as "killed by an elephant," and he was buried at Riverside Cemetery in Denver. The Eaton family eventually moved to Coeur d'Alene, Idaho, where Pressley farmed. In a sad coincidence, Pressley died in 1904 when he slipped on ice while hauling wood and fell over a cliff onto some rocks, his head "mashed to a jelly."[24]

Several people who were present at Manhattan Beach the day that George Eaton died defended Roger after the tragic accident. Jacob Sackett said he had known Roger since he was with Cole's Circus and never knew him to have an "ugly trait." W. A. Conklin, the manager of the Central Park Zoo, where Roger had lived before arriving at Manhattan Beach, said he had known the elephant for fifteen years in addition to having been his handler for five years, and described him as being as "gentle as a human being" and of the "kindest dispositions." Even the *Times* had to admit that Roger was a "mild eyed, good natured looking animal, who has been known for years to showmen as one of the most admirable and harmless beasts of his kind."[25]

The most enduring legend connected to Manhattan Beach is that Roger the elephant was put to death after causing George Eaton's death and buried in a swamp near the park. The simple fact is that no such thing ever happened. Roger was not, in fact, the property of Manhattan Beach, meaning they had no right to destroy him. And, if it had happened, it would have been made into a public spectacle. There are several well-documented cases of hard-to-control elephants being executed at amusement parks and zoos in the late 1890s and early 1900s, the most famous of which was Topsy, who was electrocuted at Coney Island in 1903. Instead, Roger remained a star attraction at Manhattan Beach until 1892 and was present for a dispute that would arise between the park and Elitch's just two months after George Eaton's death. By February of 1892, when passions had cooled considerably, the *Rocky Mountain News* even wrote that Roger "was the innocent cause of a boy's death" the previous summer.[26]

Business quickly returned to normal at Manhattan Beach, but trouble continued to keep the park in the newspapers for the remainder of its first summer. On July 26, 1891, Samuel King, another balloon performer, attempted to make an ascension from the park as a thunderstorm approached. The *Denver Republican* reported that 10,000 people were at the park that day and the sight of King's five yellow balloons being filled with gas was a big draw. Unfortunately for King, the balloons had not been used in a while and the varnish on the outside of them was not as airtight as would have been ideal, increasing the time it took to fill them with hydrogen gas. When the balloons finally achieved liftoff, a gust of wind pushed them into a light pole near where they were being inflated. Two men climbed the pole to try to free them, and between their efforts and several men pulling on the anchor rope, the balloons broke free and King floated high above the park. King sailed northeast from the park before heading south. When he disappeared from view, the crowd figured the demonstration was over, but for King, his frightening adventure was just beginning.[27]

King had flown directly into the approaching thunderstorm and "before the roaring clouds the balloons, now like one, swept swiftly through the sky." Afraid of what could happen if he did not get out of the storm, King pulled the valve cord of one of the balloons and began his descent near University Park. But a strong wind caught the balloons and dragged them along the ground more than two miles past the park until the basket caught on the bank of an irrigation ditch. His fall from the basket knocked King unconscious, but he awoke just in time to see his balloons drifting away in the storm. King caught a nearby streetcar and intended to return to Manhattan Beach, but bruised and in great pain, he decided to go to his hotel in downtown Denver instead. Despite the lousy end to the ascension, King told the *Republican* that before the crash he could see all of Denver below him in one of the "grandest scenes" he had ever witnessed from a balloon, though he was disappointed that the storm had blocked the mountains from view. Also impressive was the lightning, which he could see leave the clouds as the result of his "uncomfortable proximity" to them.[28]

The next month, on August 16, another ascension by Samuel King proved equally dramatic. That afternoon, Mary E. Johnson and William C. Hunt of Arvada were married at Manhattan Beach by Judge Talbot. As soon as they exchanged their vows, they joined King in the basket of his balloon. When the ropes were cut, it shot into the air. At 8,000 feet, King and the newlyweds encountered a thunderstorm that burst the balloon. The balloon and its passengers fell about 5,000 feet before the silk formed itself into a parachute, saving the occupants of the basket from certain death. They crashed into a cornfield about seven miles from the park, knocking them unconscious. The *Aspen Times Weekly* reported that an ascension by Ivy Baldwin and another newly married couple at Elitch Gardens the same day was completed without incident as Baldwin's balloon reached 13,000 feet. Like George Eaton's death, the trouble-plagued balloon ascension brought Manhattan Beach more national attention.[29]

Despite the troubles that seemed to plague the first summer at the new Manhattan Beach, thousands of people still flocked to the resort, especially on weekends, and everything appeared to be successful. Behind the scenes, though, things were not going as well. In addition to two mortgages on the property, the park's owners owed $60,000 to other creditors. In August, George Darrow, as president of the park company, signed an indenture for $60,000 that gave William D. Todd control of the park. Todd, who at the time worked for the investment firm of Donald Fletcher and Company, was the former cashier of both the Denver Savings Bank and Union National Bank, the two banks that had the mortgages on the park. Under the terms of the agreement, Todd was required to continue to maintain and operate Manhattan Beach for at least the next year to pay the park's bills, for which he received a $4,000 yearly salary. Perhaps in a move to earn money for the park, Adam Graff also sold his ice company to the Colorado Ice and Cold Storage Company for $18,000 in stock. Todd was required to honor that company's right to harvest ice on Sloan's Lake as part of the new agreement.[30]

Not included in the agreement with Todd was a $7,000 mortgage on the park's animals. With that in danger of being foreclosed on, an agreement was seemingly reached in court that would place Todd in charge of the animals as well. At the beginning of September, three people connected with Elitch's bought the mortgage and demanded immediate possession of the animals, which they intended to take to the rival park. Both the sheriff and coroner (who at the time was charged with taking control of property in cases of foreclosure) refused to allow Elitch's to take the animals due to the existing court order that required the animals to stay at Manhattan Beach.[31]

Elitch's hired Ed Keith, a private detective, to take the animals from Manhattan Beach by force if necessary. Keith rounded up about thirty-five men, described by the *Denver Times* as fellow detectives, and fifteen wagons to transport the animals. They set out from Elitch's, one mile north of Manhattan Beach, shortly after 5 a.m. on September 11, 1891. Just as residents of the Highlands had watched the animals arrive at Manhattan Beach in the midnight parade three months earlier, anyone who happened to be awake at that hour "beheld the awful panoply of war" as the so-called "Zoo War" began. The *Times* wrote of the "begrimed" drivers of the wagons, led by Sam Emerich, known locally as Sheeny Sam. According to the *Republican*, "the sun glinted over the mountain tops and the hostile forces right wheeled onto Byron avenue and formed in a hollow square" in front of the gates to the animal house on the east end of the park. Everything seemed quiet, and the *Republican* said "things were looking lovely for the besiegers."[32]

As Keith approached the gate, he heard a voice say, "Well I guess you fellows had better stop," followed by the appearance of a Winchester rifle held by John Kerwin. "The first one of you who attempts to get in here will get killed," Kerwin said. Far from being taken by surprise, the Manhattan Beach officials had been warned about what was planned and were prepared to defend the animals. The *Republican* reported that about fifty armed men were inside the park's gates, but both it and the *Times* said that only ten or twelve men were guarding the animal house. According to the *Times*, "each one was fired with determination to save Roger, the elephant, or die in the attempt." Tenor Huntingdon, one of the men at the animal house, reportedly had a brace of six-shooters and a Winchester rifle. Manhattan Beach employees had also attached the fire hoses to the hydrants inside the park with the nozzles aimed at the animal house gates. Keith convinced Kerwin to step outside the gates to talk, but Kerwin refused to let Keith take the animals. Kerwin went back inside the gates, which Keith said he was preparing to charge.[33]

The *Denver Times*, humorously depicting the fight as a battle between opposing forces, reported that C. O. Hatch had also enlisted the girls of the Wilber Opera Company, which had been performing at the park, supplying each with a pair of boots in the hopes that displaying them as a "skirmish line" rather than a chorus line, would throw off the invaders. As Keith and his detectives prepared to crash through the gates, Hatch held up an axe handle and shouted "fire!" The nozzles opened up and "belched out a deadly fire of Sloan's-lake water. The havoc was terrible. The begrimed veterans from the north shrank from the withering fire, and men were bathed in water who had never had a bath before." The lawyers for Manhattan Beach later said that the park people knew that "water had more terrors" for Keith's men than firearms would. Keith and his men gave up the charge, but they remained camped around Manhattan Beach for the rest of the day, apparently waiting to be paid off by Elitch's. Hatch told a reporter for the *Times* that Manhattan Beach was in the right, and that the "animals will die of old age before they will see Elitch's Gardens." Deputy sheriff Bob Stockton, who was in charge of the deputies at the park, backed Hatch, saying that if anyone from Elitch's attempted to take possession of any property at Manhattan Beach, "there will be bloodshed."[34]

The day after the "Zoo War," the attorneys for Manhattan Beach, Pence and Pence, released a statement saying that the failed attempt to seize the animals was nothing more than an attempt to "alarm the public and create the impression that Manhattan Beach has lost its attractions" ahead of several large picnics that were scheduled at the park. Pence and Pence, in the statement, again argued that the law was on Manhattan Beach's side, and said that the park would "pay off the mortgage before the animals were sold or lose the animals, but they will not be taken by any such efforts as these made last night." The matter quickly went into court on September 12, where Judge David Graham refused "to consider charges that the animals were being mistreated, and decided that they should remain at the beach, and that the gates should be thrown open and the place conducted as usual." Roger the elephant and the other animals remained at Manhattan Beach, which quietly finished out its first season. It had been turbulent, but the park had survived. However, Elitch's was not yet done with Manhattan Beach, and in the coming year a new rival, the ongoing battle over Thomas Sloan's estate, and financial problems would cause even more trouble for the park.[35]

## CHAPTER 2

# Manhattan Beach and the Southern Investment Company

DURING THE WINTER, ICE SKATING ON SLOAN'S LAKE REMAINED a popular pastime, and Manhattan Beach tried other events to keep people coming to the grounds. On January 24, 1892, the park offered horse racing on the frozen lake. The first race was a three-minute, half-mile race with a $100 purse. The second race was a free-for-all with trotting and pacing for a half mile with a $150 purse. Ice cutters still harvested ice from the lake as well under the agreement that Adam Graff had put in place when he sold his ice company the previous year. But, overall, the year 1892 did not start well for Manhattan Beach.[1]

Financial problems continued to plague the park, and elephant trainer Fred Knight, responsible for feeding all of the animals in the zoo, had to cut expenses even there. A reporter for the *Rocky Mountain News* visited the park in late February and found Roger the elephant "surly" as he was getting only five small bales of hay and half a bushel of grain each day. The reporter wrote that Roger seemed to still feel "sorrow over the sad event [the death of George Eaton the previous July], for he swayed to and fro and shook his trunk with a vigorous swing that would have left little help for John L. if he had come within range." Recent snowstorms had also made it impossible to get Roger or any of the other animals out for exercise for fear they would sink into the soft ground. On top of those troubles, two of the park's ostriches contracted consumption and died from the disease, while a chick had to be put down after it fell through a crack in the animal house floor and broke its leg. The skins of the two adult ostriches were sent to a taxidermist to make museum displays while the meat was fed to the lions. The *News* speculated that the owner of the ostriches, who lived in Coronado, California, would demand the return of the surviving birds due to the health issues. To prevent losing some of the zoo's most popular residents, William Todd, the trustee running the park under the agreement with George Darrow, purchased the ostriches himself.[2]

The zoo remained open throughout the offseason but there were few visitors during the snowy winter. In March, baseball season started, with the Manhattan Beach team playing the Cooper Lake team at the park. The Manhattan Beach team was victorious, beating Cooper Lake by a score of 20 to 12. And, despite the financial troubles, management had a number of improvements planned or already underway for the coming season. The beach itself received a new layer of sand, new trees were planted throughout the park, and the lawns and walks were "beautified." An additional thirty-five boats joined the fleet already at the boathouse, along with several swan boats that were special-ordered from New York. Renovations also opened both ends of the boathouse, allowing access from all four sides. All of the boats used during the previous season were thoroughly overhauled, and the boiler on the *City of Denver* was "legally inspected in the interest of safety." The bathhouse was renovated as well, and the bottom of the lake sanded and graveled 100 yards out from the shore for the comfort of swimmers.[3]

All of the buildings at the park were cleaned up and restocked ahead of opening day in May, and the *Denver Republican* wrote that "the general view of the grounds, the beach and the symmetrical architecture of the buildings is the first thing that pleasantly

The *City of Denver* steamship on Sloan's Lake in the early 1890s.
*Source:* The Denver Public Library, Western History Collection, X-27720.

impresses the visitor as he enters the gateway." Under construction as opening day approached was a new summer house on the park's west lawn. Covered with English ivy, the new structure provided tables and chairs for people who brought basket lunches to the park. Also new for the 1892 season was the park's first amusement park–type attraction, a steam-powered Parisian carousel. Based on the description in the *Republican*, it was a menagerie-style carousel with a variety of animals. Some park employees were worried that the swan boats would be more popular with children than the carousel, but the two attractions seemed to be equally in demand. A newly constructed trapeze in front of the animal house would be the site of acrobatic demonstrations throughout the summer.[4]

Changes were also underway at the theater, which was "the most drawing attraction at the beach." The new paint scheme at the theater was "light and gay" and also fireproof, which, along with several other unnamed features, according to the *Republican*, made the frame building as fireproof as a frame building could be. In case there did happen to be a fire, the many exits from the building were quite large. In the west wing of the theater was a new "handsomely furnished ladies' reception room," and management also added fifteen new sets of scenery to the available stock of sets. With the owners spending almost $200,000 on the park since its opening, the *Republican* said "the resort now has excellent financial prospects."[5]

"Everything was bustle and confusion" as workers prepared for the season opener on Sunday, May 15. Opening day was "as beautiful as could be desired" and came after a week of heavy rain and a "spell of bad weather as has not been experienced in years." More than 10,000 people passed through the gates that day. Manhattan Beach's opera season opened that afternoon with a performance of *The Beggar Student* starring James Duran, Edgar Temple, Carroll Daly, Katherine McNeal, and Ethel Vincent. Also part of the company for the season were Charles Huntington (who was the park's amusement manager), Jessie and Eva Mayhew, and Mr. Rawnsley, in addition to thirty-four people in the chorus. The *Rocky Mountain News* said that the opening performance was standing room only and that the new company was much better

Looking west toward the theater and streetcar station at Manhattan Beach. The steamboat dock is on the left and the dance pavilion is on the right. *Source:* The Denver Public Library, Western History Collection, F31092.

than the previous season's. The second opera of the season was *Olivette*, followed by *Boccaccio*.[6]

After the opera performance officially opened the season, Harry Bower performed "a number of difficult aerial stunts" on the park's new trapeze. Later that month the park even brought in a sharpshooter to shoot eggs from Bower's hand while he was on the trapeze. The zoo was popular with children on opening day, especially the ostriches and monkeys, but "Old Roger . . . had his fill of peanuts and popcorn, and he seemed to be delighted to see his friends again after their long winter exile." There was no mention of any children riding on Roger, so that attraction had most likely been dropped after the tragedy the previous season. The *Rocky Mountain News* reported that no mishaps spoiled opening day and that pickpockets were scarce. The only notable incident came when Henry Howard, "a smooth worker," stole Charles Hawk's gold pocket watch near the animal house. Sam Davis, who was in charge of the police officers stationed at Manhattan Beach, spotted Howard, recovered the watch, and sent Howard to jail.[7]

As usual, the lake was a popular attraction, "dotted during the afternoon with numerous row boats" while children received free rides on the *City of Denver*. That summer the park instituted Children's Day every Saturday, which allowed all children under 12 a free ride on the steamboat and free admission to the theater. Three bands provided live entertainment at the café throughout the summer: Professor Richter's military band, the Hungarian Girls Band, and the Sanford Sisters band from Boston. Achille Philon, who was famous in the 1890s for his spiral tower performances, replaced Harry Bower on the park's trapeze, performing two shows a day. Professor Belden and Lady Gray also regularly performed balloon ascension and parachute drops at the park.[8]

Still under construction on opening day was a new water toboggan, which advertisements described as "something entirely new" but was most likely a waterslide, and the park's new bowling alley was ready for opening day. Ready by early July was another

Looking east toward the zoo building at Manhattan Beach. The steamboat dock and dance pavilion are in the foreground, and the white-roofed structure behind and to the left of the steamboat dock is the merry-go-round building. The small brick structure between the steamboat dock and zoo building is a gent's bathroom. *Source:* The Denver Public Library, Western History Collection, F5867.

amusement attraction, the park's new camera obscura, which proved a popular advertising point throughout the summer. While those new attractions were still being readied, in June, the opera company staged *The Mikado*, *The Mascot*, and *The Gondoliers* at the theater. Despite the ever-increasing number of attractions, the park's theater remained its primary draw and the primary focus in advertising. Always looking to find more uses for Sloan's Lake, the park also held its first swimming competition that summer between the champions of Colorado and California. Although the Denver newspapers did not report the names of the contestants, they did say that both men were members of trade unions, which brought heavy union patronage to the park for the contest.[9]

Manhattan Beach's Fourth of July celebration included a morning balloon ascension by Belden and an afternoon ascension by Lady Gray. Instead of rides on Roger, visitors to the park got to watch him receive his annual bath. There were also a number of athletic events to mark the day, including a 120-yard foot race, a sack race, and a hammer-throwing contest that included a $25 prize. On the lake there were four-oared and double-oared scull races, each one mile in length. The day ended with a "grand display of fireworks on the lake." One advertisement in the *Rocky Mountain News* for the day proclaimed that "this afternoon you can see more interesting and amusing things at Manhattan Beach than you can see anywhere in this city." For July, the operas at the park included *Giroflé-Girofla*, *Bohemian Girl*, *Princess Trebizonde*, *Amorita*, and *The Grand Duchess*. July also brought a new star, Adelaide Randall, who was especially popular with Denver audiences.[10]

Near the end of July, the *Rocky Mountain News* wrote that "there are in all probability very few residents of the city to whom the attractions of this resort are unknown." The newspaper credited the lake and opera company with most of that success, but park management continued to bring in new attractions to keep people coming back. That month the Gillette Family replaced Achille Philon on the trapeze. The three members of the family performed twice daily. In addition to their acrobatic act, they also performed a bicycle act, though whether it was on the trapeze or on the ground is unclear. To remind people of just how much there was to do at the park, one ad told readers there were "Cool Breezes, Good Fishing, Boat Rides, Clear Bathing, the Electric Fountain, the Elephants and Tigers, a Magnificent Zoo, the Camera Obscura and a million things to amuse." The park even began to attract company picnics. On July 11, 1892, the May Shoe and Clothing Company hosted its annual employee picnic at Manhattan Beach. Nearly 4,000 people were in attendance, watching performances of *Bohemian Girl*, dancing in the café to the music of the Sanders Sisters after dinner, and watching a "magnificent display" of fireworks on the lake at midnight.[11]

August's operas included a repeat of *The Gondoliers* in addition to *Pinafore* and *Falks*, but there was a noticeable decrease in the amount of new offerings at the park. Other than Spanish and Gypsy dances by Frances Grey, park management relied on the standbys of Lady Gray's balloon ascensions and "boating, bathing, fishing." On September 7, the *Rocky Mountain News* announced that the opera season at the park was closing after an unprofitable few weeks, and the park seemingly closed for the season along with the opera, although the *City of Denver* continued to operate on Sloan's Lake into November. While publicly Manhattan Beach had seemed successful in 1892, behind the scenes things had been messy.[12]

As trustee, William Todd had done his best to get the park ready for the 1892 season, but a new player became involved in the park's finances in February. Captain William D. Bethell was born in Louisiana in 1840. He was a farmer there before joining the Confederate Army during the Civil War. After the war he resumed farming, but in 1883 he moved to Memphis and started investing in a variety of businesses. He also became politically active and was elected mayor of Memphis in 1891, a largely symbolic position that he filled while living in Denver. Bethell suffered a physical breakdown in 1891, and he and his family moved to Denver, where they built a large mansion at Colfax and Marion (it was later the home of Senator Lawrence Phipps).[13]

In February of 1892, Bethell bought $85,000 worth of Manhattan Beach bonds, followed by $15,000 more in March as well as the $10,000 mortgage on the park's animals. Samuel Rose, Bethell's lawyer, denied all knowledge of the transactions, but brokers who were aware of the large sale told the *Rocky Mountain News* that Bethell was "so well satisfied" with the purchase that he told his agents to buy as many of the bonds as possible. Bethell's bonds essentially gave him control of the park company, and he added four new members to the board of directors: his son-in-law Dr. John M. Foster, Roger Woodbury, M. J. McNamara, and Joseph Creswell. Adam Graff remained as treasurer.[14]

In July, the bonds that Bethell held on the park came due and, with Graff and the other original owners of the park unable to pay them, they went up for auction on July 9. Bethell was the only bidder on them, giving him further control over the park's operation. Ownership of the bonds went to Bethell's newly formed Southern Investment Company, which was organized on June 25. Bethell himself was not personally involved with this new company, but the founders and first board of directors included his son Pinckney, son-in-law John P. Edrington, his lawyer and former Memphis resident Samuel Rose, and future Manhattan Beach manager Robert L. Giffen. The purpose of the new company was to invest in and loan money on real estate and stocks, and its first big investment was Manhattan Beach. A little over a month later, on July 29, William Todd resigned as trustee of Manhattan Beach for health reasons. Under the terms of the trustee agreement, a committee made up of M. J. McNamara, W. W. Borst, and Joseph Creswell had to appoint a new trustee. They chose Bethell's son-in-law, Dr. Foster. By the end of July, Bethell's grip on Manhattan Beach was getting tighter and tighter.[15]

In mid-September, a little more than a week after Manhattan Beach closed for the season, Bethell insisted that the park property be sold to pay its debts. He, of course, intended to buy it at auction, giving him total ownership of it. At that point, Theodore Schrott and Ernst Steinke, who held a mortgage on Manhattan Beach and were two of the original partners when Adam Graff opened Sloan's Park in 1890, filed a lawsuit trying to stop the sale. Both Captain Bethell and Dr. Foster claimed that Bethell had nothing to do with operating the park while Todd was in charge of it. But, in a deposition taken on September 19, 1892, F. E. Wilcox testified that he had tried to rent the park the previous April and that the one sticking point had been his insistence that Todd pay one-half the cost of having an orchestra at the café. Todd said, according to Wilcox, that he could not agree to that without first talking to Bethell. Todd went on to say that Bethell was supplying the money to run Manhattan Beach, which the *Rocky Mountain News* had also reported as far back as March of that year when Bethell had increased the size of the board of directors. Todd had also approached Bethell for money to run the park in April of that year, writing to him that he would need $8,000 to pay for labor, fuel, and feed in order to keep the park running.[16]

Several other park employees also testified to Bethell's role in the park. John C. Houber, a bookkeeper at the park, testified on September 19 that Bethell had been in full control of Manhattan Beach since July 19. Between July and September, the park had made $18,461, and had expenses of $14,300, leaving a profit of a little over $4,100. Edgar Temple, a tenor with the opera, testified that Bethell had told him, however, that he "did not care whether Manhattan Beach made money or not, that he did not care to have it make any money at that time, and that he . . . wanted said Manhattan Beach property and would get it." By apparently preventing the park from paying its debts, Bethell seemed to be guaranteeing that the park would have to be sold at auction. After securing testimony from several people connected with the park, Schrott and Steinke's lawsuit stalled. In fact, in 1914, Dr. Foster asked the court to finally dismiss the suit as Schrott, Steinke, and their lawyer had all long since died. By the end of 1893, Adam Graff was also gone from his role as treasurer at the park.[17]

When Captain Bethell effectively took control of Manhattan Beach in July, he arranged a surprise meeting with A. B. McGaffey and John Carleton, the president and general manager of Elitch Gardens, on the evening of July 22, to discuss a joint management agreement between the two parks. The men agreed that each park would charge twenty-five cents for admission, twenty-five cents for parquet seats, and fifteen cents for dress circle seats and give free admission to the balconies at their theaters. The new agreement also put Mary Elitch in charge of the Manhattan Beach theater. Ownership of the parks remained separate, and both John Foster and McGaffey were firm in their denials that the two park companies were merging. Management at both parks viewed the new agreement as a chance to present a united front to the streetcar companies and try to force a change in fares so that people did not have to pay two fares to reach both parks. Elitch's and Manhattan Beach had both lost money that summer, according to the *Rocky Mountain News*, as they attempted to one-up each other with new attractions at the parks. The new agreement also presented an opportunity to not have to constantly compete with each other through newer and bigger attractions. With the new agreement, Charles Huntington resigned from the opera company and as manager of the park. Richard B. Mays took over as the new manager.[18]

In addition to trying to save money at each park, the new joint agreement may have also come about as a result of a new rival for the two parks. Arlington Park occupied thirty acres of land located along the banks of Cherry Creek, with the main entrance on Corona Street. The creation of Denver's police commissioner (and future mayor) Robert Speer, postmaster John Corcoran, and businessman Henry W. Michael, the park's main feature was a half-mile long man-made lake with a floating stage that would feature pyrotechnic shows produced by James Pain. Other attractions at the park included a baseball field, tennis court, and summer theater. Opening Day on July 4 drew 13,000 people to the new park, overwhelming Denver's streetcar lines. The 11,000-seat grandstand was packed to capacity for the inaugural production of *The Last Days of Pompeii*, which ended with Mt. Vesuvius erupting and the entire stage sinking (on purpose) into the lake. By the beginning of August, more than 45,000 people had seen the *Pompeii* production and had enjoyed the park's concerts and other plays. Although it lacked a zoo, Arlington Park promised to be a worthy rival to Elitch's and Manhattan Beach.[19]

Aside from financial difficulties and ownership changes, Manhattan Beach also faced trouble that summer from the bars that sprang up in Edgewater across Sheridan Boulevard from the park. One of the worst offenders, according to many residents, was Ernst Steinke's Golden Gate, a large outdoor beer garden operated by the one-time owner of Sloan's Park. The Golden

Gate was surrounded by a wooden fence that "shut in the celebrants but not the loud music, obscenities, and roisterings" of the customers. A Denver brewery, according to Edgewater historian Alice Coleman, sponsored a contest to see which saloon could sell the most beer, resulting in "towering pyramids of empty wooden beer kegs" outside the doors of most of the saloons. Mixed in with the saloons were gambling dens and, according to one history of Edgewater, a brothel operated by famed Denver madam Mattie Silks. On occasion a customer at Manhattan Beach, which did not serve liquor, would slip through the fence around the park and bring beer back from one of the saloons. Alice Coleman writes that these customers then rented rowboats and "from an advantageous position out on the lake, bombarded the Park and its patrons with empty bottles."[20]

By the summer of 1892 the saloons had become such a nuisance that people were begging the Highlands City Council, which then had control of the area, to do something about them. William Todd told Highlands officials on June 13 "these joints were a great nuisance and should be rigidly exterminated at once and by all means. The resort management . . . would be glad to see it done, and would do all in their power to aid the movement." Jefferson County residents circulated a petition asking the Highlands City Council to close the bars. Sheriff Samuel Poe vowed to arrest "lawless saloonkeepers" and, on July 5, the Highlands City Council vowed to wage a "vigorous war" against the saloons. Despite the pledge, the trouble with the saloons around the park would continue for many years.[21]

With his ownership of the park seemingly secure, and government officials vowing to fight the saloons, Captain Bethell and the Southern Investment Company began work on a new round of changes at Manhattan Beach in October of 1892. The new owners ordered twenty-five new boats for the lake, and also started working on a new electric plant and waterworks at a cost of $15,000. Also under construction was a new 60-foot by

100-foot animal house with a "lofty roof and most modern exhibition interior arrangements." The *Rocky Mountain News* reported that with the new changes the park "will be in better condition than ever before to fill the needs of a first class suburban resort by the time spring comes again." But there was one last surprise in store for 1892 as the legal trouble over Thomas Sloan's estate threatened to derail Bethell's plans for the park.[22]

In December of 1892, Thomas Sloan's son William, who was a lawyer and a retired judge living in Santa Fe, New Mexico, announced that he had found his sister Clarissa's daughter, Ida W. Chambers, a long-lost heir to the Sloan estate. Clarissa Sloan Fitch had died in 1860 and the Sloan family had lost touch with her husband Edward and daughter Ida. Judge Sloan announced that he was helping Ida and several other heirs prepare a lawsuit over the 160 acres around Sloan's Lake that included Manhattan Beach in addition to thirty-seven and one-half acres in Highlands.

Looking west across Sloan's Lake toward Manhattan Beach with the theater about in the center. The roller coaster barely visible to the left of the building behind the boater might be the park's 1893 coaster. *Source:* The Denver Public Library, Western History Department, F7357.

Ida Chambers and five other Sloan heirs were reportedly hiring General Benjamin Butler as their legal counsel with plans to file a lawsuit in February of 1893.[23]

News of the discovery of the lost Sloan heir made headlines in Denver and Iowa. The *Rocky Mountain News* referred to Ida Chambers as "an heiress," while the *Quad-City Times* of Davenport, Iowa, called her "a child of fortune." Judge Sloan's threatened lawsuit was just the latest in a long line of lawsuits over title to the land around Sloan's Lake that had been raging since 1883. The Arapahoe County Probate Court had appointed James Strickler as executor of Thomas Sloan's estate when he died in 1874. In 1877 Strickler asked the court for permission to sell the land around Sloan's Lake to settle the estate's debts. With court approval granted, Strickler sold the land to Margaret Higgins of Rio Grande County for $5,900. The Sloan family, guided by Thomas Sloan's daughter Amanda Lockwood, filed the first lawsuit seeking to overturn the sale in 1883. The Colorado Supreme Court ruled in favor of the Sloan family in 1884 and again in 1885 and 1888 when Strickler appealed the decision. Then, in 1889, the court reversed itself and found in favor of Strickler. The Sloan family then appealed the case to the United States Supreme Court which, in October of 1891, ruled in favor of Strickler and his sale of the property. The matter seemed to rest there until William Sloan, taking over the fight for his sister Amanda, who had died in April of 1892, found his missing niece and threatened another lawsuit in December of 1892.[24]

Much of the Sloan family's argument for overturning Strickler's sale of the property centered on the heirs not receiving proper notice of the 1877 hearing when he had asked for permission to do so. With the appearance of Ida Chambers, the Sloans must have hoped that the presence of a new heir—whom no one knew about and who had obviously not been notified about the hearing— might change the outcome of the recent Supreme Court decision. Even though the family promised to get high-profile attorneys involved in the case, and the Denver newspapers suggested that the suit might be successful, there is no evidence to indicate that Judge Sloan ever actually filed his lawsuit. Perhaps eight years of battling, and a defeat in the United States Supreme Court, finally convinced the Sloan family that their fight was hopeless. After 1892, Sloan's Lake and the land around it remained firmly in the hands of the Bethell family.[25]

# CHAPTER 3

# A Fine Outing

WHILE THE SLOAN FAMILY THREATENED TO FILE THEIR LAW-
suit to recover ownership of Sloan's Lake, in mid-January 1893,
Manhattan Beach's management announced that professor Frank
Saase, who had led the Silver Dollar band in Boulder, would be
in charge of the park's orchestra for the coming summer. The park
had also added two new bears to the zoo over the winter. The cin-
namon bear, kept in a cage outside the main animal house, immediately dug his way out of the cage, dug a hole under the building,
crawled in, and went into hibernation. Unfortunately, tragedy
claimed the park's new black bear. While it was being transferred
from its temporary cage to the new bear den at the zoo, the keeper
had some trouble with it. Enraged, he picked up an iron bar and
struck the bear several times, fracturing its skull and killing it. He
was immediately discharged and the park secured a new black
bear before opening for the summer.[1]

Ice skating remained a popular winter attraction on Sloan's
Lake, with the *West Side Citizen* calling the lake "a positive mag-
net these times to the many lovers of the pastime of skating." Ice
skating also kept people coming to Manhattan Beach, where the
zoo again remained open for the winter. The park also became
the winter quarters for Raymond's Circus, which kept its animals
at the zoo. During their winter stay they did lose one of their

elephants to old age (one article claimed it was the oldest elephant in the world at age 112), but they also had a lion cub born at the park.[2]

As Manhattan Beach prepared to open for the summer on May 28, 1893, the *Rocky Mountain News* declared that it "was in better shape and prettier than ever." Management enlarged the lawns throughout the park grounds and put out thousands of blooming flowers. New swings and other free amusements for children were scattered throughout the grounds, and the *West Side Citizen* said that women and children would especially appreciate the new seating areas and the shade from trees, arbors, and summer houses. Workers gave all of the park's buildings and the park's fleet of boats a fresh coat of paint.[3]

The park's new opera company for the summer, its first under the creative control of Mary Elitch, included prima donnas Beatrice Goldie and Pattie Henry, contralto Gertrude Eastman, tenors Hamilton Perley and Will A. Collins, baritone Mack Charles, and comedians George M. Herbert and James Doran. The first production of the season was *Fatinitza* followed by *The*

A group, including two Black children, ice skating on Sloan's Lake in the early 1900s. The Figure 8 Toboggan Roller Coaster is next to the zoo building in the background. *Source:* History Colorado, Object # HC 89.570.2.

*Black Hussar*. New costumes and sets at the theater, added to those from the 1892 season, made for an impressive array of stage effects and the *West Side Citizen* said the theater would "merit the approval and patronage of the Denver amusement loving public."[4]

With Denver's streetcar companies providing extra cars to handle the crowds, thousands of people once again turned out to enjoy Manhattan Beach on opening day of its third season. The *Rocky Mountain News* called the performance of *Fatinitza* "charming," with the cast "thoroughly able" to do it justice. An added musical attraction for opening weekend were two daily concerts by Denver's Philharmonic Society that included some of the best-known soloists in the city. After successful productions of *Fatinitza* and *The Black Hussar*, the opera company staged *The Musketeers*, which proved another popular draw.[5]

While Mary Elitch's management of the theater resulted in highly praised productions, by mid-June Manhattan Beach's management suggested that it did not need to rely on operas at the theater to draw visitors to the park. The *Rocky Mountain News* hinted that the opera season might even end early that summer and said that the "great charm" of Manhattan Beach over Denver's other summer resorts was the lake and the boating, bathing, and fishing that guests could engage in. While Arlington Park did have its man-made lake, it never offered boating or fishing, with management instead using the lake for productions on the stage and other special events such as diving elk or bicycle jumps. In 1898 new management at Arlington Park built a shoot-the-chutes that ended in the lake, but that was the extent of amusement attractions on that park's lake. Elitch's also had a lake, located at the southwest corner of the park, but it was not a major part of their entertainment offerings during the years it existed. However, any plans to close Manhattan Beach's theater early during the 1893 season quickly disappeared. Over the next few weeks *Iolanthe* and *The Pirates of Penzance* drew large crowds to the theater and customers went away "praising the way the operas are produced."[6]

Manhattan Beach continued to offer balloon ascensions and parachute jumps, as usual, but Lady Gray and Professor Belden made no appearances in 1893. They were replaced by a team that included Professor Hutchinson, Ruby DeVeau, Little Daisy, Tiffany, and Mr. Clew. Ruby DeVeau was the best known of the group, having made her first ascension and jump the year before at age 15. For the group's appearance at Manhattan Beach, they performed two different stunts. In one, Hutchinson, Ruby DeVeau, and Tiffany ascended together in one balloon and then parachuted out, one after the other. (Ruby sometimes performed this stunt with Little Daisy and Clew at Manhattan Beach that summer as well.) In their other stunt, three members of the group would go up in separate balloons and, presumably, parachute out of them. Ruby DeVeau's parachute jumping career came to an end in 1895 when she broke her back after crashing into a chimney during a jump in Canada. She later became a stenographer.[7]

The theater, the lake, and balloon ascensions were popular draws as usual for Manhattan Beach that summer, but people found another amusement attraction under construction for most of the summer far more interesting. On June 22, the *Rocky Mountain News* reported that "interest just now" was focused on Denver's first roller coaster, which was quickly taking shape at the park. The world's first roller coaster was built in France in 1804, and refinements and new inventions in the years that followed continued to transform the ride. Roller coasters began appearing at pleasure resorts in the United States in the 1870s. Further changes to the ride in the 1880s by inventors at Coney Island led to the form familiar to most people with an oval track and hills and dips. William Guigon, a roller coaster builder from Coney Island, had visited Manhattan Beach and Elitch's in March of 1893 looking for a place to build a new coaster that would be the "greatest chute west of New York, and a credit to the city."

While it is unclear if Guigon was involved with the ride at Manhattan Beach, the *News* said that the new coaster would be a "great attraction" and reported on July 2 that it was being built "as fast as possible." On August 4 the newspaper said it was being "rapidly finished," and soon after that management announced that the roller coaster would be free on Saturdays and Sundays to anyone who paid gate admission. Management carried over free Sunday rides on the steamboat, free carousel rides every day, and free seats in the theater balcony from the previous season, all in an effort to draw customers to the park. The roller coaster carried its first passengers in mid-August, and the park's ads proclaimed "the roller coaster craze is on." The *Rocky Mountain News* wrote "the roller coaster is the biggest thing out. It works like a charm and will please everybody who tries it." Rival Elitch Gardens was also reported throughout the summer to be building its own roller coaster, but it apparently never came to be. The park would have to wait until 1904 to get its first coaster.[8]

Aside from the roller coaster, Manhattan Beach's management constantly looked for new ways to draw customers to the park. Nightly fireworks displays, band concerts three times per week, and Saza the lioness and her three cubs at the zoo all helped to bring people through the gates. In July, the *Rocky Mountain News* described the visitors to the park as "a continuous parade of prettily attired girls, with their beaux" and said that they made the walks at Manhattan Beach "resemble a boulevard in some foreign city, so cosmopolitan were they in appearance." Opera performances for July included *The Chimes of Normandy*, *Olivette*, and *Amorita*. The *Colorado Daily Farmer* said on July 26 that Manhattan Beach "makes a fine outing trip any time. Go out and try it," but by then Denver and all of Colorado were deep in a depression caused by the collapse of the silver market.[9]

Since 1890, the federal government had been purchasing silver for coinage under the Sherman Silver Purchase Act. A series of economic problems led to a drain on American gold reserves in 1893, which in turn led to Congress repealing the Sherman Silver Purchase Act on June 27, 1893. Within two days, the price of silver dropped twenty cents to sixty-two cents per ounce. Silver mines throughout the state closed, putting thousands of miners out of work. With the state's economy largely dependent on silver, Colorado found itself in deep trouble economically. Elitch Gardens reportedly enjoyed record crowds seeking an escape from the hard times, but Arlington Park and Manhattan Beach took hits from the bad times. William Bethell was not invested in mining so the downturn did not hurt him personally, but with so many people in Denver dependent on the mining industry, it did hurt the park's customer base.[10]

Manhattan Beach's management carried on throughout the downturn, providing an escape for Denverites who could afford to come to the park during the economic troubles. In August they staged *The Grand Duchess*, a repeat performance of *Giroflé-Girofla*, *Fra Diavolo*, and *Dorothy* at the theater. They also added athletic events that included boat races, sack races, potato races, tub races, and foot races on Sundays. The foot races included $200 in prizes, welcome money for many at the time. Saza the lioness and her three cubs made their debut at the end of August, much to the delight of many who were uncertain if the cubs would survive. As Labor Day and the end of the season approached, the *Rocky Mountain News* wrote that "lovers of aquatic pastimes, fresh breezes and well-rendered light opera are availing themselves of the few days which remain to enjoy themselves." Denver's trade and labor unions took over the park on Labor Day with speeches, parades, and races (including a fat men's race where competitors had to be 5'9" or shorter and weight at least 215 pounds). When the festivities concluded the park closed for the winter.[11]

While it had been a relatively subdued summer at Manhattan Beach, in large part due to the silver crash, it was not without its share of trouble. As part of the joint operating agreement the two parks had worked out the previous year, Elitch's and Manhattan

Beach had stopped giving free park passes to members of the press. This particularly upset the *West Side Citizen*, which on August 4, 1893, wrote "respectable people will hesitate to take their families to Manhattan beach, where all hard characters congregate." Two weeks later, the editors of the newspaper wrote "Elitch's gardens and the chippie Manhattan beach have become so tough that respectable people hesitate to go there any more." The following year, as Manhattan Beach prepared to open for the summer, the editors publicly revealed the cause of their sudden turn against the park they had once praised as they wrote that they hoped management would "realize the benefits of liberality to the press which they last year ignored." The helpful suggestion apparently fell on deaf ears, though, as the newspaper continued its attacks on the park into 1895. Outside of the newspaper's editors, no one seemed to care. At the beginning of July 1893, two orphanages and a Sunday School brought their children to the park for two large picnics. The outings led the *Rocky Mountain News* to write that it was "an unusual scene of brilliancy and color" and the children "made all the noise their little lungs could produce" as they swarmed the ice cream stand, rowboats, and steamship and "simply filled this delightful place with all sorts of gay and laughing scenes."[12]

The saloons, gambling halls, and other such establishments around Manhattan Beach remained a problem throughout the 1893 season. Questionable and colorful characters frequented the area, such as a man who showed up in early July and called himself Sheriff Duckett of Aspen. After carefully sizing up the crowd at one of the saloons, he bet them that he could eat a live chicken, feathers and all, in less than fifteen minutes. Once the terms were settled, someone purchased a chicken from a nearby grocer. Ten minutes later, the chicken consumed, the man collected his $50 in winnings, drank a cold beer, and disappeared. Disgusted by this and other antics at the saloons, on the morning of September 8, 1893, just a few days after Manhattan Beach closed for the season, someone set fire to Ernst Steinke's Golden Gate saloon and Jim Hawley's saloon. Fanned by a strong wind, the fire quickly spread to the other saloons, destroying the Electric Palace and Free Coinage along with the Golden Gate and Hawley's place. The fire then swept across Sheridan Boulevard in "big sheets of flame," destroying the streetcar station and restaurant at the entrance to Manhattan Beach. Firemen arriving on the scene quickly realized the saloons were a total loss and turned their efforts to saving Manhattan Beach where the theater, despite a thick coating of asbestos paint, was smoking and had several small fires on its roof. Through quick work the firemen managed to save the building, and when a reporter for the *Colorado Evening Sun* encountered Captain Bethell at the park later that morning, he found him "congratulating himself on escaping with so slight a loss."[13]

Little changed at Manhattan Beach over the winter, and management decided to open the park at the end of April for the 1894 season after initially planning to open in June. The theater, where Robert Giffen planned to start a new comedy company to replace Mary Elitch's company, remained closed until June, however. Several new animals had taken up residence in the zoo over the winter, including mountain lions, monkeys, and baby lions. The park's other attractions, including the roller coaster, carousel, and swings, were available but the bathing beach remained closed until later in the season due to sometimes chilly weather. The members of the theater company, including leading lady Henrietta Crossman, arrived at the park at the end of May to begin rehearsals for the first production, *The Galley Slave.* The play would feature new scenery constructed by the theater manager, who was also overseeing extensive renovations to the inside of the theater. Other members of the company included comedian Harry Corson Clarke, the Blancke sisters, Franklin Roberts, and Mamie Ryan.[14]

The theater finally opened for the summer on June 3, 1894, and the *Rocky Mountain News* reported that the production of *The*

*Galley Slave* was well received by the public, "and the staging of the bright little play was well all that could be desired." The park itself was packed as well, especially after a week of bad weather that had preceded the day. The following week, the play *An Unequal Match* replaced *The Galley Slave* and brought the Bethell family to the park, where they hosted a theater party for fifty people. After a week's run, the plays *Not If I Know It* and *Broken Ties* replaced *An Unequal Match* at the theater with Harry Corson Clarke taking on the lead roles in both plays. A few weeks after opening, management decided to allow children into the theater for free, which resulted in large numbers of children attending nearly every performance after that.[15]

While the theater was the top draw, management continued to stage other events to help attract visitors. Near the end of June, E. P. Hastings, a bridge diver, agreed to appear at the park for a series of diving and swimming events. Hastings had already achieved some fame for his dives from the Brooklyn Bridge as well as bridges in Memphis and Peoria. Hastings and his team constructed a 100-foot-high tower near the park's boathouse. The *Rocky Mountain News* reported that the highest dive on record at the time was by a man named Burn, who leapt from a 96-foot-high tower into the Thames River in London. Hastings was clearly hoping to break that record, and he tested the tower for safety several times before his first dive on June 24, 1894. A large crowd turned out to watch. After successfully making his dive, Hastings performed several "difficult aquatic feats," including "fancy, trick and scientific work in the water, showing the new methods of swimming, in which both safety and ease are explained."[16]

In the week after Hastings's first dive, the park staged a combination of more tower dives by Hastings and balloon ascensions by La Reine. Near the beginning of July, La Reine added a parachute drop to his ascensions, but it was the ascensions by Stinson and Graves in the middle of that month that proved to be the most popular of the summer. The *News* described Stinson and Graves as "two men with more daring than is ordinarily displayed even by martyrs to heroism" when they arrived at the park with two balloons and a large cannon. Stinson and Graves had performed their act at Fairmount Park in Kansas City before arriving at Manhattan Beach. For the act, the cannon was tied to the two balloons, with one of the men in each balloon. After rising to a height of 4,000 to 5,000 feet, one of the men put on a parachute and climbed into the cannon while the other man lit the fuse. The cannon then blasted the man inside it "several hundred feet into the atmosphere" before he deployed the parachute and descended to earth once again. Park management, according to the newspaper, paid a large sum to bring the act to the park, and it took place on the afternoon of July 15 immediately after the triple bill of *The Silver Lining*, *A Pair of Lunatics*, and *Little Mother* at the theater. While Manhattan Beach was hosting parachute jumps and cannon shots from balloons, management at Elitch Gardens hired Ivy Baldwin and Clara Moore to stage balloon races in an effort to draw customers to that park.[17]

The special events brought crowds to Manhattan Beach, with the *Rocky Mountain News* reporting that the "roller coaster and steamboat were kept running continuously," while rowboats cruised the lake. The zoo and refreshment stands, which were serving red lemonade (a sweet, fizzy, lemon-flavored drink from Ireland), were also constantly busy that summer. Popular among the crowds were two new traditions started by theatergoers that summer as well. For moonlight picnics, people would bring a light supper to the park with them in the afternoon. They would then row on the lake until it was time for the show, and after it was over, eat their supper on the grounds of the park. High society women also started hosting beach parties at the park, bringing their friends to the park to enjoy the grounds and the theater.[18]

Although popular with pleasure seekers, the park was also popular with special groups. Near the end of July, Cynthia Bethell

A balloon ascension and parachute jump at Manhattan Beach on July 22, 1894. This may have been one of Professor LeVan's ascensions. *Source:* History Colorado, Object # 95.200.686.

invited the twenty-nine choir boys of St. Mark's Church in Denver to be her guests at Manhattan Beach. The *Rocky Mountain News* reported that they had a "delightful time" as they "did the manifold attractions of the place thoroughly." Civic leaders also brought special groups to the park to showcase Denver's reputation as a growing city. In mid-June, the Homeopathic Institute visited Denver for its national convention. The Denver Chamber of Commerce planned several special activities for the institute's members, including a visit to the Denver Mint and a display of gold and other precious metals from the Newton Gold Mining and Milling Company of Denver, a visit to the Omaha and Grant Smelter, and visits to Manhattan Beach and Elitch Gardens. About 400 people from the convention took the streetcar to the two parks. At Elitch's they had the run of the grounds, while at Manhattan Beach the guests were serenaded by the park's band and given free access to the attractions.[19]

While the park's fame was good for business, it could sometimes work against it as well. The rowdy nature of the saloons around the park continued to be a problem during the 1894 season, and when the police raided a Sunday night dance hall near the park, the *Rocky Mountain News* mistakenly reported that the raid had been at Manhattan Beach itself. The newspaper apologized for the mistake, writing that Manhattan Beach was "conducted on the strictest lines of propriety and has no connection as a resort with any other place about the lake." The mistake, the newspaper went on, was "at least suggestive of the fact that even fame has some disadvantages."[20]

The bathing beach opened for the summer at the end of June, and while it, divers, balloon ascensions, the roller coaster, and steamboat were popular throughout the summer, it was the theater that kept Manhattan Beach in the news for the most part. Sticking with the comedic nature of the plays as promised early in the season, Robert Giffen brought *Married Life*, *Betsy*, *A Gay Deceiver*, *Bully's Betrothin'*, and *A Scrap of Paper* to the theater in July. On July 6, after the fiftieth performance of the season at the theater, Giffen hosted a dinner for the stock company and the musicians at the café on the park grounds in honor of their dedication and efficiency in the productions. About fifty people in all sat down to what the *Rocky Mountain News* described as a "royal spread." Near the end of July, the *News* reported that the theatrical productions continued to be a "grand success," proving that the plays produced at Manhattan Beach were the kind that Denverites enjoyed. The theater company closed out the 1894 season with *Happy Pair*, *Box and Cox*, and *My Uncle's Will*. After the final performance on September 3, management staged a benefit for the company on September 4. After performing two of the three final plays of the season, two special events enthralled the audience. First, stagehands set an entire scene as the audience watched, giving a behind-the-scenes look at what it took to create a production. Then, Al Hoevet, the theater's electrician, revealed a new electrical act that he had been developing. While the newspaper did not report on the details of the act, the *News* said that it was "very interesting and received with much enthusiasm." Park management, the newspaper said, "can feel proud to know that the company leaves Denver with the good wishes of everybody."[21]

During the final weeks of the 1894 season, attractions outside of the theater remained well attended, especially boating on Sloan's Lake and walking through the park's beautifully landscaped grounds. The park closed out its season on Labor Day, September 3, 1894. The official labor parade in the morning had over 2,000 men marching in it with the Elitch Gardens band in the lead. Among the groups represented in the parade were plumbers, typesetters, house painters, beer drivers, tailors, granite cutters, waiters, and even theatrical employees. In the afternoon, 6,500 people descended on the grounds of Manhattan Beach, which was chosen as the site of the official Labor Day picnic. Music and dancing at the pavilion, boating on the lake, the triple bill at the theater, and a baby beauty contest were among the entertainment for the afternoon. Sporting events included the hop, skip, and jump race; a 100-yard race; a high jump; a married ladies' race; and a fat men's race. Newspapers around the state declared the day a great success, in part thanks to the generosity shown by management at Manhattan Beach.[22]

Robert Giffen left his position as general manager of Manhattan Beach at the end of the 1894 season, moving on to manage the Lyceum Theater in Denver. In April of 1895 the owners named the previous year's assistant manager, Thomas McMechen, a former newspaper reporter and son of Denver postmaster W. M. McMechen, as the new general manager of the park. The new manager immediately started work on the park, cleaning up the grounds, having new gravel put on the walks, and painting all of the buildings in bright colors. McMechen promised the greatest stock company ever seen in Denver for the theater, which was being renovated inside and out. The steamship and rowboats were also being repainted, and McMechen ordered new canvas tops for the rowboats to protect occupants from "the blistering rays of the sun." The *Denver Post* also reported that the zoo had been "greatly strengthened" during the winter. McMechen had originally hoped to open for the 1895 season in May, but the extensive renovations underway pushed opening day out to June 1.[23]

Both the park's management and the newspapers were hopeful that the long-standing nuisance of the nearby saloons had been solved by the start of the 1895 season. A series of court cases in late 1894 had resulted in a ruling in early January 1895 that the strip of land the saloons stood on, across Sheridan Boulevard from Manhattan Beach, was not part of Denver and was in fact under the jurisdiction of Jefferson County. The ruling meant that all of the saloons were in violation of an ordinance from the town of Highlands that forbade any saloon to open within a mile of the city limits unless it was in an incorporated city or town. Most of the saloons in question closed, although the owner of the rebuilt Electric Palace refused to close his bar and was promptly arrested. The saloon owners appealed to the state Supreme Court, but without success, and in late April the saloons remained closed. The *Denver Post* hoped that the "midnight brawls" that intruded on Manhattan Beach the previous summer were a thing of the past as county officials refused to grant new liquor licenses.[24]

While renovations at the park progressed, the new theater stock company arrived in Denver at the end of May. Under the direction of George R. Edeson, the *Denver Post* proclaimed that it was the "strongest organization of this character ever brought to Denver for a season of stock work." The 1895 company was made up of Jennie Kennark, Madge Carr Cook, Sarah Truax, Zenaide Williams, Daisy Lovering, William Ingersoll, Walter Edwards, Tom Ricketts, Augustus Halbach, and Charles Lothian. Jennie Kennark, who in 1897 would become the first leading lady in Elitch's new summer stock theater season, had started her acting career in Denver before moving on to other cities, and the newspapers were especially happy to see her back on a local stage. Several other members of the company would also go on to work at Elitch's theater in future seasons. Among the plays already scheduled for the 1895 season were *The Private Secretary*, *Wilkinson's Widows*, *Niobe*, *Humbug*, *Woman Against Woman*, and *Love on Crutches*. The Manhattan Beach theater also opened a box office at Scholtz Drug Store in downtown Denver, with advance ticket sales beginning there each Monday morning during the season. The new box office displayed summaries of each play along with a seating chart for the theater, allowing, as the *Post* said, "all the bother of waiting at the Beach to be avoided." Pinney's Orchestra, under the direction of Charles Horst, provided music for all of the theatrical productions, as well as other special events at the park, which included afternoon concerts in the theater on Mondays, Tuesdays, Thursdays, and Fridays when there were not matinee performances. The *Rocky Mountain News* called the concerts a "pleasing innovation."[25]

Manhattan Beach's 1895 theater company seated on a bench at the park. *Source:* History Colorado, Object # 89.451.3043.

When opening day finally arrived, the *Denver Post* said that the buildings and grounds of Manhattan Beach had been cleaned up so much "they fairly shine in the sunlight." The grounds, with more mature trees and carefully planted flower gardens, were especially beautiful, and the expanded zoo delighted visitors. Among the new residents was a baby leopard, which had adopted a bird dog as its mother. Also new that summer was a special parking area for bicycles, which had become a popular way to reach the park. An attendant checked in each bicycle brought to the gates and guarded them while the owners were in the park. As usual, the lake was one of the most popular attractions and when the rowboats were out on it, the "bright costumes and gay colors formed a picturesque scene on the lake." The opening production of the comedy *Betsy* at the theater received glowing reviews from Denver's newspapers, with the *Post* calling it "one of the most satisfactory bills ever presented" at Manhattan Beach. Unfortunately, heavy rainstorms throughout much of the day dampened the enthusiasm for the opening of the season and even canceled the evening performance of *Betsy*.[26]

Throughout much of June, as the weather warmed up, the theater remained the top draw at Manhattan Beach with productions of *Moths*, *Dream Faces*, *The Private Secretary*, and *Niobe* among others. The *City of Denver* made its half-hour trips around the lake regularly, and children spent hours in front of the monkey cage at the zoo. Management abandoned a fireworks show at the lake for the Fourth of July, but the *Denver Post* reported that Manhattan Beach was the best place in the city to watch the displays from Arlington Park and homes around the city. Somewhere between 8,000 and 10,000 people packed the park for the holiday, arriving early in the morning with picnic lunches, enjoying boating and fishing on the lake, and staying until the last of the fireworks had gone off that night. The *Rocky Mountain News* wrote that "a steady stream of humanity filled the walks and there were no merrier groups thoroughly enjoying the quiet and beautiful scene than" at Manhattan Beach.[27]

In mid-July the park hired Professor Brady to make a series of jumps from a seventy-two-foot-high tower constructed on the shore of Sloan's Lake, and he delighted the crowd with every leap from the platform. Large crowds came every day to watch Brady during the week that he was at the park, and his appearance was followed by Professor LeVan who did balloon ascension and parachute jumps. LeVan was famous on the East coast for what was called "high flying." Joining him for one of his ascensions and jumps at Manhattan Beach was Pie, a Scotch terrier who called the park home. According to the *Rocky Mountain News*, Pie had already made five ascensions and parachute drops at the time that LeVan arrived at the park, much to the delight of the crowds who watched. The park paid LeVan $65 for his three ascensions.[28]

After a busy July, the park relied on the theater to draw customers for most of August with plays including *Woman to Woman*, *Not Such a Fool as He Looks*, *In the Web*, and *Who Killed Cock Robin?* There was only one balloon ascension near the end of the month, but bigger things were in store for September. Late in August, management announced that the searchlight that had been on top of the Manufacturer's Building at the 1893 Columbian Exposition in Chicago would be at the park in September. The lens of the searchlight was thirty inches in diameter and the Denver Tramway Company had to supply the fifty to sixty amps of electricity that it took to run the light. The *Denver Post* wrote that if the light worked as it should, it would make "bogus moonlight from Manhattan to the foot of Pike's peak." The park offered nightly demonstrations of the light, and to make it even more impressive, management lured the famous Ivy Baldwin to the park to make nighttime jumps illuminated by the searchlight, paying him $80 for his appearances. On Wednesdays, Saturdays, and Sundays through the first three weeks of September, Baldwin ascended to 2,000 feet in his balloon and then cut loose and descended by parachute, the searchlight following him as he went up and came down. The *Denver Post* found the exhibition so thrilling that it wrote "this most interesting and novel exhibition should be witnessed by every one [sic], as it will be the last opportunity in this city to behold such a thrilling sight."[29]

While diving, balloon ascensions, and giant searchlights brought customers to the park by the thousands, management at Manhattan Beach did not neglect more civic-minded activities. In late May, before the park officially opened for the summer, management welcomed members of the Arkansas Press Association who were visiting Colorado. On their first night in Denver, they had dinner at the Windsor Hotel and saw a play at the Curtis Street theater. On their second day in town, the group visited both Elitch's and Manhattan Beach, spending about an hour at each park. The Philistona Literary Club and the members of Denver's Royal Arcanum club visited in July, and the Colorado State Pharmaceutical Association and the children of the St. Vincent's Orphanage came in August. Writing of the children's visit to the park, the *Denver Post* noted of the ice cream and cake, rides on the merry-go-round, and visit to the theater, "it costs so little to give

The newly renovated *City of Denver* steamboat is in dry dock in this view of the western part of the Manhattan Beach grounds. *Source:* The Denver Public Library, Western History Collection, X-29818.

pleasure in this world" and "those motherless children will long look on that day with feelings of the most keen delight."[30]

The biggest charitable social event of the season, however, was a fundraiser for the YWCA in late June. Captain Bethell offered the free use of the park to the association, which was raising money for its building fund. The society women of Denver worked for several weeks to put the event together, including building a shooting gallery supervised by Eliza Whitehead and Mary Addoms, who the *Rocky Mountain News* said "since childhood has been a crack shot." On June 22, the day of the event, the park was packed full of children, and the *Denver Post* reported that the lemonade stand, shooting gallery, merry-go-round, and café were "doing a rushing business." Former United States senator Nathaniel P. Hill donated $500 to the cause, and along with other donations, the group had already raised $900 by the time the park opened that day. The YWCA raised an additional $1,200 with their day at the Beach.[31]

While Labor Day traditionally marked the end of the season at Manhattan Beach, the appearance of the searchlight and Ivy Baldwin's balloon ascensions extended the season until nearly the end of September. The plays in the theater included *Forget-Me-Not*, *A Bed of Roses*, *Elopement*, and *Home*. With the season winding down, the *Denver Post* wrote that Denver was sad to see the members of the stock company leave as they had been the "most painstaking ministers to hours of enjoyment," and had by "conscientious study and talent of high order" won many admirers in the city. The last major event at the park was a visit from the members of Colorado's Populist party, who held a fundraiser on September 21. Manhattan Beach closed for the season the next day.[32]

For the previous three seasons Manhattan Beach had largely relied on its theater to bring visitors to the park. While they got to enjoy boating on Sloan's Lake, a merry-go-round, Denver's first roller coaster, and a zoo, it was the theater that received the majority of attention from Denver's press, and management worked hard to make sure it met high standards. But major changes were underway in the amusement world as the 1895 season wound down, and by the time Manhattan Beach was ready to open for the 1896 season, those changes would be starting to make themselves felt even in Denver.

CHAPTER 4

# Beautiful and Genuine Novelties

On July 4, 1895, Captain Paul Boyton, a legendary swimmer, opened Sea Lion Park on Coney Island in New York. The new park featured a shoot-the-chutes, a flip-flap roller coaster, an old mill water ride, and forty trained sea lions among its offerings. Located on sixteen fenced acres and requiring an admission fee to enter, Sea Lion became the first enclosed amusement park in the United States. Two years later, George C. Tilyou opened Steeplechase Park on Coney Island, taking Boyton's modest park and running wild with it. The park offered the human roulette wheel, the Wedding Ring swing, a booth that allowed customers to smash dishes, and the Steeplechase, the horse-racing ride that gave the park its name. The amusement park had grown out of the Midway at the 1893 Columbian Exposition in Chicago, which grouped all of the amusement attractions, including the Ferris wheel, in one location. The amusement park took the concept of the Midway and, combined with the amusement resorts and beer gardens and other forms of public recreation that existed before, created a new amusement option for the American public.[1]

With the opening of Steeplechase Park in 1897, and the rapid spread of amusement parks that would see almost 5,000 such parks built in the United States between 1895 and 1920, the owners of two of Denver's three amusement resorts took notice of the new trend. In 1896, Mary Elitch installed a Thomas Edison Vitascope at Elitch's. Essentially an enlarged kinescope, the Vitascope projected images onto a screen and was the first amusement-type attraction offered at the park. In 1899, a new penny arcade and a reenactment of the Civil War battle between the *Monitor* and the *Merrimack* (this was later replaced with the sinking of the *Titanic*) joined the park's lineup. At Arlington Park, owner Robert Speer and his associates leased the park to Henry Harris and John Baumann in December 1897. The new operators quickly announced plans to remodel the park into a true amusement park. Soon under construction at the park was a miniature railroad, merry-go-round, shooting gallery, palace of illusions, haunted swing, and a ride called Trip the Trolley. The park was renamed Chutes Park because of the large shoot-the-chutes the new operators built that ended in the park's lake. Denver's first scenic railway, a covered version of the roller coaster invented by LaMarcus A. Thompson, opened at Chutes Park in the summer of 1898, shortly after the park opened for the season. A scenic railway was essentially a roller coaster with tunnels over parts of the track; before entering a tunnel, the train would trip a switch that would light the interior. William F. Mangels, an amusement ride manufacturer and amusement park historian, wrote that Thompson put "pretty scenery, startling grottos, and historical tableaus" inside the tunnels. At Chutes Park, the scenic railway depicted the journey to the Klondike and was an instant hit with Denver's amusement-seeking public.[2]

While Elitch's and Arlington Park worked to become true amusement parks, Manhattan Beach, with its merry-go-round running since 1892 and roller coaster since 1893, carried on with business as usual. Robert Giffen returned as general manager of the park in 1896, replacing Thomas McMechen. The new theater company of James Neill, Edwin M. Arden, John B. Maher, George Edeson (who had been the stage manager the previous season), Walter Edwards, Wallace Bruce, Rebecca Warren, Annie

Blancke, Mattie Earle, and Sara Stafford arrived at the park near the end of May and began preparing for the first production of the season, *My Partner*, which would open on May 30. The *Rocky Mountain News* expected the company to "compare favorably with New York's stock companies." No major changes took place to the park's grounds, where even the Columbian Exposition searchlight remained on display and in use throughout the 1896 season.[3]

For much of the 1890s, the newspapers reported on Manhattan Beach almost as if it was primarily a theater that happened to have an amusement park attached to it, and the 1896 season was no exception. The plays *The Private Secretary* and *7-20-8* followed the opening production of *My Partner*, and the newspapers found both plays extremely funny in the hands of the talented actors. The productions of *Gloriana* and *London Assurance* near the end of June also received high praise from the papers. Charles Horst and his orchestra provided daily afternoon band concerts on the grounds of Manhattan Beach for the 1896 season, and they quickly proved popular with the park's visitors. Professor

Flowerbeds near the boathouse at Manhattan Beach, with Sloan's Lake in the background. *Source:* Author's collection.

Darling began his daily balloon ascensions and parachute jumps over Sloan's Lake at the end of June as well, continuing another standard attraction for the park. The park paid him $10 per jump.[4]

After skipping Fourth of July fireworks the previous year, management at Manhattan Beach brought them back to the park in 1896 in a big way. They hired famed fireworks expert James Pain, who had been producing shows at Arlington Park since 1892, to put on the same display he had done at the Columbian Exposition in 1893. The fireworks on the lake included flying devils, flying fish, and submarine torpedoes, while the aerial display included what the *Denver Post* described as the "latest novelties in rockets, batteries and bombs beside a beautiful hanging parachute and weeping willow." The *Rocky Mountain News* assured readers that the scene "would be a brilliant one." Also, in honor of the day, Professor Darling gave two balloon ascensions and parachute jumps, one in the afternoon and one at night illuminated by the searchlight. Manhattan Beach was packed that day with people who brought picnic lunches, watched the matinee performance of *London Assurance*, and then enjoyed the fireworks that night. The next day the Independent Order of Red Men, a fraternal organization formed in the 1830s by and for white men that based their rituals on those of Native Americans, hosted a large gathering at the park. After a day of boating, music, and foot races that included a lame men's race, potato race, ladies' race, and fat men's race, the crowd got to enjoy another balloon ascension by Darling and more fireworks.[5]

Near the end of July, a special event at the park finally managed to push the theater out of the spotlight. Samuel Lockhart was born into a circus family in England. He performed a variety of acts with his brother George until a hip injury ended George's career. Samuel then went to Burma with another circus, and while there he saw two baby elephants that he purchased and shipped back to England. He named the elephants Jock and Jenny and they began his career as an elephant trainer. His most famous elephants were Wilhelmina, Trilby, and Haddie, who were known as the Three Graces. Other elephants that were part of his act included Romeo, Charley, and Salt and Sauce. In all, Lockhart had more than a dozen trained elephants in his troupe. He traveled the world performing with them, including appearances with Buffalo Bill's Wild West show and the Ringling Brothers Circus.[6]

Lockhart and his elephants Jenny, Charley, Nellie, Harry, and Romeo made their first appearance at Manhattan Beach on July 26, 1896. Within three days, according to the *Rocky Mountain News*, nearly everyone in Denver was asking "Have you seen the elephants?" In addition to their various tricks, on the afternoon of July 28 Lockhart gave them a bath in Sloan's Lake for two hours. The elephants did several tricks in the water, and the *News* reported that Lockhart had no trouble getting them into the lake. Getting them out, though, was another matter as they "did about as they pleased and came out when they got ready." On August 6, park manager Robert Giffen invited a group of special guests to the park to watch one of the trainers trim the elephants' hoofs and tusks. While each elephant put their feet up on a tub for trimming, Lockhart told the invited guests how he had obtained and trained each of the elephants and even persuaded one of them to perform a hoochie-coochie dance for the crowd. The elephants drew such large crowds that Giffen convinced Lockhart to stay for an additional week, and he finally left the park in mid-August. The park paid Lockhart $2,100 for his appearance.[7]

With Lockhart's elephants gone, attention once again turned to the theater for the concluding weeks of the 1896 season. Among the final plays were *The Jilt*, *Niobe*, *The Club Friend*, *Her First Offense*, and to close out the season, *Turned Up*, a play the *Denver Post* wrote was "said to abound in absurd situations." Although the *Rocky Mountain News* said the theatrical season at Manhattan Beach was successful, the *Post* reported that the last week was "almost disastrous," with near empty houses at Manhattan and several other Denver theaters, including Elitch

A crowd enjoying the lake at Manhattan Beach with the boathouse and theater behind them. *Source:* Author's collection.

Gardens. The newspaper speculated that Denver's audiences may have simply been losing their taste for modern comedies and dramas. While the theater lurched toward the end of the season, Giffen scheduled several more balloon ascensions and parachute drops with Professor Darling. His nighttime performances were especially popular, with the *News* writing that "a balloon ascension by search light is one of the most beautiful and genuine novelties imaginable." In late August the park also paid $400 to book a phantoscope, which was a film projector created by Charles Francis Jenkins and Thomas Armat, for two weeks. Promoted as the first phantoscope used in the western United States, the *News* said the film shows met with "good success."[8]

The 1896 season ended quietly and, during the offseason, John Foster and his brother-in-law J. P. Edrington discussed taking over the park themselves and operating it for the 1897 season. Edrington seemed supportive of the idea, writing to Foster on February 10 that the park had made a profit of $9,000 the previous season and was a "good luck producer." On February 25, Edrington wrote to Foster that the park needed to be kept in "first class style" to keep people coming back year after year because once they abandoned the park for somewhere else it would be hard to get them back. He said that people came to the park "certainly not because they love us, but for the reason it is at Manhattan they have been in the habit of getting the most for their money." If the park was allowed to become run down, he argued, the customers would "run away, and the place is not good for a truck patch." With Edrington and Foster unable to reach a decision before opening day, Robert Giffen remained manager of the park. With bicycling gaining in popularity in Denver in the 1890s, Giffen told the *Rocky Mountain News* that the park was considering building a bicycle track around Sloan's Lake, but it never happened. The only major change to the grounds for the 1897 season was construction of a covered walkway from the streetcar station to the entrance of the theater to keep theatergoers out of the rain. Management also purchased six new aluminum rowboats for the lake. Otherwise, only the usual maintenance and beautification of the grounds took place before opening day.[9]

Captain Bethell helped choose the members of the new stock company for the 1897 season, arriving with them on a train from New York in mid-May. The members of the company included comedian Frank M. Kendrick, Julia Marlowe, Hannah May Inghram, Florida Kingsley, and Edward P. Mawson. The *Rocky Mountain News* said "Every member of the company is capable for the position chosen," and that the season at the theater should be a good one. It opened with *A Modern Match*, and among the other plays put on that summer were *Helene*, *Looking for a Wife*, *The Serious Family*, *Dora*, *Camille*, and *East Lynne*, which closed out the season. The theatrical productions again dominated coverage of the park for the season.[10]

Charles Horst's afternoon band concerts at the park were always popular with customers, and a three-week appearance by

Professor Fred Macart and his trained dogs and monkeys began in mid-June. Among Macart's animals were several Chacma baboons, and according to the *Rocky Mountain News* "their antics would . . . provoke the proverbial horse laugh." Macart had trained two of the dogs to stage a boxing match, which was just one of many stunts they performed. Assisting Macart was his wife Josephine, who the *News* said was one of the best dog trainers in the world. Macart was related to the Genet family of England, which at one time owned the largest circus there. He traveled with some of the best-known circuses of the late 1800s, including the Old Dan Rice Show and Barnum & Bailey, before going out on his own with his animal act. The park also hosted several special gatherings that summer, including the Colorado State Medical Society, newspaper editors from Montana (who also went to Elitch's), and a Grand Patriotic Celebration sponsored by St. Leo's, St. Patrick's, Sacred Heart, and Annunciation Catholic Churches on July 5. Nearly 200 people took part in the athletic events that day, but the highlight, as reported by the *Denver Post*, was a boat race between Fathers Robinson, Corrigan, Bruner, and O'Ryan. The paper reported that the race was close, but Father Robinson was ultimately victorious. The final special event of the season was a flag festival, picnic, and cantata hosted by Trinity Methodist Church and Central Christian Church on September 4, with 125 children singing.[11]

The 1897 season at Manhattan Beach was relatively quiet when compared with earlier seasons at the park, but it was not without its share of problems. The saloons and gambling dens around the park were once again a source of trouble. At the end of July, George L'Abbe, Joe Gavin, Jim Marshall, "and other leaders of the short-haired fraternity" attempted to open a Monte Carlo in the back of a pool room operated by men from Leadville across Sheridan Boulevard from the park. Sheriff George Kelly of Jefferson County said that he would not tolerate such a place and that he would "land every man in jail who attempts to start a game of any kind." Denver police commissioner (and Arlington Park co-owner) Robert Speer told the *Rocky Mountain News* that Denver had ordered all of the pool rooms in the city to close. The bars around the park that were selling liquor on Sundays in violation of state law, without any attempted action by police, also continued to draw unwelcome attention to the area around Manhattan Beach. At the park itself in early July, six-year-old Gilbert Uielling got too close to the cage holding the zoo's black leopard, which struck the boy on the head, causing five deep wounds. He was taken to nearby St. Anthony's Hospital for treatment.[12]

Manhattan Beach also found itself drawn into a naval battle of sorts with James J. Bemis, a former special officer with the Denver Police Department who was also in charge of boat rentals at the park. After being relieved of both positions, Bemis bought some rowboats and leased Cooper Lake and the southern portion of Sloan's Lake. Bemis and the management of Manhattan Beach issued instructions to their customers that they were forbidden from crossing the boundaries that marked each side's property on Sloan's Lake. According to Bemis, a Manhattan Beach employee even captured one of his boats, towed it and the occupants back to the Manhattan Beach boathouse, and had the occupants arrested for trespassing. Bemis took the case to court but lost. According to the *Denver Post*, the battle between the two sides got so intense that both sides pulled guns and exchanged "direful threats . . . over the water." When Bemis wanted to open a flume between the two lakes to lower the level of Cooper Lake, Manhattan Beach got a court order to stop it. After heavy rains a short time later, Manhattan Beach attempted to open the flume to lower the level of Sloan's Lake, but Bemis insisted on observing the court order, saying that it went both ways. The battle finally ended on July 29 when, despite objections from Captain Bethell and Manhattan Beach, the Denver fire and police board reappointed Bemis as a special policeman at Cooper Lake.[13]

After Manhattan Beach closed for the season, J. P. Edrington and John Foster continued their ongoing discussion about taking over the park. But by February of 1898, Edrington had completely changed his mind and no longer wanted anything to do with the park, writing to Foster that it was unprofitable in the offseason. On February 18 he wrote to Foster that he believed "the streetcar companies should contribute something to its support," but he was willing to go along with whatever Foster decided, as Captain Bethell was in no condition to be bothered with it. In March, Edrington wrote to Foster that he hoped the park would at least be rented out for the 1898 season and meet expenses. Robert Giffen was once again in charge of the park for the season, and one of his first decisions was to close the park's zoo and sell the animals. He told the *Rocky Mountain News* that it cost $300 a month just to feed and care for the animals, even during the off-season when the park did not make any money. The park had a mortgage of $2,200 on the animals, and by May 21, 1898, it still owed $1,700 on them. By the time the park opened, the monkeys were among the few animals still in the zoo. Frank C. Bostock of Hagenbeck's Wild Animal Show of Charleston, West Virginia, and Omaha, Nebraska, wrote to John Foster offering to buy the monkeys for $120 (the park had paid $68.15 for them in 1895). Bostock wrote that Foster "would surely see them kept together [rather] than divided amongst opposing amusement caterers in your own city," and promised to take good care of them until the end of the Trans-Mississippi Exposition when they would go to Europe. The park finally sold the monkeys to Bostock on September 6, 1898. With the zoo closed, Giffen told the *News* that his "aim will be to provide much more for the people than simply the animals," seemingly ignoring the many other attractions the park offered. In fact, not one of them, including the always popular boating on Sloan's Lake, was ever mentioned by the newspapers throughout the summer.[14]

Giffen had the theater and café at the park remodeled and planted several new trees on the grounds. The new theater company was made up of fourteen people, including leading man Hobart Bosworth and leading lady Amelia Bingham, along with Emmett Corrigan, Frederick Parry, and Nell Madeline Davis, a Colorado native. The park opened for the season on June 12 with the play *The Wife*. All of Denver's theaters and amusement places experienced a noticeable decrease in business during the early part of the summer, which the newspapers blamed on the war with Spain, which lasted from April through December that year. Other plays staged that summer at Manhattan Beach included *The Countess of Gucki*, *The Bauble Shop*, *A Bachelor's Honeymoon*, *A Social Highwayman*, *The Banker's Daughter*, and *A Southern Romance*, before closing the season with *Diversions*. Giffen also introduced free vaudeville acts between the matinees and evening performances. The *Denver Post* said the acts were "excellent," while the *Rocky Mountain News* said they quickly became a popular feature. The vaudeville acts appearing at the park included the Jose Quintette, musical comedians Hall and Staley, Josephine (known as the queen of vaudeville according to the *News*), Montgomery and Stone, and Madame Irma Orbasang and her trained cockatoos.[15]

As was often the case, the season was not without a few problems. Two employees at the park became victims of a sneak thief in July. Police arrested Eugene "Skip" Smith near the end of the month for stealing $40 from Ruben Tuck, a worker at the park who had hung his pants on a hook in the oil room of the park's power plant in order to put on his work overalls. Police suspected Smith was the same man who had stolen $20 from Miss Roemer, the ticket seller at the park's main gate, the week before. The park also had a near miss with a fire in June. A phonograph team was in the theater recording the Jose Quintette and xylophone players Adelman and Lowe when Richard Jose came into the theater and noticed smoke. He summoned Robert Giffen and Sammy

Amberg, the gas man at the park. Amberg grabbed a ladder and several members of the park's band (the *Denver Times* said their red coats were fitting for the situation), and they connected the fire hose kept at the back of the theater. The fire was soon traced to a drainpipe on the roof that drained into the canal that ran through the park. Picnickers had thrown pieces of lit paper at the end of the drainpipe, and a breeze spread the fire up it. Within three minutes of the first alarm the fire was dealt with, and the phonograph team never even knew there was a problem.[16]

After Manhattan Beach closed for the season in September, the battle against the saloons surrounding the park continued when Jefferson County resident Lizzie McIntosh began circulating a petition calling for two of the bars in Edgewater to be closed. Enough people signed it that the county commissioners had no choice but to take away the liquor licenses for the two bars and deny the application for a new one, somewhat easing the problem. Park officials also had to battle duck hunters, who were using dynamite to clear Sloan's Lake of fish and other debris. By the end of March 1899, according to the *Rocky Mountain News*, there were dead fish "six inches deep, a mass of putrid matter that smells like an old glue factory," on the shores of the lake. The park also received better fire protection over the offseason when, on April 25, 1899, two Denver aldermen, Harry Petrie and Matthew F. Murray, received permission to form two volunteer fire companies to protect the theaters at Manhattan Beach and Elitch Gardens.[17]

With Robert Giffen in charge of his own stock theater company for the 1899 season, John Foster took over management of Manhattan Beach himself for the summer. The lake received a great deal of attention as the park prepared for opening day, with workers clearing it of any weeds and debris not removed by the dynamite-tossing duck hunters. The *City of Denver* steamship was completely overhauled, and several new rowboats joined the fleet already on the lake. Workers also cleaned and re-sanded the park's bathing beach. Gardeners were hard at work on the grounds, with the *Denver Times* writing that "with the profusion of flowers and green trees" the park never looked better, and the lake "swept by the cool breezes from the magnificent range of mountains looming in the distance, forms an alluring picture." Although the park did not officially open until June 12, the public got a chance to enjoy it when the South Broadway Christian Church held a summer festival on the grounds on June 10. Events for the day included military drills by the girls of the church, acrobatic demonstrations by the YMCA, and cavalry drills by the Colorado National Guard. Governor Charles S. Thomas was a special guest of the church that day.[18]

The theater was once again the star of the season. Aside from repainting the entrance to the building, during the offseason crews had built all new scenery and, according to the *Rocky Mountain News*, "for the first time in the history of a local stock company the management has provided furniture, bric-a-brac and stage settings entirely and exclusively for their performances" in an effort to set the stage "in a manner suitable to the high class character of the plays to be presented." The leading lady for the season was Minnie Seligman and the leading man was Robert Drouet. Other members of the company included Emmet King, John Findlay, Percy Winter (who was also stage manager), Charlotte Deane, Agnes Findlay, and Florence Rolland. The theater season opened with *Lady Windemere's Fan*, and the *Denver Post* wrote that Dr. Foster and his associates were to be "congratulated upon their stock company. Taking all things into consideration it is the best stock company in Denver today, which is rather high praise." Other plays for the 1899 season included *Captain Lettarblair*, *The Three Musketeers*, *Lost-24 Hours*, *The Prodigal Daughter*, *The Prisoner of Zenda*, and, to close out the season, *My Wife's Mother*. The *Rocky Mountain News* heaped praise on the theater company, writing that "During the twelve weeks the management has presented a series of plays seldom, if ever, equalled [sic] within the same length of time in this city."[19]

The park hosted several special events throughout the summer. At the end of June, the Colorado Medical Society once again visited the park, ending the first day of their conference with a visit to Manhattan Beach. Box parties also became popular among Denver's high society set, and the *Denver Post* described the one hosted by Charles Taylor in honor of his birthday on September 1 as "one of the jolliest little affairs of the week." The park worked toward more civic-minded purposes as well. In August, pastors throughout Colorado began raising money to help bring the First

Looking north at Manhattan Beach from Sheridan Boulevard, with the theater, a dining area, and the boathouse on the left side of the park. There are two streetcars in the distance traveling on Sheridan. *Source:* The Denver Public Library, Western History Collection, X-27724.

Colorado regiment home from San Francisco. Manhattan Beach's management pledged to donate the gate receipts for August 8 to the fund and put on a special fireworks show that night in order to help increase attendance.[20]

Rumors circulated throughout the summer that Manhattan Beach was not for long, especially when Captain Bethell sold his interest in the Leavenworth Street Railway Company in Kansas for $200,000 in July. The story was that Bethell intended to drain Sloan's Lake, fill it with dirt, and divide it into building lots. His son-in-law, Dr. Foster, told the *Rocky Mountain News* that no such plan was ever under consideration, saying "The property is more valuable as a summer resort than as platted land, and Captain Bethell has entertained no such idea although it has been suggested to him several times. Manhattan Beach will not be abolished but it will rather be extended if the present income keeps up." At the end of September, the *News* reported that Walter Clarke Bellows, whose stock company had played at Elitch Gardens that summer, had leased Manhattan Beach for the 1900 season for $5,000. John Foster denied the story, saying that while the Southern Investment Company had talked with Bellows, no deal had been made. The truth was actually more interesting, as the manager of Manhattan Beach for the 1900 season would be Mary Elitch herself.[21]

The official announcement that Mary Elitch was once again taking over Manhattan Beach came in January of 1900. Under the terms of the lease, Elitch was to operate Manhattan Beach as a "high-class amusement resort" and was to operate "first-class operatic and theatrical companies and in every way conscientiously endeavor to maintain a high standard" in the theater. Walter Clarke Bellows would manage the theater and park for Mary Elitch. Praising the deal, theater critic Frank W. White wrote in the *Denver Post* that Elitch's and Manhattan Beach would "no longer be rival resorts, but friendly ones, and the establishments will be of a widely opposite character."[22]

As preparations for opening day of the new season were underway, the *Denver Post* speculated that the theater at Elitch's would rely on its stock company while Manhattan Beach would have light opera. By opening day, Elitch and Bellows had settled on melodramas for Manhattan, with *Cumberland '61* as the first play. As opening day approached, the *Denver Times* said "principal interest, of course, attaches to the theater." In addition to the nightly performances, there were matinees on Thursdays, Saturdays, and Sundays throughout the summer. Elitch and Bellows called the Thursday afternoon matinees "people's popular" matinees, with admission to the theater reduced to fifteen cents. The leading lady of the new theater company was Mary Hampton and the leading man was Eugene Ormond. Also in the company were Hardee Kirkland, Asa Lee Willard, Ethelyn Clemens, Mary Louise Aiger, and Fred Perry.[23]

The opening of *Cumberland '61* was generally well received, although one critic noted that "the audience was not large . . . and the poor lighting of the theater, due to unforeseen causes, robbed the affair of the brilliance which is popularly supposed to characterize openings." When Elitch's second play at the Beach, *Mr. Barnes of New York*, failed to cause much excitement, she and Bellows switched to offering comedies instead. As part of what the *Denver Times* said was a "bold bid for popularity," they also reduced admission to the theater, with seats in the balcony costing ten cents, general admission seats fifteen cents, and 800 reserved seats on the main level costing a quarter. Among the plays offered after the change were *Imogene*, *The Lost Paradise*, and *The County Fair*. The *Denver Post* reported that the change in plays and prices seemed to be drawing more people, with the balcony always crowded.[24]

While Mary Elitch staged special band concerts and had Ivy Baldwin doing balloon ascensions at Elitch's, the only attraction outside of the theater at Manhattan Beach that received any attention during the 1900 season was the lake, and even then, only on the Fourth of July. To start the day's celebration, Elitch staged a naval battle on Sloan's Lake that recreated the storming of the Taku Forts in China that had just taken place the previous month as part of the Boxer Rebellion. Crews made two boats look like the USS *New Orleans* and *Monocacy*, and the Chaffee Light Artillery supplied several guns and soldiers for the day. After the bombardment and taking of the fort, visitors got to see a $1,500 fireworks show under the direction of Ellsmere Sullivan of New York. The display included floral bombs, multicolored stars, a Niagara Falls, and Old Glory in fire suspended from chains 500 feet in the air. The *Rocky Mountain News* reported that about 2,000 people were at the park that day. At Elitch's, offerings for the Fourth included vaudeville shows, band concerts, dancing, and a balloon ascension.[25]

After staging *Niobe* and *The Sporting Duchess* at Manhattan Beach, the theater company shut down rather abruptly and the *Denver Post* said there were "signs of disintegration" at the park. Bellows and Elitch moved the stock company to Elitch Gardens in a production of *As You Like It*, which Mary Elitch later told Caroline Dier was a "masterpiece of staging and theatrical art." At Manhattan, Bellows and Elitch switched to vaudeville for the theater. According to the *Denver Post*, "all summer long it has been the cry that Denver had no amusements upon the musical line," so Elitch and Bellows tried to fill that need. For the first vaudeville performance on August 5, the acts included actor and singer Will S. Rising, comedian Lillian Komble, Japanese juggler Sats Zoroni, Teddy de Luc and his dancing dog Mubbs, and whistler Virginia Shaeffer. Acts for the second week included Stauffer and Witter in the Tuneful Tars, acrobatic comedians Roberts, Smilax and Company, and the Morrison Sisters in "soubrette specialties." Despite booking nine new acts each week, even the vaudeville did not catch on. On August 20, the *Rocky Mountain News* reported that Manhattan Beach and its theater had "pursued a rather doubtful season." According to the *News*, only the heat of summer and the fact that the downtown theaters were closed for the season brought people to Manhattan Beach's theater, which "led the managers to believe that the programmes were so pleasing that they threatened to repeat the old-time worn bills next season." The only thing left for the park to do, said the newspaper, was to "keep up the appearance of courage and rush the torture through as quickly as possible." It was harsh criticism at a time when the operation at Elitch's theater usually received high praise from Denver's newspapers.[26]

In November of 1900, Mary Elitch married Thomas D. Long, the longtime manager of Elitch Gardens. The following March they formed the Elitch-Long Opera Company to manage both Elitch's and Manhattan Beach. Although they had not yet made any firm plans for Manhattan Beach, the *Denver Times* reported that they expected to revitalize the bathing beach, build a new bathhouse, and bring more aluminum boats to the lake. There was also talk of engaging a new military band to provide music at the park. In the theater, the plan was to stage light opera.[27]

On May 18, 1901, about a month before the park officially opened, the *Denver Times* rented it for a May Festival. About 5,000 people entered the park that day, reportedly jamming the streetcar lines. The festival was so popular, said the *Times*, that "From every part of town was heard the cry to the conductors, 'Give me a transfer to Manhattan beach . . .'" A concert by Satriano's Band began in the theater at 1 p.m., followed by a theatrical program at 2 p.m. that began with film of the Passion Play from Oberammergau, Germany, filmed by Thomas Edison himself the previous July. This was followed by a high wire act starring Mademoiselle Adele, singing by Denver native Grace Smith, humorous recitations by William "Bill Nye" Hamilton and his daughter Grace, dancing by Denver resident Lucille Chesley, and a one act play starring Bessie McCarron and Leon Chapman. The theatrical production ended with a biograph of scenes from American history. The most popular outdoor attractions that day were the merry-go-round and steamship.[28]

The forty-eight members of the Elitch-Long Opera Company who would spend the summer at Manhattan Beach arrived at the park on June 19. The principals included William Blaisdell, Arthur Donaldson, Henry Gonson, Hermann Hirshberg, Frances Graham, Florence Walcott, Julia Cotte, Mayme Taylor, and Jesse Fahnstock. The park finally opened for the season on June 29 with a production of *Wizard of the Nile*. The *Denver Post* said the opera was "particularly good" but long, not ending until almost midnight. The play remained at the theater through the Fourth of July, when the park once again shot fireworks over the lake, although the display was not as elaborate as the year before.[29]

After the *Wizard of the Nile*, the plays at the theater included *Marita Bound*, *The Wedding Day* (which was credited as the biggest production of the season), *The Idol's Eye*, and *Madeline, or the Magic Kiss*. At the beginning of July, the *Rocky Mountain News* wrote that "Mrs. Elitch Long is to be given the utmost credit for the really splendid comic opera company she has placed at Manhattan Beach. It is immeasurably superior to what anyone had looked for or expected." The praise continued throughout the remainder of the season, which ended with *The Jolly Musketeer* in mid-August. Remarking on the approaching end of the season, the *Denver Post* wrote that it was "with sincere regret" that the end neared, a far better verdict on the season than that of the year before.[30]

Although Denver's newspapers enjoyed Manhattan Beach's offerings during the 1901 season, not everyone was as complimentary. Writing in his 1901 *History of Denver*, Jerome Smiley briefly commented on the city's amusement resorts. Of Chutes Park, Smiley wrote it was "designed for those who enjoy spectacular things, and have a fondness for 'roller coasters,' a playground for grown-up boys and girls." Elitch Gardens was "a worthily popular place of summer amusements" in a "handsomely improved enclosure," with a theater "conducted upon a high plane." Manhattan Beach, according to Smiley, strained "a point to be entitled to its name," though he grudgingly admitted it was located on the beach at Sloan's Lake, which he said "does what it can toward justifying the name its associate bears." Seemingly ignoring the fact that Mary Elitch Long had been managing the park for two years at that point, Smiley wrote simply that "Summer theatricals go on there."[31]

By the end of the 1901 season, the Arapahoe County assessor had also become interested in both Elitch Gardens (valued at $9,000) and Manhattan Beach (valued at $12,000). With no one seemingly able to explain both the low figures and why Manhattan Beach was valued higher than Elitch's, the assessor revalued Elitch's at $30,000 and Manhattan Beach at $20,000. By then, Mary Elitch Long had also decided to give up her lease on Manhattan Beach, though whether it was willingly or if the Southern Investment Company forced her hand is unclear. On August 5, the *Rocky Mountain News* reported that a "capitalist" from Kansas City was interested in leasing the park for three years. Mary Elitch Long denied the story was true, but on August 10 the *Denver Times* announced that Joseph Hellbrun of Kansas City had secured an option on the park and was already planning extensive renovations and improvements. After a relationship dating back to 1892, Mary Elitch Long's only association with Manhattan Beach going forward would be as a rival.[32]

Joining Joseph Hellbrun in managing Manhattan Beach was Max Mayer. As soon as the two men signed the lease, Mayer and Hellbrun began making changes at the park. All of the buildings were repaired and repainted. The theater, which the *Denver Post* said was "woefully neglected," was completely remodeled. Painted ivory and gold inside, the theater also got new carpets and curtains that were "rich red, with artistic dashes of buff and green." The *Rocky Mountain News* said the effect was "simply dazzling."

The theater roof, which had apparently been badly leaking for quite a while, was replaced as well.[33]

Mayer and Hellbrun tore down the park's nine-year-old roller coaster and the empty zoo buildings, replacing them with a midway that had a shooting gallery, cane and doll racks, and baby incubators. Dr. Martin A. Couney would become famous for exhibiting working baby incubators at Coney Island and other amusement parks throughout the country, as well as World's Fairs from the early 1900s to the 1940s in his effort to gain widespread acceptance of the devices among the medical community. Couney is credited with saving the lives of anywhere from 6,500 to 7,000 premature babies with his incubators. Although he was the main exhibitor of baby incubators, and he would appear at Manhattan Beach rival Lakeside Amusement Park in 1913, there is nothing to indicate whether or not Couney was the one displaying incubators at Manhattan Beach in 1902. The park's new miniature railway was near the midway, although it was not complete by opening day. As opening day neared, Mayer and Hellbrun found themselves having to deny rumors that the new midway would feature female hoochie-coochie dancers, as had been the case with the midway at the 1901 Pan-American Exposition in Buffalo, New York. The men told the *Rocky Mountain News* that "nothing savoring of, nor bordering on, vulgarity will be permitted on any part of the grounds." In addition to the new midway, the new managers were also trying to buy the electric prismatic fountain that had been at the Pan-American Exposition. When they were unable to do so, the men hired Professor DeVry, who had operated the first electric fountain in Chicago, to build one at Manhattan Beach. New swings and merry-go-rounds for children dotted the grounds, as did hammocks and chairs in shady areas throughout the park. Mayer and Hellbrun also moved the entrance, which had been rebuilt closer to the theater, back to its original location at Zenobia Street on the north side of the park. A new restaurant, two new picnic stands, and ice cream stands and soda fountains throughout the grounds provided refreshments and places to eat for park visitors. The *Rocky Mountain News* reported that the establishments would charge "popular prices" so that it would "not be necessary to be a multi-millionaire" to eat at the park. To further beautify the grounds, Mayer and Hellbrun purchased 15,000 plants.[34]

At the lake, Mayer and Hellbrun re-sanded the beach and built new bathhouses. They also dredged the lake, something they planned to do regularly throughout the season to make it better for boating and fishing. They added several new rowboats to the park's fleet, and got rid of the sidewheels on the steamship, saying they were "relics of the past." They replaced them with a screw drive to give the boat a more modern feel. A new floating dance floor on the lake replaced the park's old dance pavilion, which was converted to a large bandstand. Samuel Koenigsburg and his band performed three times a day in the new bandstand.[35]

Ahead of opening day, Mayer and Hellbrun booked several special acts to help entertain visitors to the park. They built a special platform near the side of the zoo for Ben Bowen and his friend Walter J. Flexon to use to perform balloon ascensions and aerial stunts. They also booked a human cannonball and Professor Clark and his dog and monkey show, which included two gorillas. The star of the season, though, was bicycle rider and daredevil Charles Marsh, known as "Marvelous Marsh." He had made a name for himself performing with circuses and at the Pan-American Exposition in Buffalo, riding his bicycle down a steep ramp and jumped into a water tank. For his appearance at Manhattan Beach, he originally intended to jump into the lake but, after looking over the grounds, decided to stick with the tank. The ramp built at the park under Marsh's direction was 150 feet long and 30 inches wide, with a height of 70 feet in the back and 50 feet in the front. The tank, which was located 50 feet away from the end of the ramp, was 25 feet long by 10 feet wide and 3 feet deep.[36]

Joseph Hellbrun and the members of the new Manhattan Beach Opera Company arrived in Denver from New York on May 16, 1902. The members of the company included Laura Millard, Lee Hobbs Martin, Laura Denio Jaffray, Katheryn Bradbury, Jessie Fahnstock, William T. Prizer, Robert Parkins, and A. Edward Archard. In all, according to the *Rocky Mountain News*, there were sixty members of the company, and all were favorites in Eastern theater circles. They began rehearsals for their first production of the season, *The Amer*, on May 18, with the first dress rehearsal six days later. The *News* said the company "showed off to advantage," and predicted a great season at the theater. Hellbrun and Mayer assured newspaper readers that no expenses would be spared when it came to the theatrical productions at Manhattan Beach for the 1902 season.[37]

More than 10,000 people passed through the gates of Manhattan Beach when it opened for the summer on May 25, 1902. Marvelous Marsh did his first jump after a performance by Koenigsburg's band and a demonstration by Professor Clark's dogs and monkeys. Marsh, described by the *Denver Post* as a "small, wiry, dark-haired man," appeared shortly after 4 p.m. Wearing a robe over his tights, he dropped his robe and climbed the ladder to the top of his ramp. After surveying the scene and checking wind conditions, with a shout he took off down the ramp on his specially constructed bicycle. About fifteen feet from the end of the ramp, he vaulted over the handlebars in a "graceful parabolic curve" and dove head-first into the tank. As he rose from the water the crowd let out a great cheer. Marsh repeated the stunt that night, accompanied by flashing lights and fire.[38]

After witnessing Marvelous Marsh's first ride at the park, the crowd headed for the theater and the first performance of *The Amer*. The *Denver Post* was less than impressed with the production, writing that "much allowance should be made for the usual disadvantages attendant upon a first night by a new company in a new place." The newspaper described the cast members as being

A button showing the bicycle stunt performed by Charles "Marvelous" Marsh. Although the button is not from his time at Manhattan Beach, it does show the steps he followed in performing his bicycle jump. *Source:* Author's collection.

weak, off-key, and passable. The *Denver Republican* found the new scenery backdrops to be "glaringly new" with a combination of colors that would "make an impressionist painter wild—perhaps not with delight." Only the *Denver Times* found the performance "entirely satisfactory." The theater company performed *Maritana* its second week, and the *Rocky Mountain News* was kinder in its review, writing that it "has hardly ever been better played and produced by a stock organization."[39]

On the night of May 26, twenty-year-old Ben Bowen performed his first balloon ascension at the park, going up at about 9 p.m. Bowen had been performing in his home state of New Jersey since he was fifteen, and had performed at the Pan-American Exposition in Buffalo prior to coming to Manhattan Beach. Several people at the park on the night of May 26, including Max Mayer and Marvelous Marsh, urged Bowen not to go up, saying it was too dark and windy. Bowen insisted, saying his ascension had been advertised for several days and that if he did not do one, people would think he was a "fakir." At the time Bowen ascended the wind had died down some, but when he was several hundred feet up the wind picked up and blew the balloon out over the lake. He started to bring the balloon down over the lake, and initially, people thought it was part of his act. However, several people on the ground noticed that he was not shooting off fireworks as originally planned during his descent. Details of what happened next are somewhat confusing and depend on which newspaper was reporting, but Bowen seems to have jumped from the balloon before it hit the lake. He was wearing heavy clothing at the time and had not taken a parachute or life preserver up with him. Some accounts stated he was shouting for help as he jumped from the balloon, while other accounts say he called for help once he hit the water. Men in two rowboats from the park's fleet immediately went to the spot where they thought he had entered the water but could find no trace of him. The steamboat and rowboats followed the balloon to the small island between Sloan's and Cooper Lakes, but found no trace of Bowen there either. George Price, the purser on the steamboat, and William Randall, the engineer, said they heard Bowen calling for help about sixty yards from the island, but after half an hour of searching, there was no trace of the balloonist.[40]

The steamship and eight rowboats dragged Sloan's Lake all night searching for Bowen. Members of the opera company helped with the search, and several people from the park went to neighboring houses on the off chance Bowen had waded ashore and gone to one of them for help. In the morning, the eight rowboats and the steamship continued the search. Balloonist Ivy Baldwin arrived at the park with bottles filled with lime and water. When submerged in the lake they would explode, and if near Bowen's body at the time would cause it to surface. When that failed, the searchers tried dynamite without success. Searchers finally recovered Bowen's body on May 31. The coroner determined that a cramp had caused the young man to drown before rescuers could get to him. One newspaper writer said that Bowen's death proved balloon ascensions should be stopped, which so angered Ivy Baldwin that he told the *Denver Post* that he was ready to "meet that 'half-baked scribbler' anytime, anywhere and with any old kind of weapons." After Ben Bowen's tragic death, his friend Walter Flexon took over balloon ascensions at the park for the summer.[41]

Marvelous Marsh was so popular at Manhattan Beach that management extended his stay until mid-June, when he had to leave due to other engagements. The electric fountain, which included animated fairy dancers, was so popular that the Denver Tramway Company had to adjust its schedules so that park visitors could stay to see the half-hour nighttime show before catching the streetcar home. With the park so popular, in early June Hellbrun and Mayer made the unusual move of dropping the gate admission price from a quarter to ten cents. Admission fees were meant to keep unruly customers out of amusement parks, so lowering it was a bold move. Hellbrun and Mayer were careful to point out to the *Denver Times* that intoxicating drinks were strictly prohibited at the park, and they also revealed a new tool for enforcing good behavior that was at their disposal. On June 5 they turned on the park's newest attraction, a searchlight. The first night in operation it picked out the state capitol building in Denver along with "other distant points" while also attracting attention to the park. But, as Hellbrun and Mayer explained to the

*Times*, the searchlight could also illuminate any part of the park grounds, "so as to insure against any infraction of the rules laid down governing the general conduct of the place." In the hopes of further making Manhattan Beach an "eminently respectable resort for families," the managers instituted free Children's Days on Thursdays throughout the summer. In addition to free admission to the park, which sent the children at "breakneck speed past the gatekeeper, whom they seemed to have a right to ignore," the children also got free rides on the steamboat, merry-go-round, and miniature train. At the end of June, Hellbrun and Mayer adopted a new slogan, naming the park "Denver's Only Summer Resort Fanned by Lake Breezes."[42]

As the summer progressed, several groups booked large picnics at the park, joining the ever-increasing crowds. In mid-June the Brotherhood of Railroad Trainmen brought 7,000 people to

Children waiting to board the miniature train at Manhattan Beach in the early 1900s. *Source:* History Colorado, Object # 89.451.3041.

the park for fishing in Sloan's Lake and dancing at the floating pavilion despite it being a chilly day. The Grocery Employees Union held its annual picnic at the park on July 4, with over 1,500 people in attendance, ending with a massive fireworks show depicting the Battle of Manila. In the middle of the month, the Ancient Order of Hibernians held its gathering at the park. The Knights of Pythias picnic in early August brought 4,000 people, while the Grand Army of the Republic picnic two weeks later brought only a few hundred people. The day featured special athletic events, including a fat ladies' race (the victor, Frances Hill, won a "fine vase"), a Civil War veterans' race, a potato race and sack race for boys, and a lemon race for girls under 18 (who had to carry a lemon on the backs of their hands to the finish line). The day ended with a dance and cakewalk on the floating pavilion. At the end of August, the Socialists of Denver held their picnic at the park. In addition to the athletic and boating competitions, the day also featured Indian club exhibitions by G. W. Patterson and his daughter. The featured speaker of the day was Socialist leader Eugene V. Debs, who delivered three speeches at the park. The day ended with a fireworks show over the lake.[43]

When Walter Flexon took over the balloon ascensions at the park, he was joined by Sappho the monkey, who also made balloon ascensions and parachute jumps. Sappho was especially popular with the children on the free Children's Days. In mid-June, Mayer and Hellbrun hired French balloonist La Gette to perform at the park for a short time. Hiring La Gette required a "special and hugely expensive contract" according to the *Rocky Mountain News*, but he was so popular that he was held over until the end of June. Throughout the summer the park brought in a number of other special acts, including mind reader Mademoiselle Orietta. To close out the season on September 14, Hellbrun and Mayer scheduled a Butcher's Contest as part of the Denver Butcher Protective Union's annual free barbecue. In June the men told the *Denver Post* that it would be their policy "to introduce at least one big sensational act, from time to time" throughout the summer, but for many the Butcher Contest went too far. The Humane Society urged Denver police to stop the event, while the butchers argued that it would determine the Western champion butcher. Despite protests, the *Longmont Ledger* reported that an "immense crowd" was at the park that day to watch Jacob Teitz win the beef dressing contest and Jacob Baer the sheep dressing.[44]

By the time of the Butcher Contest, the mood at Manhattan Beach had already soured considerably. Throughout the summer the productions at the theater had improved and won mostly high praise from audiences and Denver's newspapers. The *Denver Post* said the company's production of *The Little Trooper* in June was of "special merit" with excellent costumes and scenery, and the *Rocky Mountain News* said the chorus for the double bill of *Cavalleria Rusticana* and *Trial by Jury* was "in fine voice." That show even brought General Frederick Funston, who was a fan of *Cavalleria Rusticana*, to Manhattan Beach. The productions of *Boccaccio* and *The Grand Duchess* were highly praised, with the *Post* saying that *The Grand Duchess* brought "nightly increasing attendance" to the park. There was such high demand for Sunday matinees that management even dropped the Wednesday matinee to provide one on Sundays.[45]

By mid-August, however, things were quickly beginning to fall apart. The *Denver Post* said the August 11 performance of *Olivette* was "rather ragged," but the newspaper was sure it would improve. *Olivette* was followed by Henry W. Hunt and Charles Fonteyn Manney's *The Nameless Opera* which, despite a promised cash prize to the audience member who came up with a name for it, was dropped after only one performance and replaced by more showings of *Olivette*. The season ended abruptly with *Said Pasha* on August 25 when it was revealed that members of the chorus had not been paid for two weeks and that most of them did not have enough money to even return home. Other theaters in Denver quickly organized a benefit for the stranded chorus members, which was held at the Broadway Theater on August 29. Manager Peter McCourt offered the Boston Bijou Opera Company for the event, while Mary Elitch Long offered the services of actress Maude Fealy. The benefit raised about $250 for the actors. At the end of September, Alexander Henderson, the stage director at Manhattan Beach, filed a $1,200 lawsuit against Hellbrun and Mayer to recover back pay for himself, music conductor William T. Glover, and several members of the cast and chorus. It was an ugly end to a season that had seemed to start so well.[46]

With Hellbrun and Mayer obviously gone from Manhattan Beach ahead of the 1903 season, the Southern Investment Company hired J. Edgar Clifford, who had worked for the *Denver Post* and the Sells-Floto Circus, to manage the park. Devastating fires in 1901 and 1902 finally led to the closure of rival Arlington Park after the 1902 season, leaving only Elitch's for the time being as Manhattan Beach's only competitor. Aside from the usual repainting of the buildings, planting new flowers, and other improvements to the park grounds, Clifford made relatively few changes to the attractions at the park. Although he initially suggested there would be a new roller coaster, a crystal maze, and illustrated song machines, the only new addition was a sand bowling beach (bocce ball). Clifford also dropped the gate admission fee entirely, allowing free entry to the park. "The Point Is This," said an ad for opening day, "You get into the grounds FREE! and help yourself to the fun!" Manhattan Beach finally opened for the 1903 season on June 14.[47]

At the theater, Clifford decided to go with vaudeville acts rather than plays and a stock theater company, although later in the summer he did start the Manhattan Beach Stock Company to stage one-act plays. Initially advertised as high-class vaudeville, Clifford later settled on "polite vaudeville" as the description. Opening acts at the theater included dancer Jessie Smith Bronx (who accidentally started a fire in the building with a candle), European acrobatic comedians DeMora and Graceta, and child singer Dainty Little Doris. Acts later in the summer included ventriloquist Claude Tana (known as Clever Tana), female impersonator Charles Fox, banjo player John H. Mack, the Fay Sisters as "The Matinee Girls," and Ella Ewing, billed as the tallest woman on earth at 8 feet 4 inches. Ewing arrived at the park in mid-July, but she ended up cutting her engagement short when she left for Butte, Montana, on August 4 to marry Édouard Beaupré, who was billed as being 8 feet 6 inches tall. (It appears the marriage never actually took place.)[48]

Clifford dropped the free Children's Days of the previous season, but he regularly scheduled Punch and Judy puppet shows for the children, and Professor Rutherford offered free dance lessons for children and adults in the pavilion. At the end of June, the park began offering free moving pictures in one of the outdoor areas, as well as specialty acts on the grounds. The most popular of these acts was an appearance by Baron de Malchin of Russia, a champion broad swordsman. Among the baron's company were two women, Mary McLean and Marie Von Lake, who did fencing exhibitions. Almost 10,000 people turned out to see the baron and his company at Manhattan Beach on August 1.[49]

Denver's turnverein societies (which were German social and athletic clubs) held two massive picnics at Manhattan Beach during the 1903 season. The first, on June 28, under the Rocky Mountain Turn Berzirk, brought 15,000 people to the park for athletic events, dancing, marching and drills, dinner, speeches, and the park's amusement offerings. The only dark moment came when attendees realized there was no beer. Although beer had been ordered, the Denver fire and police boards threatened that "if the amber fluid was not moved off the grounds before noon it would all be dumped in a ditch," despite having already given permission to have it served there. At this, the crowd became somewhat upset, but the *Rocky Mountain News* reported when the crowd finally broke up around midnight it was while "vowing they had never had a better time." The second turnverein picnic,

Dancers in the dance pavilion at Manhattan Beach in the early 1900s. *Source:* Author's collection.

on September 6, under the West Denver Turnverein, brought 12,000 people to the park for the first annual Field Day. In addition to athletic events, former Denver mayor Henry Johnson gave a speech explaining the proposed new charter that would create the City and County of Denver, relieving the city from state control. The day also included special dances in the pavilion and performances in the theater.[50]

For the Fourth of July, Clifford staged an elaborate naval battle on Sloan's Lake, with the *Denver Post* reporting that "Battleships of many designs and questionable displacement" floated on the lake, but that the park's force successfully defeated the enemy. A 45-minute fireworks show followed the battle, starting with "red fire, then sizzling, crackling, screeching things of beauty that whirled and twisted and lingered in the floating colors, and things that suggested men on fire, boats in the air and balloons galore." A relatively small crowd of 5,000 people were at the park for the Fourth, but a crowd three times that size attended the official Labor Day picnic at the park on September 7. In addition to special athletic events, there were yacht races between the *Lark*, *Skylark*, and *Reliance* boats, rowing competitions, dancing in the pavilion, and continuous vaudeville in the theater. The day ended with a massive fireworks spectacle called "The Birth of the Sun." The day very nearly became a tragic one when, around 5 p.m., two men in a buggy pulled up to the fence at the northwest corner of the park and fired shotguns into the grounds. The first round sounded like firecrackers to many of the park's visitors, but several people—including two police officers, Carney and Peisse—had gone to investigate when the men fired a second round. Buckshot from the second round hit Arthur Jones, 14, in the temple and James Durmon, also 14, in the hand; luckily the injuries were not serious. Realizing what was happening, Officers Carney and Peisse went after the men, who fired one more round before fleeing in their buggy. The officers commandeered the Twenty-Third Avenue streetcar to pursue the men, directing the chase from the front of the streetcar, but obviously limited by the tracks it had to follow. The officers lost the two men as they traveled into downtown Denver. The *Denver Post* said the fence around the park likely prevented the two gunmen from causing more serious injuries and reported that the rest of the day was "unmarred by displeasing happenings." The Labor Day celebration marked the end of the 1903 season and J. Edgar Clifford's brief run as manager of Manhattan Beach as the Southern Investment Company looked for a new lessee to manage the park.[51]

CHAPTER 5

# Manhattan Beach and the People from Detroit

THE SOUTHERN INVESTMENT COMPANY LEASED MANHATTAN Beach to the Denver Recreation Company, which was a newly formed subsidiary of the Michigan Amusement Company of Detroit, for the 1904 season. Among the backers of the new company were steel magnate Allen W. Atterbury, C. W. Barker of the Detroit Stove Works, and capitalist Allenson S. Brooks. With the deal finalized in April, the new management team started an ambitious renovation program that would eventually delay the season opening for the park until June 18, more than two weeks later than normal. A crew of 150 men were hard at work on the park in the weeks before opening day.[1]

Workers completely remodeled the theater, painting it white, and installing 300 additional lights. All of the other park buildings were painted white with green trim, and the fence around the park was painted white as well, leading the *Denver Republican* to refer to the park as "the White City by the Lake." The old boathouse was converted to a dancing pavilion with a new hardwood floor, and the park's café was turned into a Japanese Tea Garden with "thousands of incandescent lights secreted in dainty Japanese lanterns" and a "wealth of flowers and plants." After the park opened, Japanese waiters served customers at the tea garden. Flowers and lights were everywhere on the park grounds, with arches covered with rows of colored lights making for a "magnificent illuminated promenade." At the bathing beach the new managers installed a children's area under the supervision of trained nurses and attendants. The *City of Denver* steamship was completely overhauled, and all of the rowboats were repainted, with several new boats joining the fleet. The merry-go-round, shooting gallery, miniature train, and bowling alley installed under previous managers were left untouched.[2]

To replace the park's original roller coaster, which had been torn down in 1902, the Denver Recreation Company spent $12,000 to build a new roller coaster, the Figure 8 Toboggan. The coaster's 2,000-foot track ran half the length of the park grounds, and according to the *Denver Republican* it was the largest in the United States. The *Rocky Mountain News*, being more modest and perhaps more accurate, said it was the longest west of St. Louis. Twelve cars, each holding four passengers in two seats, ran continuously on the coaster, making a complete trip in sixty seconds.

Looking east over the park grounds from the theater, with the Figure 8 Toboggan Coaster behind the boathouse. *Source:* Author's collection.

Another new attraction at the park was a Gypsy Camp with six tents. Also ready for opening day were the baby incubators on the midway. The *News* was careful to point out that "this feature is purely educational, and has not been secured as a freak exhibit in any way." Two doctors and a nurse were always in attendance when a baby was in the incubator, with the nurse ready to explain to visitors how the incubators worked. While this sounds very similar to the way Martin Couney operated his baby incubator displays, there is again no indication that he was the one at Manhattan Beach that summer. In all, the new company spent over $40,000 on improvements for the 1904 season. Admission to the park was set at ten cents, with separate fees for most attractions.[3]

When the park opened for the season on June 18, the featured act was Ellery's Royal Italian Band under the direction of Manfredo Chiffarelli. The band, famous throughout the United

The Figure 8 Toboggan Coaster with the Helter-Skelter slide in front of it. *Source: Denver Municipal Facts,* July 30, 1910.

States, had performed at the 1904 World's Fair in St. Louis before coming to Manhattan Beach. Considered one of the best Italian bands at the time, it was unique for its combination of brass and woodwind instruments. Ellery's Royal Italian Band gave daily afternoon and evening concerts on the park grounds and in the theater. Vaudeville acts in the theater for the park's opening included Great Leon the illusionist, the comedy teams of Swan and Bombard and Phil and Nettie Peters, and instrumentalists Almont and Dumont. The *Rocky Mountain News* said that "while no startling headliner's names appear upon the bill, yet there is not a mediocre name on the list." Each week the theater also put on a new bioscope motion picture.[4]

According to the *Denver Post*, 5,000 people passed through the park gates on opening day, and the *Rocky Mountain News* reported that "All day the resort was thronged, and at night the grounds were filled with several thousand people." The *News* went on to state that never in the history of Manhattan Beach had a season started with such bright prospects, with Helen Ring Robinson singling out Ellery's Royal Italian Band as never being in finer form and saying the vaudeville acts in the theater were of "exceptional merit." When the park's 2,000 lights were turned on at night, the *Post* described it as "an imposing spectacle" that "gave to the grounds a picturesqueness that simply beggars description." Opening day nearly turned into a disaster when, just before the gates opened, a fire broke out in a lunch stand owned by L. D. Littlefield and G. H. Powers across the street from the park. Until firefighters had it contained, the fire threatened to spread to the buildings at Manhattan Beach's entrance.[5]

Aside from Ellery's band, the new dance pavilion and roller coaster proved to be the most popular attractions at the renovated park. Describing the dancers, *Denver Post* theater critic Frank W. White wrote of the solemn looks on their faces, saying "Girls and boys seemed to feel a sort of sanctified ecstasy and most of them looked as though they were enjoying a first-class funeral rather than a gallant merrymaking." He described the embraces he spotted as the Colfax clutch, the Globeville grip, men who held their partners' arms up to their ears, and those who danced face-to-face. Above it all, White wrote, were the "soft swish of the dresses, the rhythm of the gliding feet as the silent dancers waltzed up and down in pretty and graceful measure." The crowd at the roller coaster, where hundreds waited throughout the day for their chance to ride, was far livelier. Most people took a double ride at a nickel apiece.[6]

The second week of the season brought Denver native Henry Linton and the Lawrence Sisters to the theater in an act entitled "Three of a Kind," the Robert Carter Company with their skit "The Wise Mr. Conn," prima donna Mademoiselle Avery Strakosch, and the juggling team The Mathieus. The bioscope feature of the week was pictures of the Slocum steamboat disaster in New York City. The boat caught fire and sank on June 15, 1904, killing over 1,000 of the people on board. Many park goers objected to this particular presentation given how recently it had happened, and park management quickly removed it from the show, replacing it with "some very pleasing" images.[7]

Manhattan Beach's new management made sure to provide several special events for the first Fourth of July at the new park. In the afternoon, Wayne Abbott performed a balloon ascension and parachute jump over the lake. In the evening, visitors got to see a reenactment of the storming of Port Arthur during the Russo-Japanese War on the lake. Workers had constructed a fort representing Port Arthur on the shore of Sloan's Lake, and boats on the lake represented the Russian and Japanese fleets. The evening began with a naval battle between the two fleets "in which thousands of bombs and rockets will be used, making the scene realistic in the extreme." After the naval battle, soldiers stormed the fort, firing guns and throwing bombs. The battle ended with the destruction of the fort and the sinking of one of the Russian battleships. At night, management staged an elaborate fireworks display over the lake with a number of set pieces, including a depiction of Niagara Falls. In between the naval battle and the fireworks display, visitors to the theater got to see Joe Howard and Ida Emerson in *A Night at the Opera*, trick jumper William Deengow, and comedian Dorothy Levell.[8]

Attendance at the park continued to grow as the summer progressed, with the *Denver Post* reporting large crowds and the *Rocky Mountain News* saying a "goodly number" of Denver Tramway riders were going to the park. The *Post* said a large crowd was at the park for the Fourth, and despite a run of bad weather after that, attendance was "generous." Given the late start of the Denver Recreation Company's renovations at the park, not everything was ready on opening day and new attractions continued to open throughout the summer. In early July the Ulaugh Kastle and Komedy Kave opened, with the *Post* calling the new features "decided novelties in the amusement line." No description of the two attractions survives but, given the names, they were probably fun houses. They apparently were too novel for Denver's amusement park customers at the time as they did not survive past the 1904 season.[9]

Management brought back Children's Days on Tuesdays in mid-July, and the recently installed big swings were especially popular with children, as were rides on the miniature railroad and roller coaster. Children's Days also included lawn games and wading in the lake, and ended with special dinners in the pavilion, "when the sun is setting and the resort is at its prettiest." A number of groups held special picnics at the park throughout the summer as well, including the Ladies Auxiliary of the BMH, the women in charge of the relief fund for the Grand Army of the Republic, and the Waunita Branch of the Order of Rebekah. The rides, vaudeville acts at the theater, and group outings kept attendance up throughout the season.[10]

On July 17, management staged the first of a weeklong series of bronco busting contests on the open field at the east end of the park during the day and night, with the nighttime shows illuminated by electric arc lights. The company hired ten of the "most noted and daring bronco riders of the western plains," including Jim Little of New Mexico, the Jackson brothers, Ira Wines, Texas Connors, and John Blocker. Each afternoon and evening the men gave demonstrations in riding, roping, shooting, and trick riding. The park brought in twenty of the "fiercest outlaw horses" for the men to work with. Another feature of the shows was Bucking Rastus, a famously temperamental white mule who had appeared at parks and fairs throughout the United States. Rastus took "great delight in tossing the bronco busters right and left," and volunteers from the audience could win prizes if they could ride him for two minutes. The bronco busting contests, combined with the other attractions, helped keep Manhattan Beach "filled to overflowing all day, from quite early in the morning until late at night" according to the *Denver Post*.[11]

The bronco busting contest was the last major special event scheduled by park management for the summer. After that, the vaudeville acts at the theater were the big draw. Acts for the rest of the season included Miles McCarthy and Aida Wolcott in the show *A Race Tout's Dream*, the banjo-playing Olson Brothers, snake charmer Harry Davies (who was bitten by his Texas diamondback rattler and had to be treated by the Denver police surgeon), a juggling cat, the Zeb and Zorrow bicycling troupe, singer Nora Bayes, and coronet player Alice Raymond. All of the shows were highly praised by Denver's newspapers, with the *Post* writing that Manhattan Beach's theater was "proving one of the most popular attractions in the city and is rapidly gaining a large patronage, who appreciate the good vaudeville bill presented." Each performance ended with a bioscope presentation of new pictures each week.[12]

The *Denver Post* said there was a "strong rivalry" between the indoor and outdoor attractions at Manhattan Beach with the cool breezes on the lake drawing large crowds, while "moonlight on the lake" made it "doubly attractive." For the more daring, the roller coaster, under the direction of Mr. Curry, was the top draw, and it carried "crowds running into the hundreds" each day. Close behind in popularity was the dance pavilion which, in addition to its regular business, hosted special parties for Denver area dance clubs. Claude Robey, a graduate of Villa Park High School in Denver and a member of the Trinity Methodist Church choir, even wrote a new song, "Where the Cherry Greets the Platte," that debuted at the dance pavilion and was an instant hit with the dancers. Robey dreamed of becoming a composer and would write several more songs in his short life, including "When Moonbeams Kiss the Clover" in 1909, before going into the educational field until his death in 1923.[13]

On August 6, a group of young Denver society women rented Manhattan Beach to host a fundraiser for St. Vincent's Orphanage, which had been forced to go into debt to build a new home after a fire in 1902 destroyed the previous building. It was not the orphanage's first visit to the park, but it was their first fundraiser held there. Children from the orphanage were given free rein at the park that day. Wayne Abbott agreed to do a special balloon ascension and parachute drop, which the children enjoyed, but not nearly as much as they enjoyed rides on the roller coaster where, according to the *Rocky Mountain News*, the "delighted screams as the cars rounded a sharp turn could be heard a long way off." Two special programs in the theater, dancing in the pavilion, and the "usual sideshows" of the balloon man, the returning balls, and the shooting gallery made for a full day. The women behind the event served refreshments in the Japanese Tea Garden "beneath flowered booths." An estimated 12,000 people entered Manhattan Beach that day, raising a little over $2,600 for the orphanage.[14]

The *Denver Post* said that vaudeville shows in the theater for the remainder of the season were "diversified and featureful." Heading into the last week of the summer, new acts included the comedy juggler La Toska and illusionist The Great Leon, who called his act "A Night in India." As Labor Day approached, both the *Post* and *Rocky Mountain News* urged their readers to visit the dance pavilion or get one last ride in on the roller coaster before the park closed for the season. When Labor Day finally arrived, the *News* said the season was "one of the best that has been won by the resort in years," and that the stockholders from Detroit were "more than satisfied." As soon as the park closed, officials with the Denver Recreation Company began making plans for the next year, but the park had one last event to host before all was quiet. On September 10, Manhattan Beach was the site of the Colorado Democratic Party's first annual picnic. All of the rides and concessions, including the theater, were in operation for the day and open to anyone who paid the 25-cent admission fee. Speakers for the day included former Colorado governors Charles S. Thomas and Alva Adams, *Rocky Mountain News* publisher and United States senator Thomas M. Patterson, and future United States senator Charles J. Hughes Jr.[15]

As the 1905 season approached, the Denver Recreation Company once again waited until the last minute to begin making changes at Manhattan Beach. According to legend, the *City of Denver* steamboat sank in a storm either at the end of the 1904 season or during the 1905 season and was not replaced. On April 28, 1905, the *Denver Post* announced that after long negotiations the park had signed a contract with the Richardson Ball Bearing Skate Company and Fred W. Nall of Chicago to build a new roller-skating rink at the park, located to the left inside the main gate. The newspaper said it would take about $10,000 to build the rink, with $4,000 of that going for the building that would house it. On April 29 the building permit was issued, and by mid-May construction was well underway on what Fred Nall said was the largest outdoor skating rink in the country. The 180-foot by 90-foot building had an open court in the center and was open on all sides, allowing for greater air circulation. The bandstand was in the center of the open court, and at night "hundreds of electric

Manhattan Beach's roller-skating rink. *Source:* The Denver Public Library, Western History Collection, X-19525.

lights and beautiful varicolored lanterns" made the rink glow. The 10,000–square foot skating surface was a highly polished maple floor, and there was a 20-foot-wide promenade area around the skating area. Even with the late start in construction, management promised that the rink would be ready on opening day.[16]

Replacing the Ulaugh Kastle and the Komedy Kave were the Laughing Gallery and the Temple of Mirth. The Laughing Gallery was filled with distorting mirrors to "reflect the visitors in most grotesque characters," while the Temple of Mirth housed a helter-skelter spiral-shaped slide. As work on the new buildings progressed, crews were also hard at work on the grounds. The *News* reported that "every walk and grass plot is carefully diagramed, evenly cut and trimmed and beautifully bedded with flowers of all kinds." All of the trees were trimmed, and the banks of the canal were turned into flower beds, with old rowboats buried and used as planters. Manager William Lawrence stressed, though, that there would never be "Keep Off the Grass" signs at the park because "to deprive the children of the pleasure of rolling on the grass would take from them half the pleasure of the park." The newspaper went on to say that Manhattan Beach had "taken on an appearance of fairyland." Another new feature at the park was box ball bowling, which the *Rocky Mountain News* described as a "delightful form of exercise and amusement for women and children." Management also purchased a new fleet of rowboats for the lake from a company in Detroit. However, a railroad strike in Chicago delayed the new boats from arriving at the park until the afternoon of opening day. Described as being of the latest and safest design, the new boats were wider and lighter than the older boats, had airtight compartments to make them virtually

Manhattan Beach's Laughing Gallery, which was filled with distorting mirrors. *Source:* The Denver Public Library, Western History Collection, X-19529.

unsinkable, and could hold six to eight people. The twenty-five new boats were named for the presidents from George Washington to Theodore Roosevelt.[17]

Manhattan Beach opened for the 1905 season on the afternoon of May 27. The *Rocky Mountain News* said that once the gates opened "the orchestras in the dancing and roller skating pavilions struck up, the engine of the miniature railroad tooted its whistle, the animals of the merry-go-round began cavorting to the harmony of a new organ, the concessionaries commenced their bids for patronage, and Denver's delightful summer pleasure resort was open." Even poor weather and a hailstorm over the area late in the afternoon did not drive the crowd away. Although the distorted mirrors in the laughing gallery and the four box ball alleys were popular (the *News* said it was "highly amusing" to watch people until they got the hang of the game), the new roller-skating rink was the star attraction, especially at night with the lights on. Even the highly praised vaudeville acts in the theater could not outshine the rink. Allen Atterbury and A. M. Pelletreau, investors from Detroit, were at the park for opening day, as was L. M. Richardson of the roller-skating company.[18]

By the second day of the season, the new rowboats on the lake had become so popular that management decided to add some motorboats to the fleet, ordering them from Detroit as well. The box ball alleys also continued to gain in popularity, with the *Rocky Mountain News* saying all four alleys were "constantly in use by devotees of the game." Also growing in popularity as the summer progressed was the Temple of Mirth and its helter-skelter slide. In early June the *Denver Post* reported that the "terrifying appearance" of the slide had kept many people from trying it, but once they got up the nerve to attempt it, they soon went back for another turn. The newspaper was certain the slide would "probably compete with any of the older attractions."[19]

Throughout the early weeks of the 1905 season the vaudeville acts in the theater remained highly praised, as usual. Among the acts booked through the end of June were Spaulding, who jumped with his hands, blackface storyteller Tom Ripley, comedy jugglers and singers Edward La Vine and Lillian Walton, blackface comedians Herbert and Willing, and Señor Maceo and his talking dog. One of the biggest acts to appear at the theater was Dubec's dog, monkey, and cat circus. His act was particularly popular with children who, beginning on June 15, were admitted to the park free each Children's Day to "help the children enjoy their season of rest from study." Vaudeville's run at the park came to an abrupt end in early July, however, when manager William Lawrence dropped it in favor of hourlong programs in the theater that included illustrated songs, moving pictures, "and entertainment of that character." Lawrence told the *Denver Post* that the Denver Recreation Company wanted Manhattan Beach to be known as a playground for the public rather than as a summer theater. In fact, Lawrence told *Post* theater critic Frank W. White that management preferred to keep park visitors out of the theater because

Midway at Manhattan Beach with the Box Ball Alley, Electric Studio, Ping Pong building, and other concessions. The park's observation tower is between the midway and the theater. *Source:* Author's collection.

they made more money on the other attractions than they did the theater. The change in program, according to the *Post*, would encourage visitors to enjoy the outdoor pleasures of the "Coney Island of the West."[20]

Although the nickname was coming into common use for the park by 1905, Lawrence also took issue with referring to Manhattan Beach as the Coney Island of the West. As the *Rocky Mountain News* explained, there were two sides to Coney Island in New York. One was a place of unlimited fun while the other was "a place that it isn't quite proper people should attend." The Denver Recreation Company wanted Manhattan Beach to be a place for "enjoyment and fun and freedom so far as propriety permits," and did not want to encourage people to connect it with the seedier side of the New York playground. The new attractions at the park, said the newspaper, were "all of high class," and at a time when many amusement parks used temporary materials such as staff (created for the 1893 Columbian Exposition, it was a mixture of powdered gypsum, alumina, glycerine, dextrine, and fibers) to create fantastically shaped structures that lasted only a few years, management at the Beach believed in "permanency, as is indicated by the solidity and expensiveness of the new improvements." While Lawrence most likely preferred the "White City by the Lake" nickname sometimes used that summer for the park, newspapers still frequently referred to it as the Coney Island of the West.[21]

The change in program at the theater did not seem to hurt attendance at the park, and some of the illustrated songs and motion pictures shows were quite popular. The man described by the newspapers as "Denver's musical postal clerk," Mr. Avery, was a hit with his song "The Silvery Colorado Wends Its Way," which was accompanied by stereopticon slides. Among the motion pictures offered were Long Island at night, the New York City subway system, a trip to the moon, and a series "showing the trials of a man and two girls who become acquaintances through a 'personal' in a newspaper." Management did still book the occasional vaudeville act, including the Ward Trio and their Human Bridge and the Flying Banyards, both aerial acts.[22]

The Fourth of July brought another elaborate fireworks spectacle to the park, and the *Denver Post* was justified in saying Sloan's Lake would be a "lake of fire" that day. Both the *Rocky Mountain News* and the *Post* reported that William Lawrence said that the day would not be complete without pyrotechnics and as such, he sought to get "'the best fireworks made.'" Consisting of twenty-one separate displays both in the air and on the water, it was the most elaborate fireworks show ever seen at the park. The displays included aerial maroons, star and serpent fireworks, Japanese willow tree displays, floral bombshells, a Tree of Liberty display, a piece called devils among the talon that produced "hissing dragons," batteries of Japanese electric musical fireworks, a Yankee Doodle display, a 10,000 shot Rough Riders display, and hundreds of rockets. Over 8,000 people visited the park that day, with the *News* saying the roller coaster, Temple of Mirth, dance pavilion,

A view of the grounds at Manhattan Beach. The dance pavilion and Sloan's Lake are just visible behind the trees. *Source:* Author's collection.

*Roller Rink*
*From Main Entrance looking to the left.*

Another view of the grounds with the Roller-Skating Rink on the left and the Laughing Gallery on the right. •The lake and a refreshment stand are behind the trees in the center of the photograph. *Source:* Author's collection.

and the rowboats were the most popular attractions. Once the fireworks started at night, "not until the last set piece was fired did the crowd begin to move." Only one minor accident occurred that day when an intoxicated man fell out of one of the rowboats, but he "was promptly rescued."[23]

So many groups booked private parties at Manhattan Beach during the summer of 1905 that the park sometimes hosted two or more groups at a time. Among the groups holding gatherings at the park that summer were the House of the Good Shepherd, Camp No. 4 of the Patriotic Order of America, the Royal Highlanders, the Rathbone Sisters, the Letter Carriers, the Eagles, and the Laundry Workers. The park also hosted another fundraiser for St. Vincent's Orphanage on August 5, with the children from the orphanage again having free rein at the park. Over 10,000 people paid admission that day, and one lucky visitor even won $100 in gold. Wayne Abbott once again made a balloon ascension and parachute drop for the children, rising over one mile into the air in his balloon before jumping. The special day raised about $4,000 for the orphanage. A week after the orphanage picnic, the Democratic Party held their second annual picnic at Manhattan Beach, with "Thousands of Democrats, their families and friends . . . making merry."[24]

The end of August brought the return of bronco busting contests to the park, but with a much smaller field of riders and horses so that it could all take place on the stage in the theater. Charles and Harry Tipton did the riding and busting, while Henry Brennan performed rope tricks. A specially constructed 90-foot-long curtain served as a corral to contain the horses on the stage, and a wire screen, hanging from a 3/8-inch iron cable and secured with 1/4-inch iron hooks, made the performances "absolutely safe" for audiences. The George W. Cook Drum Corps and Cooks' Ladies Drill Team provided additional entertainment during the bronco busting performances, along with illustrated songs and motion picture shows that included *The Firebug*, *The Gordon Bennet Automobile Races*, and *A Glutinous Negro*.[25]

After such a successful season, management decided to keep the park open until October 1, in part, as the *Denver Post* explained, because "usually September is the most beautiful season of the year in Denver and it is believed by the beach people that the opportunity for outdoor entertainment will be taken advantage of and they will receive some commercial return for their sense of the artistic." All of the park's attractions remained open, but after initially attracting good crowds, attendance must have dropped off dramatically as the management did not repeat the experiment again the next year.[26]

As Manhattan Beach prepared for the 1906 season, it did so knowing that it would face competition from a new rival. Tuileries Park, at Broadway and Floyd in Englewood, was built on the site of Orchard Place, a beer garden that became known as a haven for gamblers and other troublemakers. Backed by a group of men from Cripple Creek, the new park cost $140,000 and included a roller-skating rink, baseball diamond, dance hall, theater, aerodrome where balloonists and aerialists performed, and a miniature railroad. The park was patterned after Coney Island in Kansas City, and William Simpson of Kansas City was the first manager of it. The *Denver Republican* said Tuileries was "the most beautiful natural park" in Colorado. It officially opened on July 26, 1906, two months after Manhattan Beach opened for the season.[27]

Longtime rival Elitch Gardens had also become a more typical amusement park by 1906. After adding the Edison Vitascope in 1896 and the *Monitor* and *Merrimack* battle reenactment in 1899, in 1900 Mary Elitch added a miniature train, which had taken two years to build, to her park. The coal-burning engine pulled eight cars through the park on a 12-gauge track. In 1904 Elitch's finally received its first roller coaster (after a false start on one in 1893), a Figure 8 Toboggan coaster similar to the one at Manhattan Beach. And, in 1906, the park got its first merry-go-round, a menagerie-style ride manufactured by the Philadelphia Toboggan Company and modeled after the merry-go-round at Manhattan Beach at the time.[28]

Manhattan Beach had clearly been ahead of its rivals for quite a few years as it prepared to open for the 1906 season, so manager William Lawrence and the Denver Recreation Company made only a few additions to the park for the summer. A new naphtha-powered launch on the lake and the Japanese rolling ball game were the only new amusement attractions. In the rolling ball game, players rolled balls up a long board. There were pockets for the balls at one end of the board, each marked with a point value. The game first appeared in the United States at the Pan-American Exposition in Buffalo in 1901, and quickly spread to amusement parks throughout the country. In an effort to revive the theater, management hired the Augustin Daly Musical Company of New York, which started its season on June 9 and ran for ten weeks. Management also booked Horn's Zoological Arena and Professor Clark's Dog and Monkey Show for the summer. Horn's animals were located in the park's old bathhouse, which was enclosed for the purpose. Also new for the summer was the Electric Photograph Gallery, where pictures were taken "while you wait." For those needing a rest from all the fun, management installed new steel wire frame benches throughout the rounds.[29]

The new company also brought Robert Giffen back to Manhattan Beach for the first time since 1899, though only as manager of the theater company. The *Rocky Mountain News* was particularly pleased by his return, writing that "if some morning, we see the flag that swings on the capitol dome plastered with a Manhattan beach placard, blame it on the enterprise of Giffen and not on any unpatriotic motive." *Denver Post* theater critic Frank W. White was also pleased by Robert Giffen's return, writing that the one-time park manager wanted to "bring the nice people back again" to Manhattan Beach by returning the park to the days "when Manhattan Beach was a step above buttermilk; when it had a sort of aristocratic air; when the Bethells and Fosters ran it and polite society found it a favorite fad." Or, in other words, when the theater dominated all other activities at the park. White found the changes made by the Denver Recreation Company at the park particularly distasteful. Writing later of Elitch's, he said "It is a saving grace that it is not managed from Detroit or from any other distant point," an obvious knock on the Denver Recreation Company. Frank W. White's objections aside, when the park opened for the season on May 26, 1906, the *Denver Post* reported that hundreds of people poured through the gates, "flying through the tops of the trees on the blood-tingling toboggan; shooting across the lake in the cutest little launch you ever laid eyes on; gliding on a waxed floor to the strains of Strauss' seductive waltzes; matching skill at the Japanese ball game; and—oh a dozen other attractions." Crowds kept the park busy until nearly midnight on opening day, but it was the opening of the theater on June 9 that drew the most attention from Denver's newspapers.[30]

The *Rocky Mountain News* said the reason the Denver Recreation Company contracted with the Augustin Daly company was their "desire to rehabilitate the best summer theater in the country." Among the company members for the summer were Sam Collins, Adele Rafter, Eleanor Dorel, Harold Crane, Helena Byrne, and Adam Dockray (the *News* said most of the actors were unknown in Denver because musical comedy acts generally did not play west of the Mississippi River). The theater season at Manhattan Beach opened with *A Country Girl*, which *Post* theater critic Frank W. White said was very successful. *San Tay*, *The Geisha*, *The Circus Girl*, *The Silver Slipper*, and *The Cingalee* were among the other plays staged during the company's twelve-week run. The run of *The Cingalee* in August dragged the theater into a major scandal in Denver society involving lawyer Tyson Dines and millionaire businessman and philanthropist J. K. Mullen.[31]

Dines and Mullen, who were neighbors, shared a two-party telephone line. While trying to call a doctor for what he said was a life-or-death situation, Mullen found that Dines's daughter Virginia was engaged in a conversation with a young man. After waiting more than half an hour, Mullen reportedly asked if he could use the phone. Virginia Dines responded "impertinently" by telling Mullen not to "butt in." Mullen then said he would hold the line until she allowed him to use it. Virginia's brother Courtland then got on the phone and insulted Mullen, who responded that no lady would tie up the line under such circumstances. Courtland Dines and a friend then went to Mullen's house, where they apparently settled the matter. But as soon as they left, Tyson Dines appeared and demanded to see Mullen. As soon as he saw Mullen, Dines attacked him with a heavy dog whip while Mullen's wife and daughters attempted to pull the lawyer off of him. In the struggle a revolver fell out of Dines's pocket, which he then waved around the room before leaving. Mullen had Dines arrested for assault and also sued him for $50,000 in damages. During the performance of *The Cingalee* at Manhattan Beach, part of one song was changed to include the lyrics: "When our millionaires go into battle over two-dollar two-party lines / And all our risibles-rattle / With the merry skit 'Mullen and Dines' / With charge, countercharge, allegation / And complaints of attacking to kill / We wonder, now, what in the nation / Will be the next thing on the bill?" Friends of Dines demanded removal of the lines. Management refused, saying that national figures had found themselves put into topical songs, so local figures were fair game as well. (The following December, Dines apologized and Mullen dropped the charges and lawsuit.)[32]

The Dines and Mullen fight was not the only problem to confront the theater company that summer. Unfortunately, an outbreak of typhoid fever among the Augustin Daly Company members in mid-July claimed the lives of Cleo Spruin and Katherine Brown and severely sickened Francis Hartly and Robert Nash. Cleo Spruin's mother, May, charged Dr. Everett Brandt, who ran the sanitarium near the park where Cleo died, with malpractice. Dr. Brandt immediately fled to Chicago when the Denver district attorney issued a warrant for his arrest. Nothing must have come of the charges, as a year later Brandt was still running his sanitarium and facing new charges from another patient.[33]

While news of the theater once again dominated coverage of Manhattan Beach for the season, there were occasional glimpses of other activities at the park. Every Friday and Saturday night brought Pain's Fireworks displays, but there were no special fireworks for July 4. Still, 13,000 people visited the park that day, which was near the end of a special two-week engagement of Liberati's Band. Early July also brought the opening of the park's new steel observation tower, which the Denver Post said attracted large crowds of "those wishing to view the country o'er." Management also added an attraction named Trip Around the World Car, which was described as a world journey. This was most likely an illusion ride, where riders entered a familiar looking vehicle, such as a train car. A film projector showed moving scenery, visible through the open front end of the car and along the sides, which gave the car the appearance of movement. (Elitch Gardens also had a Tour of the World attraction around this time, and riders entered through the back end of two train cars.) The *Rocky Mountain News* said "The host of attractions at Manhattan seems to increase in popularity as the season advances and there will soon be several new ones to join the already large membership in the fun family."[34]

Manhattan Beach once again hosted a fundraiser for the St. Vincent's Children's Home in August, while the *Denver Post* hosted a picnic for newsboys at the end of July. About 200 newsboys attended the picnic, with Shorty, Pie-Face, and Freckles competing for the first ride on the roller coaster. (Freckles won even though he was nursing a broken arm at the time.) Professor Clark gave a special performance of his dog and monkey show, and then the boys chased a greased pig around the athletic field before Lemon eventually caught it. The day ended with the boys getting front row seats at the theater, and the *Post* reported "'Wasn't it great?' sighed the tired and happy newsboys as they trailed wearily out of the gate toward home" at the end of the day. Near the end of August, the Democrats held their third annual picnic at the park, which even attracted mayor Robert Speer of Denver. Leading Democrats took over all of the park's attractions and concessions, acting as carnival barkers in an effort to get attendees to spend their money. The money raised that day went to the general fund of the Democratic Club of Denver.[35]

For all of the fun and games, there were some very serious and controversial moments during the 1906 season. On June 23, 1906, the *Denver Times* reported that three people, described by the newspaper as a well-dressed young man and two young women, drowned in Sloan's Lake when one of the new unsinkable boats overturned during a sudden squall on the night of June 22. Workers at the boathouse discovered the boat late in the evening when it floated back near the pier. But, as the *Denver Post* reported the next day, no such tragedy had occurred. There was indeed a storm that forced the three people in the boat to the opposite shore from the boathouse, but they had walked back to the boathouse and told the attendant what had happened. The *Post* reported that the *Times* was well aware of the truth, and headlined the article about the incident "Times Clinches Record as Most Fearless Faker."[36]

In mid-August, a Denver police officer on duty at the park noticed a couple engaged in a "spasm of intense love-making" under the branches of a tree. Attracted by what he thought was the odd appearance of the man, the patrolman discovered that the man was in fact 24-year-old Grace Evangelisto dressed in overalls, a dark coat, and a sailor cap. The other woman was identified as Catherine Jones, a 72-year-old widow from Denver. At the police station, according to the Denver newspapers, Jones insisted that her companion was a man and that the police had no cause to arrest them. Evangelisto also insisted she was a man, identifying herself as James Roosevelt, a distant relative of Theodore Roosevelt, and said she was going to marry Jones. Further investigation revealed that Evangelisto had been arrested two months earlier for abandoning her two children. Jones was let go, and Evangelisto was released to her husband, Vetal, after police sent him the message "'If you want your wife come after her.'"[37]

Just a few days later on August 19, Captain William D. Bethell, the owner of Manhattan Beach, died at age 66 in Denver at the home of his son-in-law, Dr. John Foster. Bethell had been in poor health for a few years and had been spending time in California and the south in hopes of recovering. After Captain Bethell's death, Dr. Foster remained the driving force keeping Manhattan Beach alive. Manhattan Beach closed for the season on September 9, and the *Denver Times* said the park's attractions had "enjoyed the most popular season they have ever known," while the *Rocky Mountain News* said the roller coaster and skating rink were the clear favorites among park visitors. As soon as the park closed, preparations began for the 1907 season. The Denver

Recreation Company decided to make the lake the focal point of the park for the upcoming year. The old boathouse and several smaller concessions were torn down, creating an unobstructed view of Sloan's Lake from the front of the theater. The *News* said that Manhattan Beach was trying to keep up with Denver's growing reputation as the city of lights, so workers installed twelve new arc lights on the park grounds, and strung lights on poles around the entire lake. In fact, Manhattan Beach was the first of Denver's amusement parks to adopt an elaborate lighting scheme in its design, something that would soon become standard at the other parks. The *Denver Republican* said that "the effect of the thousands of incandescent lights on the water is beautiful in the extreme." The grounds crew planted "flowers in profusion" throughout the park along with bushes and grass in any bare spots. The work, said the *Republican*, created "a delightful air of restfulness."[38]

In the theater, workers installed four new banks of 120 lights each on the edge of the stage, more footlights, and a new row of lights on the proscenium arch. The Augustin Daly Company once again appeared at the theater, but for 1906 their run lasted only until the end of June. Among the plays they performed were *A Country Girl*, *The Cingalee*, *San Tay*, *A Circus Girl*, and *A Runaway Girl*. The John C. Fisher Opera Company replaced the Augustin Daly Company at the end of June, staging *Florodona* and *Miss Pocahontas*, but after only two weeks Fisher and park management began to argue about the shows. Fisher staged what newspapers described as old favorites, but the park management insisted people wanted to see new shows. Fisher left the park, taking his company to the Tabor Grand in Denver where their production of *Florodona*, according to the *Rocky Mountain News*, drew "capacity houses at every performance." To fill the gap, Robert Giffen brought the Comedy Opera Company of New York to Manhattan Beach for the remainder of the season. Among the shows they staged were *Two Little Girls*, *Baron Humbug*, *Down on the Cape*, *Boodle and Co.*, and *La Poupee*.[39]

Management installed a new Double Whirl ride at the park (the ride was similar to a Ferris wheel but also spun horizontally as it rotated), but the star attraction of the 1907 season was the Fighting the Flames show. A hit at the 1904 World's Fair in St. Louis, Fighting the Flames shows soon began appearing at amusement parks throughout the country, with Dreamland and Luna Park on Coney Island opening their versions of the show within a few weeks of each other in 1904. The set for such a show typically consisted of a realistic looking city block or other appropriate scene that could be engulfed in flames, allowing firefighters to perform heroic rescues of trapped townsfolk and put out fires, multiple times a day.[40]

At Manhattan Beach, the set was named Fire City and, in addition to a number of buildings, also included moving trolley cars and automobiles. The early Fighting the Flames productions at the park were fairly simple. As the fire spread and the walls of buildings began to crumble, firemen rushed onto the set to battle the flames and rescue the "distressed maidens" trapped on the tops of buildings. The *Denver Republican* reported that management initially had a hard time finding actresses who were willing to stay on the tops of the burning buildings, but as the actresses became more comfortable, they trained them to do more complex stunts. (One actress, Anna Loehr, successfully sued the park for $1,000 when one of the firemen dropped her and broke her ankle.) Near the end of June, a new safe-blowing story debuted in Fire City. The act began with five robbers riding into the town on horseback, guns blazing as residents dove for cover. Three of the gunmen then entered the hotel, which was soon followed by a "terrific explosion" as they dynamited the safe. The five bandits rode out of town, guns blazing again, as the fire from the explosion consumed the town. Among the stunts performed as the firemen battled the blaze was a high dive from one of the windows by John C. Farrell. In mid-July, management staged carnival week in Fire City, with "new and amusing acts," including the "death defying

Wheelock," who slid down a wire from the highest point of the theater into the lake, holding onto the wire with his teeth. Professor Nixus Frostus, a fire eater, also performed in the carnival. In August, the fire broke out after an actress playing Carrie Nation raided the saloons and gambling halls of Fire City, which the *Republican* said made the production "humorous and exciting." To close out the season, legendary Denver Fire Department horses Pete and Con joined Carrie Nation in Fire City, performing their "wonderful ground hitch" at each show. Throughout the summer, firemen fought the flames each night at 7:45 and 9:00 p.m. with afternoon matinees at 3:00 and 4:30 p.m. on Sundays and holidays. Attendance at the Fighting the Flames shows remained heavy throughout the summer, with the *Republican* saying the shows were so realistic that some audience members wanted to "dash forth and lend a hand."[41]

Manhattan Beach's regular attractions received far less attention from Denver's newspapers during the summer of 1907. Workers installed a new floor in the dance pavilion, but it and the other attractions were mentioned almost as afterthoughts in articles about the theater and the Fighting the Flames show. There was also little coverage of special events at the park that summer, such as the Festival of Lights that ran from July 20 to 28 and included 16,000 electric lights, 2,500 Japanese lanterns, and fireworks. The event that received the most attention was when park management hid $350 in cash (consisting of one $100 bill, two $50s, three $20s, four $10s, and ten $5s) on the grounds for visitors to find on August 4. After advertising on August 18 that there were "only two weeks more of opportunity then nine months of deprivation," Manhattan Beach closed for the season on September 2. By the time the park closed, management knew that they would be facing their biggest competitor yet when they opened in 1908.[42]

On September 1, 1907, the *Denver Republican* reported that architect Edward H. Moorman had finished his design for the new Lakeside Amusement Park and that construction would soon begin. Located on the shores of Sylvan Lake at 46th and Sheridan Boulevard, just two miles north of Manhattan Beach, Lakeside was the creation of Denver brewer Adolph Zang, his stepbrother William Buck, step brother-in-law Peter J. Friederich, and several other Zang family members and longtime business associates. Zang's father, Philip, had moved to Denver in 1869, and soon after started the Philip Zang Brewing Company. Although Philip Zang had sold the brewery to an English syndicate in 1895, Adolph Zang stayed with the brewery as manager. One of his duties was to create new outlets for Zang Beer, and among his best-known before Lakeside was the Oxford Hotel in Denver. On March 20, 1907, Zang and his associates incorporated the Lakeside Realty and Amusement Company to build an amusement park in the new Jefferson County town of Lakeside, which they also incorporated.[43]

As built, Lakeside Amusement Park included two roller coasters, a miniature railroad, shoot-the-chutes, circle swing, merry-go-round, double whirl, indoor swimming pool, theater, roller-skating rink, ballroom, restaurants, and boating on the lake. Construction on the park began as mayor Robert Speer was hard at work implementing his City Beautiful program for Denver. An outgrowth of the Court of Honor at the 1893 Columbian Exposition in Chicago, the City Beautiful movement sought to clean up dirty, badly planned cities through the use of unified architecture (especially for government and civic buildings), parks and open space, and moral uplift. With Lakeside demonstrating those ideals in its design, rides, and other attractions, Speer, himself once the owner of the old Arlington Park, happily adopted Lakeside as part of Denver's City Beautiful program. He took part in opening day ceremonies at the park and hosted a dinner there for delegates to the 1908 Democratic National Convention, which was held in Denver that year. Construction costs for Lakeside ranged from $750,000 to $1,000,000, and it was quickly nicknamed both the

White City (for the 100,000 lights used throughout the grounds and the white paint used on the buildings) and the Coney Island of the West, both nicknames that had been used to describe Manhattan Beach. Zang and his associates hired Albert Lewin as the first general manager of the park.[44]

Lewin was a German immigrant who became involved in the liquor business after arriving in Colorado in the 1880s. He and his partner, Lesser Levy, frequently did business with the Zang Brewery, which brought him to the attention of Adolph Zang. According to his daughter, Mildred Sweet, Lewin was also involved in building the Mammoth Skating Rink at Colfax and Clarkson in Denver in 1905 (it later became the Fillmore Auditorium), so he had some experience with amusement venues.[45]

Lakeside Amusement Park opened its gates on May 30, 1908, with a crowd of 50,000 people, far more than Manhattan Beach had ever attracted. Unsurprisingly, Lakeside dominated the

Julia Rhoads, wife of longtime *Rocky Mountain News* photographer Harry Rhoads, riding the 1908 merry-go-round at Manhattan Beach. *Source:* The Denver Public Library, Western History Collection, Rh-627.

amusement park coverage in Denver's newspapers that summer, but the Denver Recreation Company did their best to give visitors to Manhattan Beach a good show when it opened on the same day as Lakeside. There were only minor changes to the park for the season. One was a new dancing pavilion built out "over the limid waters of Sloan lake." Named Sans-Souci, the *Rocky Mountain News* said it was the chief innovation for the year at the park. Management also installed a new $30,000 merry-go-round from the Philadelphia Toboggan Company at the park, replacing the park's original carousel. The *News* reported that the new ride was "elaborately decorated and will be illuminated by over 500 electric bulbs." To handle the new lighting system, management completely rewired the park.[46]

The 1908 merry-go-round at Manhattan Beach with Sloan's Lake visible behind it. *Source:* The Denver Public Library, Western History Collection, X-19526.

The Fighting the Flames show was gone from the park for the 1908 season. In its place was a new baseball stadium that was home to the City Baseball league and other athletic events. The William G. Stewart Opera Company took over at the theater, with the fifty-member company staging a "series of standard successes in the musical comedy line." The theater opened with *The Mikado*, followed by *Babette* and *Robin Hood*. The theater once again received the most attention of any of the park's attractions from Denver's newspapers in their brief coverage that summer, with the *Denver Post* writing that only one week into the season the operas offered at the park were "setting a new standard of summer musical entertainment" for the city. The park also began offering free gate admission to anyone who purchased a theater ticket in advance at the Gano-Downs store in Denver.[47]

Aside from the opening of Lakeside, the other big news in Denver for the summer of 1908 was the city's hosting of the Democratic National Convention, held at the Auditorium Theater. The Denver Convention League raised $15,000 to help entertain the visitors through two big benefit programs. The first took place at Manhattan Beach on June 27, followed by a concert in the Auditorium Theater on July 5, the day before the convention began. There were no official visits to Manhattan Beach for convention attendees as there were to Lakeside, but at the evening performance of *Erminie* on July 8, according to the *Post*, delegates made up over half of the audience. Later in the summer the Denver Democrats and the Brotherhood of Railroad Trainmen again held their annual picnics at the park.[48]

Bronco busting returned to Manhattan Beach for the Fourth of July weekend, with fifty horses going up against the field of riders. The grand prize was a belt decorated with twenty-five $20 gold pieces and silver buckle engraved with the words "World's Champion Broncho Buster, Denver, U.S.A., July, 1908." The first round of the contests from July 4–6 was so popular that the park delayed the championship event until July 12, when a crowd of 3,000 people watched Hugo Clark of Wyoming win first place and Harry Tipton of Denver take second place. But even though the *Rocky Mountain News* said the contests drew thousands, the theater still remained the most talked-about attraction, with productions of *The Bohemian Girl* and *The Pirates of Penzance*. Because the Denver newspapers largely focused on Lakeside and its first season, the *Jewish Outlook* attempted to keep the public interested in Manhattan Beach. Noting its location on beautiful Sloan's Lake, the newspaper said the park "with its shady lanes and velvet lawns, its myriad of recreative attractions, its theater and its lake, offers the maximum degree of rest and recreation at minimum outlay to the tired business man, city-wearied family, pleasure-seeking youth, or the observing tourist." More than its lake, new dance pavilion, grounds for picnicking, or the other attractions, according to the *Outlook*, it was "the touch of human sympathy between the public and Manhattan" that had drawn thousands of people to the park over the years.[49]

In early August, after productions of *Dorothy* and *The Chimes of Normandy*, the *Rocky Mountain News* wrote that the Stewart Opera Company had "done all things pleasantly, many things well, and nothing badly" at the Manhattan Beach theater that summer. Near the end of August, readers of the *Denver Post* became caught up in the story of Anita, an orphaned girl from Rivenada, New Mexico. As told by *Post* reporter Winifred Black, Anita had once had a wheelchair and a pair of crutches to get around, but after the death of both of her parents, the wheelchair and crutches broke. The story was so compelling that the Stewart Opera Company and Manhattan Beach agreed to donate the proceeds from the August 25 performance to a fund to bring Anita to Denver, much to the delight of the newspaper's readers. Before the theater season closed on August 29, the company staged *Martha*, which starred Denver native Pauline Perry, *Iolanthe*, *The Beggar Student*, and *The Black Huzzar*. After the theater closed for the season, the end of the park's season on Labor Day received almost no attention from Denver's newspapers. However, the park would soon make front page news once again.[50]

Shortly after 8 p.m. on December 26, 1908, fire broke out in the Manhattan Beach theater, starting in the roof above the stage. Nearby residents rushed to the park and formed a bucket brigade, primarily to keep the fire from spreading to neighboring buildings. Young boys on the scene threw snow onto the fire as well. By the time the fire department arrived, about fifteen minutes after the fire was first reported, the theater was "practically level with the ground" and the fire had spread to the nearby observation tower and two small buildings. Firemen worked hard to save those structures, fearing that if the fire spread from them to the dance pavilion, the entire park would be lost. The crew saved the observation tower, but had to then turn their attention to the fences on the north and west sides of the park which had caught fire. Fearful that the fire could spread from the fences to the row of buildings in Edgewater across Sheridan Boulevard, it took crews several minutes to put them out. The *Denver Post* reported that the fire "lighted up the western sky in one great lurid blaze."[51]

The Denver Recreation Company did not have any insurance on the park or its buildings. The Southern Investment Company did have some insurance, but since all of the buildings at the park were constructed of wood, they were not insured for as much as they should have been because they were considered such a fire risk. Captain Carlin of the Denver Fire Department told the *Post* that he had long dreaded the prospect of a fire at Manhattan Beach, saying "I have figured out time and again how I would go after this fire. I remembered every calculation and followed them up in detail."[52]

While the ruins of the theater were still smoldering, Jennie Beck of the Denver Recreation Company told the *Denver Post* that they were uncertain as to whether or not they would rebuild the theater, or even if it was their responsibility to rebuild it or that of the Southern Investment Company. A little over two weeks later, the two sides were still debating whether or not to rebuild the theater and who was responsible. The Denver Recreation Company lease, according to the *Denver Post*, required the Southern Investment Company to build a new theater, which was estimated would cost $30,000. But the park had proven less than profitable for the last few years. The Detroit group, which was paying $5,000 a year to rent the park, seemed willing to let the Southern Investment Company skip building a new theater as long as their lease was canceled without any penalty. The *Post* reported that a group of Eastern investors was eager to buy the park property for as much as $250,000 for development. The newspaper said that if the lease was indeed cancelled, "then Manhattan Beach, long a familiar place of amusement to Denverites, will be a memory."[53]

What the *Denver Post* had neglected to take into account in its reporting about the potential demise of Manhattan Beach was Dr. John Foster's commitment to the park, which went back to the earliest days of his father-in-law's ownership of the property. By February of 1909, the lease with the Denver Recreation Company was canceled and Dr. Foster told the *Post* that he would soon be making arrangements to rebuild the burned portion of the park. However, nothing had been accomplished by the end of May, the typical opening date for Denver's amusement parks. The Denver Recreation Company was formally dissolved on November 24, 1909, in Detroit.[54]

While Lakeside, Elitch's, and Tuileries opened for their seasons at the end of May, Manhattan Beach remained closed. The park finally opened for the 1909 season on the Fourth of July. Gone was the admission fee, allowing anyone to enter the park grounds for free, making it the only park in Denver to do so that year. Also gone were the elaborate Fourth of July celebrations and fireworks shows of past years, with management instead inviting "the little ones to bring their Fourth of July fireworks this evening." In addition to the observation tower, roller coaster, and merry-go-round, the park offered the usual boating, fishing, dancing in the pavilion, and the Japanese tea garden. As the *Rocky Mountain News* said, "there is no cooler resort than the beach, at which there is always a pleasant breeze from the lake," which was nearly identical to the way it described Lakeside Amusement Park as well that summer.[55]

Aside from special dances in the pavilion on Saturdays and Sundays (advertised as the "finest pavilion with the best music and floor"), the only special attractions during the shortened 1909 season at Manhattan Beach were bronco busting demonstrations. On July 18, Lola Bennett Fara, a champion bronco buster, took on Pride of Clear Creek, a "vicious sorrell," at the park, in addition to demonstrating lariat throwing and bareback bronco busting. Gone, however, were the large newspaper ads that had once promoted such events at the park. Instead, management was reduced to placing ads in the want ads section of the newspapers, such as the one on July 31, 1909, that read "WANTED—1,000 people to see ball games and wild west show at Manhattan Beach Sundays, 1:30 p.m." The future of the park definitely looked bleak as the 1909 season wound down.[56]

There had also been some staff changes at Lakeside prior to the start of the 1909 season. After successfully guiding the park through its first season, Albert Lewin was replaced by Frank Burt as general manager for 1909. Lewin's daughter, Mildred Sweet, said that a dispute over beer destroyed the longtime friendship and business relationship between her father and Lakeside owner Adolph Zang. But Lewin's successful run at Lakeside had given him a taste for the amusement business, and in September of 1909 he signed a fifteen-year lease on Manhattan Beach and immediately announced plans to begin a major renovation of the park ahead of the 1910 season.[57]

# CHAPTER 6

# Luna Park, Denver's Prettiest Resort

AFTER LEASING MANHATTAN BEACH, ALBERT LEWIN IMMEDI-
ately announced two of his planned changes to the park. The
first was the reintroduction of steamboat rides on Sloan's Lake
with the construction of a new side-wheel steamboat capable of
carrying 1,000 passengers. The second was changing the name
from Manhattan Beach to Luna Park. Lewin's partners in the
new venture were Carl Lindquist, head of the Lindquist Cracker
Company of Denver, Peter Hansen, a contractor and builder,
and S. K. Howe, the chief accountant at Lakeside. At the end of
October 1909, the men incorporated the Luna Park Amusement
Company with $100,000 in stock.[1]

The following month, Lewin and Hansen went to Dubuque,
Iowa, to sign the contract for construction of the $25,000 three-deck
steamboat that would carry passengers around Sloan's Lake. By
then, Lewin and his associates had also announced that they
would not serve any intoxicating beverages at Luna Park, which
was perhaps meant as a critique of Lakeside, where Zang Beer
flowed freely. Shortly after Lewin and Hansen returned to Denver, the fractured business relationship between Zang and Lewin,
along with their new rivalry, erupted in a fight over a restaurant
the two were associated in.[2]

Albert Lewin, who reinvented Manhattan Beach as Luna Park in 1910, is in the center of this group of five men standing at the park in May 1911. *Source:* Beck Archives, Special Collections, University of Denver Libraries.

Lewin and his longtime business partner Lesser Levy had operated The Famous saloon and café at Fifteenth and Curtis Streets in Denver since 1904. The building that housed the restaurant was owned by the Teutonic Investment Company, which was owned by Adolph Zang, Peter Friederich, and Godfrey Schirmer, who also owned Lakeside. Marvin Adams, head waiter at The Famous, was the first mayor of the town of Lakeside. Lewin and Levy had a ten-year lease on the building, and during the first five years rent was $475 a month. Under the lease terms, a board of arbitration was responsible for determining rent for the last five years of the lease. When the initial five-year term expired in December 1909, the Teutonic Investment Company demanded rent of $1,000 per month. Lewin, of course, objected, telling the *Denver Post* that "the Zang interests are doing all they can to put us out of business" because of his involvement with Luna Park. While there appear to be no surviving records of the outcome of the case between Lewin and Zang, The Famous remained in business after 1909.[3]

Despite the trouble with Zang, work on the new Luna Park proceeded rapidly during the first months of 1910. The biggest attention getter was the steamboat, which was under construction at a temporary shipyard built at the west end of the park grounds near the dancing pavilion. The boat drew so much attention that in February, Lewin decided to open the park grounds on Saturday afternoons to any school children who wanted to check on the progress made during the previous week. In the weeks leading up to the launch of the boat, both the *Denver Times* and *Rocky Mountain News* held contests to name it and choose who would christen it. Eleanor Christian came up with the winning name, *Frolic*, while Cordelia Hamlin won the popularity contest and the right to christen the boat. In April, Lewin advertised in *Billboard* magazine that the park was looking for concessionaries and was interested in "anything that will bring in the money." *Billboard* later noted that many of the concessions secured for the park were "new to Denver and the West." They included boxball games, boomerang games, ping pong booths, a Coney Island cow (a statue that dispensed sweet and buttermilk), a shooting gallery, and a photo gallery.[4]

On April 17, 1910, more than 14,000 people entered the gates at Luna Park to watch the launch of *Frolic*, which had been "raised high on the ways at the shipyard . . . covered with flags, which waved gayly in the wind, the great vessel loomed high above the heads of the throng." While the crowd inspected the ship, Barkell's band played several selections. Supervisor A. J. Spengel, representing the city of Denver, delivered a brief speech, pointing out how fortunate it was that Colorado had adopted the same navigation laws as the state of Illinois when writing its constitution. After Spengel's speech, Winona Hall, dressed in full Indian costume, sang "Ogallala" and "America." Then, with a signal from Albert Lewin, who was on board the *Frolic* along with Carl

Lindquist, Peter Hansen, and other guests, M. J. Godfrey, who was in charge of construction of the boat, cut the ropes holding it in place. As the boat began to slide down the ways, Cordelia Hamlin smashed a bottle of champagne against the bow and said "I christen thee Frolic." The *Rocky Mountain News* reported that "the boat slid gracefully down the ways and out upon Sloan's lake with a big splash." Denver's newspapers made sure to point out that the champagne used to christen the boat was sent by the Italian-Swiss Colony Company of California, the first American company to make champagne, because they "declared it would never do to christen the Frolic with the imported article." At the time of the launch, the boat had been completed to the point of the hull and the woodwork on the first deck, so it was moved to the east side of the lake while work on it continued.[5]

After the launch, visitors to the new park enjoyed rides on the roller coaster, a baseball game, dancing in the pavilion, and rowboat rides on the lake. Lewin planned to keep the park open

Launching the not-yet-completed *Frolic* steamboat at Luna Park on April 17, 1910. *Source: Denver Republican*, April 18, 1910.

on weekends for the rest of April and into May, weather permitting, although the official grand opening of the park was set for May 28. Over the next few weeks, workers installed the engine and other machinery on the *Frolic* and finished the woodwork on the other two decks. When completed, the boat was 110 feet long and had three decks (roughly the size of the *Mark Twain* riverboat at Disneyland in California). The engines and concession stand, where passengers could purchase soda water, Coney Island sandwiches (hot dogs), and "cornucopias of ice cream," were on the first deck. The middle deck housed the bandstand and a "perfectly waxed" dance floor which charged a separate admission fee, along with walkways and seats for people to enjoy the views around the lake. The top deck offered the best views of the park and surrounding area. In all, the *Frolic* could carry between 700 and 800 passengers. Almost lost in the coverage of the steamboat was the launch of two new sailboats for races at the park.[6]

To replace the destroyed Manhattan Beach theater, Lewin and his associates remodeled one of the larger existing buildings, which stood across from the steamboat dock, into what the *Denver Republican* said would be a "pretty but modest sized playhouse." When finished, it could hold an audience of 800 people and had a 25-foot by 25-foot stage with "complete scenic equipment and adequate space for all but the most elaborate vaudeville acts." Admission to the new theater was free, and it would present short vaudeville acts and motion pictures. The goal was to keep the shows short, according to the *Republican*, so the "public may enjoy the numerous open-air features of Luna Park." For almost the first time since Manhattan Beach opened, the theater would not be the focus of the park.[7]

Also under construction by the end of April was a new $15,000 Circle Dips roller coaster. The *Republican* said the new coaster was "entirely different from any other device in the city," which included the existing Toboggan coaster at the park. According to the *Denver Post*, the new coaster had three dips and numerous loops (meaning turns). The newspaper noted that the ride was much more thrilling than the already existing Toboggan coaster but was "absolutely safe." The *Republican* said that another new roller coaster was also under construction at the park. Named the Aero Coaster and designed by Denverites Harry L. Weber, Theodore Nollenberger, and W. W. McFarland, the new ride was supposed to have a 60-foot-high conical tower that was 120 feet around at the base. Miniature hot-air balloons inside the tower, which was to be decorated with "scenic effects," would lift riders to the top of the tower, where they would then board cars that descended on the track wrapped around the outside of the tower, making the descent in six revolutions. The men planned to build their ride at parks throughout the country, but it does not appear that they ever finished the first one at Luna Park.[8]

Across from the main entrance to the park, in the remodeled carousel building, Lewin and his partners built a new Eskimo Village (spelled Esquimaux at the park) and Arctic Museum. The residents of the village came from the Labrador area, but the star of the village was 16-year-old Columbia, who was born at the Eskimo Village at the 1893 Columbian Exposition in Chicago. One of the highlights of the season was the birth of a baby in the village on June 10 to Esther Dnutseak. The *Denver Republican* said that a visit to the Eskimo Village was "as educational as it is diverting." A group of Roma (then called Gypsies) also set up camp, which the *Republican* said was "picturesque," at the park for the summer. The newspaper noted that they were "quite willing to tell one's fortune in the accepted way." Another Romani group, made up of the Adams and Buffalo families, set up camp at Lakeside Amusement Park that same summer. Lewin kept the skating rink, dance pavilion, athletic field, and the existing midway that were already at the park when he took over.[9]

One of mayor Robert Speer's many innovations in Denver as part of his City Beautiful program was *Denver Municipal Facts*, a city-published magazine that he viewed as a means to disseminate good news about what was happening in the city, as opposed to what he thought was the bad news frequently reported by Denver's newspapers. Because Lakeside was such an important part of Denver's City Beautiful movement during its first years in operation, it received far more attention in *Denver Municipal Facts* than the other amusement parks in the city. However, the magazine always spoke kindly of Luna. In its coverage of the park in 1910, the magazine said that Luna had a "pretentious stadium" on its athletic field, and that children could enjoy the "well equipped" children's playground at the park. The magazine also occasionally featured pictures of the park and its attractions.[10]

Luna Park, which the *Denver Post* said was the "precocious youngster of Denver's summer amusement resorts," officially opened its gates on May 29, 1910. While the newspapers reported that all of the attractions were popular, the steamboat was the clear favorite. The *Telluride Journal*, which was not as enthusiastic about the park and the steamboat as the Denver newspapers, wrote that "It is hoped that her next bid for notoriety may not be through the medium of the sinking of the ship and the drowning of her cargo of human freight, due to overloading, which greed almost inevitably begets in such enterprises." Enjoying the day a bit more, the *Republican* wrote that "There were hundreds at Luna Park in the afternoon, thousands in the evening. And everybody found the place delightful." After a month in operation, the *Denver Post* said Luna Park was a place where "every member of the family may find recreation and exhilarating, but harmless diversion; where the rich and poor, the young and old may spend a merry afternoon or the evening; in other words a distinctly outdoor amusement park for all the people."[11]

On opening day and Memorial Day and then on Saturdays, Sundays, and holidays throughout the summer, management staged four vaudeville shows in the new theater, two in the afternoon and two at night. Motion pictures ran continuously in the theater at all other times. Winona Hall, who had sung at the

A postcard showing the completed *Frolic* out for a cruise on Sloan's Lake in 1910. *Source:* Author's collection.

christening of *Frolic* in April, regularly performed in the theater, while the Henry Curtis Orchestra provided music for dances on the *Frolic*. Aside from the steamboat, visitors to the park could rent sailboats and rowboats as usual, or ride on a smaller gasoline-powered launch which "had always a merry crowd of passengers." The *Republican* reported that the skating rink and the park's two roller coasters were "decidedly popular" on opening day. And, for those who needed a rest from all the fun, there was "plenty of shade. There are lawns and benches and nooks for lovers; lights and laughter and gay music for those who have passed or not yet reached the age of romance."[12]

As general manager of the park, Albert Lewin immediately launched into special events, with a yacht race on Sloan's Lake on the afternoon of May 29. On May 30, any member of the Grand Army of the Republic received free admission to the park, as many times as they wanted in one day. June 12 started the free Children's Days at the park, which continued every Wednesday throughout the summer. Once in the park, children could take a ride on the *Frolic* and enter the children's playground section, both for free. The days also included free entertainment and half-price admission to all the other rides and concessions at Luna Park. Midweek offerings at the park that summer included special club nights in the dance pavilion on Wednesdays and Thursdays with club dances, prize waltzes, schottisches, and confetti dances. Skating contests in the skating rink on Mondays, Wednesdays, and Fridays and skating races on Saturday nights also helped to draw in bigger crowds. In late June, Luna Park hosted a wrestling match that began with two preliminary rounds before the main event between F. P. Walton of Erie, Pennsylvania, and George Gerig of Cleveland, Ohio (Gehrig was the victor).While the special events were small compared to those taking place at Lakeside, which had massive free barbecues and illuminated boat parades on its lake, the events did draw people to Luna. On June 19, the *Denver Republican* reported that crowds at Luna were increasing to the point that the Denver Tramway Company was improving its streetcar service to the park, with West Twenty-Third and West Twenty-Ninth Avenue cars running to the park more frequently. A number of groups also started holding picnics at the park, such as the Farragut Women's Relief Corps in late June.[13]

For Luna Park's first Fourth of July, Albert Lewin brought back the bronco busting contests of the past and staged an elaborate fireworks display. The bronco busting contests began on July 3, with contestants competing over the next two days for a world championship title and $1,000 in prizes. More than 100 people and 150 horses took part in the events, which included busting and riding, steer roping, fancy and trick lariat throwing by Jane Bernoudy, a cowgirl relay and wild horse races, Roman standing races between Bessie Prentis and Warren La Vergne, and the holdup of the Deadwood Stage. Ten events took place on each of the two days, with the ultimate winner of the bronco busting contest claiming $100 and a $300 silver-mounted saddle. On the afternoon of the Fourth, there was swimming in the lake, canoe and sailboat races, high-diving competitions, and other aquatic sports. Throughout the afternoon, visitors could also get updates by telegram on the fight between Jack Johnson and James Jeffries in Reno, Nevada. To end the day, a "gorgeous" fireworks display was launched over the lake from the *Frolic*. According to the *Republican*, it had "many novel effects," including the Flight of Death. The park narrowly avoided a tragedy on the night of the Fourth when a sudden squall overturned several rowboats on the lake. Will and Henry Carston, employees at the park, rescued the man and two women who were in one of the boats, leading them to the *Frolic* before rescuing two more women who were clinging to their overturned boat at the west end of the lake. The *Denver Post* said the searchlight on the steamship "proved of exceptional value in the emergency."[14]

On July 15, 1,500 veterans of the Cuban and Philippine campaigns of the Spanish-American War arrived at Luna Park to recreate the Battle of El Caney, assisted by the Colorado National Guard. Taking place on the athletic field and the lake, the spectacular show involved military maneuvers and fireworks. The *Frolic* served as a military transport ship, and the reenactment included landing the troops, rushing the trenches, cutting the fences, and assaulting the blockhouse. Denver balloonist Wayne Abbott oversaw the pyrotechnic effects for the day. The battle recreation was very similar to the elaborate productions that Arlington Park had staged in the 1890s, and the *Republican* wrote that "Denver has not witnessed a big sham battle in a great many years." Ahead of the show, workers tripled the size of the grandstands around the lake to accommodate the expected crowds. Proceeds from the event went to the entertainment fund for the United Spanish War Veterans' National Encampment that would take place in Denver that fall. Sherman Bell, who as adjutant general of the Colorado National Guard, had helped crush a miner's strike in Cripple Creek in 1904, took part in the day's exercises. Editors of the *United Labor Bulletin* felt it was fitting that the event took place "at unfair Luna Park," which union members were not supposed to visit, so that they would not have to "see his hated countenance protruding from a freeman's uniform." Denver's trade unions had declared Luna Park unfair to labor the previous May, with Albert Parrish of the Cooks' Union stating that the park was an unfair resort and urging all union members to visit Elitch's, Lakeside, or Tuileries instead. The unions adopted the motto "Pass up Luna Park" to remind members to stay away from it.[15]

The recreation of the Battle of El Caney was so popular that the park soon announced plans to stage the Battle of Manila in August, with Lewin assuring the Denver newspapers that the Manila production "will eclipse El Caney." Members of the First Colorado Regiment took part in the day's events, with only men who had actually served in the battle playing parts. Brigadier General Irving Hale was in command. Dick Holmes, the flag bearer, carried the battle-scarred flag of the regiment along with the Spanish flag taken down from the fort during the battle, and two Spanish guns presented to the regiment after the fight were also brought to the park. The regiment's band even marched through shallow portions of Sloan's Lake playing "Hot Time," which they had done at the battle. The first half of the program depicted life at Camp Dewey, including soldiers bringing in the wounded, preparing a meal, and enjoying a cock fight and dice games. For the battle, infantry units were deployed on the left and right in trenches, while Battery A of Denver had the center position. Picket firing by sharpshooters was followed by heavy cannon fire during the general engagement. In addition to the first production August 13, two more were held on August 14, with filming taking place during the matinee that day.[16]

The bronco busting contests over the Fourth of July proved so popular that the park delayed the final championship match to later in the month to give more people a chance to see it. The expanded grandstands from the Battle of El Caney production provided more seating. The championship match took place during two programs on July 17, one in the afternoon and one at night, with illumination provided by the searchlight on top of the observation tower. Among the new events included for keeping the crowds entertained that day was a "realistic representation" of the capture of a horse thief. The bronco busting contests and other Wild West shows were so popular that management continued them throughout the rest of the 1910 season.[17]

On July 31, the park held its first annual Sunday School Day, with over 3,000 children, parents, and teachers in attendance. Special athletic events for the gathering included 50-yard races for boys and girls under age 6, ages 7–8, and ages 9–12, sack races with high jumps, and 100-yard, 200-yard, and quarter-mile races. The day ended with a greased pig race with over 500 children chasing the "brown streak of squeals" around the athletic field. In the end, although seven children had hold of the pig, Calvin Martin of Denver was declared the winner. Soon after, the Salvation Army hosted a free day at the park for the poor of Denver. The Denver Tramway Company offered free rides to the park, and visitors received free admission and a free ride on the *Frolic* in addition to a free dinner at night.[18]

Aside from the Battle of Manila show, August brought even more special events to the park, including a kayak-diving demonstration by Zed, one of the residents of Eskimo Village. According to the *Denver Republican*, Zed was famous in Alaska for his skill with a kayak, and part of the demonstration involved him performing a complete somersault by flipping his kayak on the lake. The newspaper said the event would be an "absolute and interesting novelty" for Denverites and was "another evidence of the high class and the general merit of the Luna park Eskimo village as an instructive and thoroughly entertaining park attraction." A mask carnival at the skating rink on August 4 included prizes for the most attractive, comical, and original masks. A huge fireworks show at the park on August 28 included another mask carnival for everyone at the park. Among the fireworks displays that night were representations of a naval battle, Niagara Falls, and the biblical story of Jonah and the whale. A daytime water carnival on the lake included an appearance by Alphonse King, known as "the man who walks and rides a bicycle on water," horse races, a duck chase, greased pole walking, and canoe races between "Indian," "Eskimo," American, Mexican, English, and French rowers.[19]

Two major events closed out Luna Park's first season. The Loyal Order of Moose brought their burlesque circus to the park from September 3 to 5. Under the direction of J. F. Miller and Louis Backley, the circus had already been seen at Madison Square Garden in New York City and in Seattle. A huge parade on the morning of September 3 went from downtown Denver to Luna Park, and it included more than 100 clowns, a burlesque menagerie of papier-mâché animals, fifty costumed riders, and more than forty different acts. Aside from bringing people to the park, the circus was also a fundraiser for the Moose Society Club- house Fund. On Labor Day, Albert Lewin, who had arranged a free barbecue at Lakeside two years earlier that brought in 35,000 people, hosted a similar free barbecue at the park, cooking 10,000 pounds of meat, which was served with gravy, bread, pick- les, and corn on the cob. More than 18,000 people paid admission to the park that day, closing out a successful first season.[20]

There was, however, one more special event held at Luna Park that year. The Masons of Centennial Lodge No. 4, a Black Masonic lodge, declared that it was time that Black residents of Colorado had a special celebration "as it is a well-known fact that every nation within our borders seek to celebrate some historic day connected with their freedom or victory in a crisis." Because Blacks did not have such a day, said the Masons, they decided to hold an Emancipation Day gathering at Luna Park on September 22, 1910. Throughout the summer Denver's Black newspaper, *The Statesman*, urged its readers to take part in the day, headlining its July 30 article on how plans for the day came about as "A Call to the Patriots." On September 17, *The Statesman* reminded readers that the day was the "last opportunity you will have for outdoor amusement" and the "only opportunity the people of this city have had in years for amusement in such a high-class place as Luna." At a time when all of Denver's amusement parks were segregated, it was indeed a rare opportunity to visit one of them. In fact, not since Arlington Park had hosted special cakewalk dances in the early 1890s had any of Denver's amusement parks been open to Black visitors. What remains unclear was just how segregated Luna Park actually was. There were several reports in *The Statesman* during the summer of 1910 that various groups had indeed visited the park and, in one case, went to Lakeside. Black Sunday Schools had also been invited to the special Sunday School Day on July 31, and Black and white children skated together on Sloan's Lake in the winters. But, in a May 14, 1910 article headlined "Denver's Parks Are Not for Colored," *The Statesman* said "So far there is not a park in the town where the negroes can have their summer picnics and dances, and it is impossible for us to dance at any of the big amusement parks such as the White City [Lakeside] or Luna Park." The author of the article went on to suggest that the only answer was for Denver's Black community to build a park of their own.[21]

The Elks had hosted an Emancipation Day celebration at the park in 1908, but the shortened 1909 season had not been ideal for special events. With the Masons bringing it back in 1910, Blacks would have full access to every ride and concession in the park. Other special attractions included a free barbecue under the direction of C. B. Hall, described by *The Statesman* as "the most famous barbecue cook in the west," and performances by the RMAC Quartette on the *Frolic*. About 700 people showed up for the celebration, but as *The Statesman* reported, "It rained and rained" that day. Although all of the rides were still in operation, the rain drove most of the people into the dancing pavilion, skating rink, and restaurants. The bad weather ultimately brought an early end to what was otherwise an enjoyable day.[22]

Luna Park's 1910 season was so successful that the park company was able to pay a 12-percent dividend and make plans for
more improvements in 1911. First on the list was construction of
the long-delayed new bathing beach, which was originally planned
for 1910. By late January of 1911, work on the $10,000 beach was
underway "as rapidly as the ice on the lake will permit." Lewin
also had a covered parking area under construction for customers
who drove their automobiles to the park. When Lakeside opened
in 1908, its covered parking area was unique among amusement parks. It was a sign of that park's efforts to attract mainly
upper-class customers, since it was primarily Denver's elites who
owned cars at the time. That had not changed much by 1911, and
by building a covered parking area at Luna, Lewin was clearly
trying to tempt some of those customers to try out his new park.
One of the garages was complete by the end of January. Lewin
also told the *Denver Post* that he was working on another project that would cost $25,000 and bring 100 men to Denver for
the summer, but he remained secretive about the details. While
Lewin worked on his project, Carl Lindquist, along with Henry
Niederhut, Charles Anderson, Albert Heintz, Pete Peterson, Emil
Walter, and several others incorporated the Colorado Amusement
Company with plans to spend at least $50,000 to install new rides
at Luna Park.[23]

During the next few months, work on the new bathing beach
continued, and work also started on a new bandshell and garden
for Lewin's still mysterious $25,000 project. As later revealed, the
project was a season-long engagement of the Banda Mexicana. Led
by Captain Jesse E. Roach, the band was made up of more than
fifty performers from army and police bands recruited throughout
Mexico, along with singers and dancers. The band performed both
traditional Mexican music and popular music of the day. Banda
Mexicana had spent the summer of 1910 at the Million Dollar
Pier in Atlantic City, New Jersey, and its appearance at Luna Park

would be the first in the West. Roach rented a large house near the park to house the band for the summer.[24]

Luna Park opened on Sundays in April and May as work on the improvements progressed, which by then included a new carousel for children and a Joy Wheel (also known as the Human Roulette Wheel). But, as opening day approached, it looked very much as if the Banda Mexicana would not be a part of the season. Manuel Gutierreze, assistant director of the band, had assembled the members in Juárez and was making arrangements to travel across the border when the Battle of Ciudad Juárez broke out in early April. Gutierreze and the band managed to escape Juárez and get back to Mexico City, but their departure for Denver was delayed by treaty negotiations between the successful rebels and Mexican president Porfirio Díaz. Once the treaty was signed, Roach wired money for transportation and the members of the band hurriedly boarded a special train chartered to take them to Denver.[25]

When the park opened for the 1911 season, visitors got to witness balloon ascensions, dance at the pavilion, skate in the rink, and enjoy rides on the *Frolic*, the roller coasters, and the new Joy Wheel. Opening Day was May 27, and the *Rocky Mountain News* said the grounds were "prettier than ever," but the big hit was the new bathing beach, with its imported ocean sand, water slide, dive tower, and new dressing rooms with hot and cold showers. The *News* called the new bathing beach "an expensive innovation," while the *Republican* said it was "the only real bathing beach in the Rocky mountain west." The *News* praised the park's other attractions as well, saying the children's carousel was "new and up-to-date, for the little folk," and the Joy Wheel was "one big laugh." Equally well received were the old favorites, including the two coasters, the skating rink (which had a new floor), and the dance pavilion, which was "conducted on the same orderly lines" as in the past.[26]

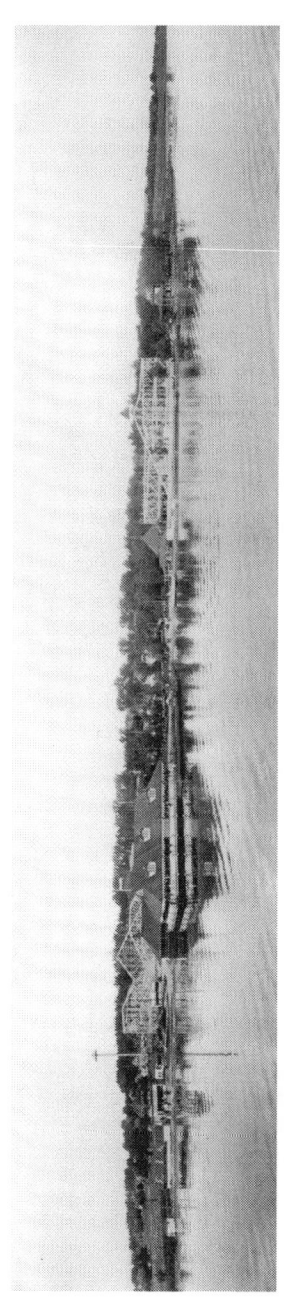

Luna Park in 1910. The midway and observation tower are on the left next to the Circle Dips Roller Coaster, and the Figure 8 Toboggan Coaster is on the right side of the park next to the old zoo building. The boathouse is still in its original location on the lake. *Source:* The Denver Public Library, Western History Collection, X-27722.

The new bathing beach at Luna Park in 1911 with the bathhouse on the left and the slide and diving tower on the right. The *Frolic* is visible behind the barrier that separated the swimming area from the rest of the lake. *Source: Denver Municipal Facts*, August 5, 1911.

The Banda Mexicana finally made its debut at Luna Park on June 3 with selections from Verdi's *Ernani*, the *Blue Danube* by Strauss, and "several dainty Chaminade numbers." The band's debut drew mixed reviews. The *Rocky Mountain News* referred to the band as one of the park's chief attractions, but *Denver Post* theater critic Frank W. White found the show, which started an hour later than scheduled, disorganized. While he did not doubt the skills of the band members, he wrote that it should play dreamier music and that both Captain Roach and the park management needed to keep in mind "the novelty of real Mexican music, of the native atmosphere of the lure of the castanets and the fandango should be borne in mind." As it was, wrote White, there was an "unfinished and also a rather uncertain air about the whole thing" and the prettiest sight during the concert was the unexpected appearance of the "gorgeously lighted steamer, Frolic, which now and then would come out of the purple night like a giant of gold, and gliding on the placid waters would make a reflection radiantly beautiful, adding a decided touch of splendor to the evening that was more attractive from the fact that it was unexpected and unplanned."[27]

While White admitted in his review that the entire band was not present the first night, and that the arrival of the missing members would likely cure some of the defects he saw, the Banda Mexicana faced an even bigger problem during their time at Luna, but not because, as the *Denver Post* wrote, "the band was not a good one, or that Roach was not a capable director." Rather, union musicians in Denver disliked the band because its members were not part of the union. Denver's union musicians managed to get all of Denver's other trade union members to boycott the concerts. With Luna Park already not a favorite with Denver's unions, the boycott was a big blow to attendance at the concerts. The *United Labor Bulletin* was particularly brutal in its criticism, referring to Roach as a "professional scab-herder" and the members of the band as an aggregation of cheap artists into a "Mongrel Mexican band," and as "Mexican peons" who threatened free American labor. The *Bulletin* also printed what it said were pictures of shacks built to house the musicians, rather than the big house Roach was supposed to have rented. By June 18, management had canceled the band's contract, a major setback to both Lewin and the members of the band who were counting on the money they would have earned. To raise funds to send the band back to Mexico, organized labor allowed Roach to rent Denver's Auditorium Theater for a series of fundraising concerts. The *Denver Post* urged its readers to attend the concerts as the band played "excellent music" and was "well worth hearing." With a 10-cent admission fee, the concerts raised some money, but even the benefit concerts fell apart and were canceled after only a few days. "Destitute and strictly up against it," the band started to tour the West in hopes of raising money. Its last known appearance was at American Fork and Salt Lake City, Utah, in August of 1911.[28]

To replace the canceled Banda Mexicana programs, Lewin brought back bronco busting contests. On July 4, in addition to bronco busting, visitors to the park could see cowboy and cowgirl races, steer roping and riding, a stagecoach holdup, and special appearances by the Miller sisters and child bronco rider Edna Rooney. The *Denver Times* said "never before in Denver was there a greater gathering of fine riders and bad horses than can be seen in the hippodrome of Luna park." After the bronco busting, the program concluded with a free steak broil for all park guests served in the cowboy camp of the arena. While Denver's newspapers proclaimed there was no finer place in the city to spend the Fourth, absent from the day's festivities were any fireworks displays.[29]

Lewin continued to hold bronco busting competitions and free barbecues over the next several weeks to keep people coming to the park. Surprisingly, the *United Labor Bulletin* was complimentary of the barbecues, writing that they were delicious and wholesome with the "choice meat cooked and broiled to the proper turn . . . taste it once and you will be convinced that it could not be better cooked in your own home." Although the barbecues were costly, wrote the newspaper, Lewin did not care about the expense so long as the customers were happy. The bronco busting contest on July 9 featured a potato race on horseback while the July 16 barbecue was German style. Another special event on the 16th was a duck-throwing contest with live ducks released into Sloan's Lake. The prize, wrote the *Rocky Mountain News*, was "a nice fat duck for Monday's dinner." Also at the lake that day was the greased pole with special prizes for the first swimmer who could climb it. The *Denver Post* proclaimed "in other words, Luna park has prepared a gala day for visitors today." The park hosted another free barbecue on July 23, followed by a watermelon feast on July 30. In August, the park hosted a broadsword competition with Captain Duncan Ross. Prior to the event, Ross issued a challenge to meet any Denver man in broadsword combat on horseback. Five men accepted—Lieutenant C. C. McKinney, Count Rico Rahini Cafrini, Sergeant E. Davis, August Von Schmidt, and Lucien S. Fournier. Ross did battle with Fournier first, and then with the winner of a contest between the other four. Unfortunately, Denver's newspapers did not report on who the victor of the final battle was.[30]

The park heavily promoted the bathing beach and dance pavilion throughout the summer, especially after a new set of chimes was added to the orchestra at the pavilion near the end of July. The *Denver Post* said the chimes were "sweet sounding" and were the only such set of chimes in any dance hall in Denver, while the *Republican* said the chimes were a "decided improvement for the benefit of the dancing public." The pavilion and orchestra were under the direction of Louis Kreamer, whose "one hobby is decorum on the floor, and he enforces this rule firmly," according to the *Rocky Mountain News*. The Wednesday night feature at the pavilion was a prize waltz contest. The free Children's Days also continued on Wednesdays "when special effort is made to give the youngsters an enjoyable time."[31]

Noticeably down was the park's picnic business. Only one major special picnic made the newspapers, that of the Columbian Camp of the Royal Neighbors of America held on July 30. The day featured nail-driving contests, egg and sack races, and a clothes-pin scramble, but it was a rare occurrence that summer. Numerous newspaper articles reminded readers that the *Frolic* could be rented for private excursions and that "the shade makes Luna an ideal place for such outings in the afternoon, and the cool breezes from the mountains make it a desirable place in the evening." The *Rocky Mountain News* said "the flowers are beautiful and the atmosphere is the pure breath of the nearby mountains." Despite high praise from the newspapers, the picnic business remained down for the summer, with Luna simply unable to compete with Lakeside and Elitch's.[32]

While management promoted Luna Park as a happy, family-friendly place, behind the scenes things were not as happy or friendly. According to the *Denver Post*, there had been serious disagreements between the park's financial backers and management all summer. The newspaper did not elaborate on what those disagreements might have been, but the expensive failure of the Banda Mexicana appearance must have been a major one. On August 23, Albert Lewin resigned as general manager of Luna Park and was replaced by S. K. Howe, the company secretary. Over the next few days, Carl Lindquist and Peter Hansen, who had joined with Lewin in forming the Luna Park Company in 1910, purged all of Lewin's friends from management positions at the park, filling the jobs with people friendly to them.[33]

With only a couple of weeks left in the season after Albert Lewin's departure, the new management team carried on with the same programs. On August 27, the park provided free box lunches to all visitors between 4 and 8 p.m. Visitors could then spend the day at the park with "no necessity of planning to go home for supper," with special music at the pavilion and "exercise for all who enjoy this kind of amusement" at the skating rink. Labor

Day weekend began with a bronco busting contest between the Great Athos and a local wild bull. Labor Day itself, the last day of the season, began with a gold hunt at the park, with coupons for a total of $500 in gold hidden in tin boxes throughout the grounds. A free barbecue followed, and then a special contest with prizes for women skaters at the rink. The day ended with what the *Denver Republican* called a "beautiful and costly array of fireworks" over Sloan's Lake, and special tickets were available that allowed people to stay on the *Frolic* as it cruised the lake during the show.[34]

The Mason's Centennial Lodge again rented Luna Park for an Emancipation Day celebration on September 21. Park management also leased the skating rink to an unnamed person, who then sublet it to C. B. Hill and C. Allen. Beginning in October, Hill and Allen opened the rink to Black skaters. Twice a month they hosted special prize skating days and mask skating parties. *The Statesman* reported near the end of October that the skating rink was "proving a success and the crowds run large." In December, Joe Williams, described by *The Statesman* as "one of Denver's best colored roller skaters" began skating at the Luna rink and announced that he had "a neat side bet" waiting for any challenger who thought they could skate better. Denver's Black community enjoyed skating in the "heated and enclosed" rink, and on March 15 management held a Masquerade Roller Skating Carnival, with plans for a ten-hour duration race in the future. Unfortunately, skating came to an abrupt end in April when the original lessee failed to keep up the terms of his lease, forcing the park company to close the rink.[35]

As soon as Luna Park closed for the season, Carl Lindquist, Peter Hansen, and Omar Garwood incorporated a new Luna Park Company with the three men as directors and a capital stock of $50,000. With the new corporation in charge of Luna Park, the three men made plans for a number of changes ahead of the 1912 season. Among the first was reverting to the name Manhattan Beach. They also started work on a new open-air theater for

vaudeville acts booked by the Western Vaudeville Managers Association of Chicago. The new theater had 2,200 seats, forty boxes,
and 400 opera chairs, and "from pit to dome the cool, refreshing
breezes from the lake will reach every spot in the house." Management hired a twelve-piece orchestra for the theater, and the
*Denver Post* assured its readers that "patrons of the park are guar-
anteed the highest class vaudeville attractions obtainable free."
The dancing pavilion and skating rink got new oak floors (the
rink also got 600 new ball-bearing skates), and at the beginning
of June crews were rushing to get a mass of vines, shady trees, and
other plants in the ground.[36]

Lindquist and the other new owners told the Denver newspapers that they were bringing fourteen new sideshows and fifty
new attractions to Manhattan Beach for the 1912 season. Among
the new attractions was a recreation of Robert Peary's trip to the
North Pole, "during which one will travel from tropical clime to
the cold and frozen North, 'where the wind blows fiercely and
snow falls continuously.'" The Sioux Village housed fifty people of
the Lakota/Dakota/Nakota Nation "eating, cooking and living as
they do at home," and Ye Olde Plantation Village provided the
best "Southern melody and Negro plantation songs" in Denver.
A new hydroplane was supposed to give rides over Sloan's Lake,
but the plans for it seemed to fall apart fairly quickly. Satriano's
Concert Band gave daily performances throughout the park
grounds. Lindquist hired Earl Gandy, who for several years had
managed parks in Europe, as the new general manager of Manhattan Beach.[37]

Work on the planned changes soon fell behind, and when
rivals Lakeside, Elitch's, and Tuileries opened for the summer at
the end of May, Manhattan Beach remained closed. Crowds still
swarmed the park during the early days of June, enjoying picnics
on the grounds and boating on the lake, but none of the concessions or rides were open. With opening day scheduled for June
9, in a first for Denver's amusement parks, Gandy began offering

season tickets for $2, which would allow two people admission to the park every day of the season. The park also began to advertise itself as the "Cut Rate Amusement Park," a far cry from the loftier slogans of previous years. Opening day attracted little notice from Denver's newspapers.[38]

Business was somewhat slow during the first days of the season for the new Manhattan Beach, but several clubs did book picnics at the park, including the Central Tramway Club, which held a two-day carnival at the park on June 15 and 16, and the North Side Women's Club on June 23. The *Denver Post* hosted a Children's Carnival on June 17, granting free admission to the park and one free ride on the merry-go-round and roller coasters to any child under 15 who clipped the coupon from the newspaper. Other special attractions for that day included a special vaudeville program in the theater and athletic events under the direction of A. C. Thompson, head instructor of Denver's playgrounds. The day was so successful that Earl Gandy decided to bring back Children's Days on Wednesdays for the rest of the season.[39]

The free vaudeville acts at the park, which included the singing and dancing of the Two Grahams, singers Doris Little and the La Delle sisters, the Four Wonderful Benos gymnastic act, and Charles Hughes and Company, received high praise, but some of the park's offerings proved more controversial. On June 16 the park staged the Sinking of the *Titanic* on Sloan's Lake, just two months after the real *Titanic* went down, claiming over 1,500 lives. *Denver Post* theater critic Frank W. White found the spectacle particularly offensive, writing "It is not only abnormal, offensive and foolish as an entertainment, but an exhibition that must violate the most tender sentiment of humanity." White wrote that if it were up to him, he would cancel the performance, but he was sure it would draw a crowd and might even please viewers. He went on to compare it to announcing that a hanging would take place on the state capitol lawn. While that would draw a crowd, he wrote, "it would be none the less horrible—none the less hideously wrong, would it?"[40]

The staging of the Sinking of the *Titanic* went ahead as planned, with, according to the *Denver Republican*, "all the thrills and perilous rescues reproduced as truly realistic as possible." The show did indeed draw a crowd, and the park staged it again several times over the next few days. For the Fourth of July, the *Titanic* became the battleship *Maine*, blown up and sunk in the lake as part of the day's special events. The *Rocky Mountain News* wrote that the demonstration included "real and sensational rescues from the burning vessel," with life preservers, rafts, and life buoys used to rescue passengers from the ship. The cannonading, the newspaper proclaimed, could be heard for miles around. The naval shows were so popular that park management vowed to carry them out weekly for the rest of the summer, and the sinking of the *Titanic* would become a standard show at amusement parks throughout the country, including Elitch's, where it replaced the *Battle of the Monitor and Merrimac*.[41]

The Fourth of July also brought the debut of the park's long-delayed hydroplane, captained by A. C. Wagner. Built by the General Aviation Company in a shed at the park, construction of the plane was delayed when parts failed to arrive from the east. The first passenger on the Fourth was Wanda Mundy of Denver. The plane and its first flight must not have been a great success as it was never mentioned again after the Fourth. Sun dances and sporting events by the Native Americans living at the park in the Sioux Village, and the debut of Florence Gale and Company at the theater, rounded out the offerings for the holiday. Florence Gale and her troupe turned out to be so popular that management booked them for the rest of the summer.[42]

After the delayed start, Denver's newspapers reported that attendance at Manhattan Beach grew steadily throughout the 1912 season. The *Denver Post*'s Children's Day brought between 12,000 and 15,000 children to the park, while another Central

Tramway Club picnic at the end of June brought 12,000 people. The vaudeville acts in the theater, rides on the *Frolic*, and beautiful grounds were heavily promoted by the newspapers, with the *Denver Times* writing near the end of June "daily and nightly family parties in large numbers gathered under the luxurious shade trees and enjoyed picnic baskets on the beautiful lawns."[43]

On July 28, Manhattan Beach played host to Colorado's Socialist Party for its annual picnic. Advertisements stated that Eugene Debs would be the special guest speaker at the picnic as he had been in 1902, but he never appeared. Instead, the day's speakers were William Rodriguez, one of the owners of Chicago's *Daily World* newspaper and a one-time candidate for mayor of Chicago, and Joseph Cannon. The picnic came just as *Denver Post* publisher Frederick Bonfils was sentenced to sixty days in jail and fined $5,000 for being in contempt of court by judge Hubert Shattuck. Bonfils had printed a story in the *Post* stating that Shattuck and Denver Tramway Company president William G. Evans were lifelong friends. Evans filed a complaint alleging Bonfils was in contempt over the story, and Shattuck sentenced the newspaper publisher without a trial. Labor organizations throughout the state protested the sentence, and it was a hot topic among speakers at the Socialist picnic. Rodriguez told the *Denver Post* that the case showed the "court has taken unto itself powers that it does not possess," and he was outraged that after imposing the sentence, Shattuck had a Bible sent to Bonfils in jail as either a joke or an insult. The *United Labor Bulletin* declared the picnic a success even though only 4,000 people paid admission to the park, with children 12 and under admitted free. The Socialist Party made about $150 from the gathering according to the newspapers.[44]

The 1912 season at Manhattan Beach ended quietly. The park hosted a watermelon festival on August 4, followed by a Rocky Ford cantaloupe festival on August 18. August 25 brought a special appearance by Mademoiselle Yvonne, billed as Europe's lightweight champion wrestler. She offered to meet any challenger and give $25 to anyone she could not throw in thirty minutes or less. Children's Days continued through the end of August, with a free bonbon lunch for them on August 28. Another free barbecue on Labor Day marked the end of the season. At the end of September, Manhattan Beach became a mock courtroom for famed Denver juvenile court judge Benjamin Lindsey. A motion picture company had approached Lindsey about filming one of his court sessions, but Lindsey decided that the children he regularly dealt with could not appear without their parents' permission. Instead, the film company put out a casting call for volunteers, and more than 100 boys offered to appear. All of the furniture from Lindsey's courtroom, "even to the pictures on the wall," was moved to a three-walled canvas room at the park, and the judge, his clerk, Ida Gregory, and his bailiff, Patrick O'Brien, held a mock court session for the cameras.[45]

The Centennial Lodge hosted its third annual Emancipation Day celebration at the park on September 12. *The Statesman* noted that the day had become "a sure rain maker," and despite the day living up to this reputation, there was a good crowd and everyone had a good time. After the end of the season, park management also once again leased the skating rink to C. B. Hill, who named it the Bull Moose Skating Rink for its winter operation. Events at the rink during the winter included prize nights, a seven-mile racing contest for men and a mile-and-a-half contest for women, and a masked carnival on Valentine's Day 1913. The Bull Moose Skating Rink closed for the season on May 16, 1913, just ahead of Manhattan Beach's regular season.[46]

As the opening of the 1913 season approached, it was obvious that Manhattan Beach and Tuileries were losing ground to rivals Lakeside Amusement Park and Elitch Gardens. After the 1912 season, Tuileries focused most of its attention on motorcycle races, vaudeville in its theater, and its ballroom and skating rink. At Manhattan Beach, Lindquist and the park's other owners hired

Cinta Dillon, who was always referred to in newspaper articles about the park as Mrs. W. Edward Dillon, as the new manager for the season. Near the end of the season, the *Rocky Mountain News* even referred to her as the first woman to manage an amusement park west of the Missouri River, seemingly forgetting about Mary Elitch Long, who had been managing one in Denver since 1891. Opening day at Manhattan Beach attracted little attention from Denver's newspapers, but Dillon continued the park's Children's Days on Wednesdays, with free dance lessons from Professor Kreamer and vaudeville acts in the theater. She booked Balfe's Band to provide music throughout the summer. The dance pavilion and skating rink remained popular, as did rides on the *Frolic* and the park's merry-go-round, roller coasters, and other attractions. Dillon also brought in a number of special attractions, including Mademoiselle La Bella, who performed a "sensational automobile act" twice a day. Named the "Automobile Accident," Mademoiselle La Bella, seated in a car, accelerated down an incline at sixty miles per hour. In the middle of the incline, the car wrecked, throwing La Bella into the air. Hanging from a trapeze, her partner in the act, Dare Devil Henly, then caught her. The act had caused quite a stir in New York, which is where it was performed before Dillon booked Mademoiselle La Bella for Manhattan Beach.[47]

Denver ballooning legend Ivy Baldwin, who had been performing at Elitch's since the 1890s, also joined the lineup at Manhattan Beach for the 1913 season. By 1912, Baldwin had progressed from balloons to a new hydroplane, which the General Aviation Company was building in its shed on the north side of Sloan's Lake. Baldwin's first flight on May 18, 1913, ended with him in the lake. His second flight, on June 13, started well, but as the *Denver Post* reported, "He went up as he said he would, but he came down considerably faster than he went up, and now he is nursing sundry bruises. The machine is a wreck." The accident happened after Baldwin had circled the lake several times and was attempting to go higher. On the Fourth of July, he finally went up with a passenger in a "death-defying flight" over Sloan's Lake. Baldwin did another daredevil flight on July 16. The Fourth of July brought the return of bronco busting contests as well, with forty contestants and one hundred horses (the *Denver Post* said that "never were there more skillful riders or more fractious little horses"), but no fireworks. Ivy Baldwin was not the only person injured by a fall at the park that summer either. On July 20, Genevieve Andreen of Denver became dizzy while riding one of the roller coasters and fell out of her seat in the front car while it was rounding a sharp curve. She fell more than twenty feet to the ground, but managed to escape serious injury.[48]

Throughout the summer several clubs and organizations held gatherings at the park. In June the Central Tramway Club booked the park for two days and once again staged the Fall of Port Arthur on the lake. They also held a mask carnival on the second day of the gathering, and even staged a mask parade in a mock boat through the streets of downtown Denver to draw crowds to the park. In July the members of the Order of the Eastern Star held a moonlight dance on the *Frolic*, which was followed a few days later by an aquatic carnival. The park built a new 20-foot diving tower in the lake for the carnival, which featured a diving and swimming exhibition with Denverites Mayme and Jennie Saradowski, Sophia Schwalb, Gertrude Woods, and Marion Gray. The day also featured 100-yard sprints for girls and 200-yard races for boys, swimming across the lake, and a tub race for boys under age 14. The Socialist Party picnic at the end of July featured boat races with crews trained by Captain Butterbaugh of the *Frolic*. In August the park hosted fundraisers for the Mount St. Vincent's Children's Home and St. Clara's Orphanage. The *Rocky Mountain News* hosted kiddie days on July 30 and August 27, which featured a variety of races and, at the August event, a money hunt to provide spending money for school. On both days, according to the *News*, the roller coasters and merry-go-round were at full capacity all day and the children crowded the decks of the *Frolic* for trips around the lake.[49]

At the beginning of August, the *Rocky Mountain News* said that "After many days Manhattan Beach is coming into its own. Always one of Denver's prettiest parks, it is only recently that Denver people have really appreciated it, and it has of late been receiving a share of its well-deserved patronage." The newspaper praised the bathing beach and the *Frolic*, along with the children's playground, while also saying that if a person had no interest in amusement devices the park was "a dandy place . . . to just go and sit." In mid-August the Wild West returned to Manhattan Beach with more stagecoach holdups and appearances by female riders from Buffalo Bill's recently closed Wild West show. In addition to the Wild West shows and bronco busting contests, Ivy Baldwin walked a tight rope stretched over the park grounds, and visitors got to feast on two carloads of Rocky Ford cantaloupe. Labor Day weekend brought balloon ascensions by Ivy Baldwin and a

The *Frolic* and its dock at night with all of the lights turned on. *Denver Post* theater critic Frank W. White described the illuminated boat as a "giant of gold." *Source: Denver Republican*, August 14, 1910.

large picnic, but Carl Lindquist limited attendance to grocery workers, employees of the Lindquist Cracker Factory, and their friends. Whatever attention Denverites were giving to the park that summer proved to be too little. Simply unable to compete with the bigger Lakeside Amusement Park and Elitch Gardens, the 1913 season was the last for Carl Lindquist's version of Manhattan Beach. Both it and Tuileries closed their gates for the last time at the end of their seasons.[50]

Carl Lindquist had planned to reopen Manhattan Beach for the 1914 season. As crews closed up the park's buildings for the winter, Cinta Dillon sat for an interview with the *Rocky Mountain News*. Stating that she felt managing the park had been a rewarding experience, she told the newspaper that a sense of humor, tact, and executive ability were critical to doing the job, which she highly recommended to other women. Dillon also said that the owners of the park wanted her to manage it again in 1914, and that another amusement park had also offered her a management position, but she did not think she would take either job. Even if she had been inclined to manage Manhattan Beach for another season, that possibility ended on October 1, 1913, when judge John A. Perry of the Denver District Court ordered the Luna Park Amusement Company's interest in the Manhattan Beach property sold to satisfy a $30,870 mortgage held by the Southern Investment Company and a $14,577 loan from the Continental Trust Company.[51]

A little over two weeks after the judgment against the Luna Park Company, the Denver Wrecking Company was at the park dismantling the Joy Wheel building and selling the parts for scrap. There was no mention of the human roulette wheel itself, so it was most likely sold to another park. Shortly after crews started dismantling the building, Carl Lindquist, then a state representative, told the *Rocky Mountain News* that vandals had wrecked the *Frolic*. According to Lindquist, someone opened the valves in the hull of the boat, flooding it and sending it to the bottom of

Sloan's Lake. In January of 1914 the Denver Wrecking Company also announced that they were dismantling the *Frolic* and its dock, and that the "boat contains a lot of good building material, which we are selling cheap on the grounds."[52]

There was no Emancipation Day celebration at Manhattan Beach in 1913, but C. B. Hill did once again lease the skating rink for the winter for Denver's Black roller skaters. Early in 1914, the park did play a starring role in another airplane story. For several days in February Arthur Wagner, who designed the airplane, and Chris Petersen, who would fly it, had been experimenting with the plane at the park, using the General Aviation Company's shed on the north side of the lake. Wagner drove a police car and Petersen was a licensed pilot from the Wright Brothers Flying School. On the afternoon of February 11, 1914, the men finally achieved success when Petersen reached an altitude of 190 feet and covered twenty miles by circling over Sloan's Lake for twenty minutes. A biplane modeled after the Wright Brothers' airplane, the plane was fitted with pontoons so it could land on water. The flight attracted hundreds of people to the Manhattan Beach grounds, and a photograph in the *Denver Post* showed the plane in flight over Sloan's Lake with Manhattan Beach's roller coaster visible in the background.[53]

Just as airplane enthusiasts were unwilling to give up on flying planes over Sloan's Lake, John Foster was unwilling to give up on Manhattan Beach and he worked out a plan to give the park one last chance. Over the winter he leased it to the Uno U-C Club, a Black fraternal organization in Denver, with Edward Jackson as president and Eugene Montgomery as secretary. With Denver's Black residents either excluded from the city's other amusement parks or allowed in only on special days, this was finally their chance to have a park of their own. Most of the concessions that Carl Lindquist had brought to the park were gone, and the owners of the rowboats, gasoline launch, and box ball alleys advertised them as being for sale or lease in early June "on account of other business." The park's new management advertised for concession-aires at the end of May, and by June 14, the park was ready to open for the season. According to the *Denver Post*, there was a "fine orchestra and dancing on a brand new floor," with special prize dances on Wednesdays. Denver bandleader George Morrison and his orchestra provided music at the park. On June 17, the park hosted a riding contest with "grand prizes," but unfortunately it was all downhill for the park from there. On Tuesdays, the Uno U-C Club hosted Midsummer Fests at the park, with the first one on July 14 advertised as the grand opening. The Midsummer Fests continued until August 11, when the park closed for the season. On September 12, the Masons once again hosted an Emancipa-tion Day celebration at the park, which the *Denver Star* described as bringing "one of the largest crowds of the season." It was the last official event held at Manhattan Beach. It is hard to say whether Denver's newspapers largely ignored Manhattan Beach during the 1914 season because it was meant for Black customers or because it was simply a shell of its former self, but without their help in promoting it, the park did not stand a chance.[54]

After the last Emancipation Day celebration in 1914, Man-hattan Beach sat empty for nearly a year until the Denver Wrecking Company announced on August 1, 1915, that it was beginning to dismantle the remaining parts of the park. At the time there was 30,000 feet of "extra good" lumber in various sizes from ceilings and floors at the park, and the company was willing to sell it cheaply to avoid having to move it to the wreck-ing yard. Additional items for sale included twenty-three tables, 100 chairs, and all of the park's refreshment equipment. More than a year later, the Denver Wrecking Company was still tearing down the park. In October of 1916, the company advertised that it had 200,000 feet of lumber in all sizes, roofing material, a small building, and the 61-foot by 120-foot steel trussed roof of the dancing pavilion, which "would make a good roof for [a] garage or large barn." Two months later, the Denver Wrecking Company advertised that in addition to the last 5,000 feet of boards, there were also several ticket booths remaining, as well as the roller coaster cars, which "make good sled bodies." By the end of the year, all that remained of Manhattan Beach was the fence around the property. On September 1, 1916, the *Denver Post* reported that the Manhattan Beach Amusement Company was a defunct corporation.[55]

By 1918, the Edgewater Athletic Club was using the old athletic field at the park as its baseball field. That spring, John Foster and the Southern Investment Company agreed to tear down the fence around the park grounds and make repairs to create "one of the finest corner lot baseball fields" in North Denver. The new baseball field officially opened on May 12, when the Edgewater team defeated the Priest-All-Stars by 5 to 4 in their first game on their new home field. Ten years later, in 1928, as the city of Denver was assembling the land around Sloan's Lake to make a public park, the Seventh-Day Adventists held their annual campmeeting over a nine-day period in June on the former park grounds. It was one of the last major events to be advertised as taking place at Manhattan Beach. Soon, the amusement park that had entertained Denverites for almost twenty-five years would find new life as a city park.[56]

# Conclusion

## *Sloan's Lake Park*

ALMOST FROM THE DAY IT WAS FOUNDED IN 1858, DENVER HAS tried proving that it is a sophisticated city of the world rather than a cow town. The city's streetcar system, individual houses spread out over a large area instead of tenements and apartment buildings crammed into the core of the city, beautiful parks and cemeteries, theaters, and the ability to host national conventions, among many other things, were all steps toward dispensing with the city's cow town image that so many residents seemed to be embarrassed about. The city's amusement parks were no exception. While most major cities were home to one or two amusement parks, between 1890 and 1914 Denver could proudly claim to have had five, although after 1914 only two of them remained in business.[1]

By the time Manhattan Beach closed for good in 1914, Sloan's Lake had been helping to fulfill Denver's recreational needs for more than fifty years. With residents eager to enjoy their free time, ice skating, boating, and fishing on the lake had always been popular. The steamboat and canal in 1874, along with Johnson's Park, proved a novel, but short-lived, escape. With the rise of amusement resorts and then amusement parks, Denver embraced Adam Graff's Sloan Lake Park and Manhattan Beach as wonderful and beautiful places to have a good time. Even as it struggled through different owners and changes, Denver's newspapers did their best to promote Manhattan Beach as a worthy place to visit and a sign of the city's prominence in the West. By 1914 rivals Lakeside Amusement Park and Elitch Gardens may have made it impossible for Manhattan Beach to keep amusing the public, but Sloan's Lake was far from done with entertaining people.

Denver's amusement options had come a long way since Adam Graff and John Elitch opened their parks in 1890. New theaters had spread rapidly throughout Denver during the 1890s and early 1900s. The Curtis, Denham, and Orpheum theaters played everything from melodrama to vaudeville. Curtis Street, with 10,000 electric lights, became known as Denver's Great White Way. As movies became more popular, movie theaters also spread rapidly throughout the city, including the Bluebird, Paramount, Aladdin, Mayan, and Isis. Harry Huffman, who owned the Bluebird, started buying other theaters, including the Tabor Grand, Broadway, Orpheum, and Albert Lewin's Rialto (some of them one-time rivals of Manhattan Beach's theater) and converting them to movie theaters. As part of mayor Robert Speer's City Beautiful program, Denver built its own theater, the Municipal Auditorium at Fourteenth and Curtis, finished just in time to host the Democratic National Convention in 1908. The Auditorium hosted concerts, operas, automobile shows, Boy Scout conventions, and many other events, which people were happy to attend.[2]

The city's public parks had also grown rapidly, especially under Speer, who saw parks as a vital part of his City Beautiful program. Between 1904 and 1912, Speer doubled the size of Denver's parks. At Washington Park, the city extended the park to the south and built a bathing beach on Smith Lake. City Park was home to the Denver Zoo and the Museum of Natural History (later renamed the Museum of Nature and Science). Congress Park became Cheesman Park when the Cheesman family donated $100,000 to build a pavilion in the park honoring Walter S. Cheesman. New parks added during Speer's years as mayor included Sunken Gardens, Inspiration Point (just north of Lakeside Amusement Park), and Alamo Placita, which was built on the site of Arlington Park, Manhattan Beach's one-time rival. Speer also planted the seed that became Denver's Mountain Parks system. At Berkeley Lake, where John Elitch had once planned to build his summer resort, park visitors could swim in the lake and play golf on the city's first public golf course. Speer's best-loved park project, however, was Civic Center Park, in the heart of downtown Denver. Speer hoped that Civic Center Park would be similar to the Court of Honor at the 1893 Columbian Exposition, with the park itself surrounded by architecturally similar government buildings. It took until 1912 for the city to get the money to buy the thirteen acres that would make up Civic Center Park, and it would take many years after that for Speer's vision to be realized, but Denver would have its open space in the heart of the city. Speer also wanted a network of parkways that would connect all of Denver's parks.[3]

The first proposal to turn Sloan's Lake into a public park came in 1881, but it was 1906 before the city of Denver finally acquired some of the land as part of Speer's City Beautiful program. By 1912 the city owned a little over 160 acres around the lake. The Manhattan Beach property was the last remaining piece that the city needed to get. The main reason John Foster had gone to court in 1914 to clear up the lawsuit filed by Theodore Schrott and Ernst Steinke in 1891 was to clear title to the land, making a future sale possible, although at the time he hoped that Manhattan Beach would continue as an amusement park. However, it was not until September 1936, more than twenty years later, that John Foster and J. P. Edrington, both sons-in-law of the late Captain William Bethell, reached an agreement with George Cranmer, manager of parks and improvements for Denver, to sell the Manhattan Beach property to the city for $32,500. The purchase made Sloan's Lake the second largest park in Denver after City Park.[4]

As the city of Denver slowly assembled the property needed to create the park, some Denver residents urged it to take better care of both the land it already had and the lake. In 1922, one woman, identified only as a North Side Club woman, urged the city to provide a lifeguard and a bathhouse or other building "in the name of decency," because boys and men who wanted to swim at Sloan's Lake often stood on the beach dressing and undressing in full view of women and children. She said nearby residents were "entitled to a respectable beach." The next year, the members of the Denver Municipal Trap and Skeet Club built their clubhouse on the southwest corner of Sloan's Lake, and the sounds of shooting replaced the noise of roller coasters, merry-go-rounds, fireworks, and steamboat whistles at the lake until 1969. (For years, people dredged the lake collecting the used bullets for the lead in them.) In the early 1930s, the city finally began cleaning up the land around Sloan's Lake. In 1933, officials announced plans to build a bathing beach, and around that time Sloan's and Cooper Lakes were permanently connected (with the island created when digging the canal in 1874 still there). Swimming, fishing, ice skating, and boating remained popular activities on the lake. In the late 1930s, the Works Progress Administration built a boathouse and marina on the north side of the lake on the Manhattan Beach property, which had been the stated intention for buying it in 1936.[5]

According to *Rocky Mountain Life* magazine, by the late 1940s, Sloan's Lake was "the setting for more activity and general all-around fun than a circus." Even though it was only a "little lake—a pond really," from early April to Labor Day the "midget sea" was crammed daily with boats, with more than eighty in the water on Sundays. The Mile High Boat Association was then responsible for policing the boats on the lake, and it set aside two hours each Sunday for motorboats and the water skiers they towed behind; the rest of the time rowboats and sailboats dominated the water. Young boys often gathered near the boathouse on the north side of the lake, where they offered to bail out returning boats for a quarter. Competing with the boaters on the lake were

The Denver Municipal Trap Shooting Clubhouse at Sloan's Lake. *Source:* Photo by the author.

The boathouse at Sloan's Lake built by the Works Progress Administration in the late 1930s. It is near the location of the park's second zoo building. *Source:* Photo by the author.

swimmers and those who enjoyed fishing, while a number of people also sat around the lake watching all of the activity.[6]

Much as the saloons and gambling dens had been a problem for Manhattan Beach during the 1890s and early 1900s, by the 1970s heavy automobile traffic on the roads around Sloan's Lake Park and drinking and drug use in the park became major problems. The city of Denver frequently attempted to adjust traffic routes through and around the park to cut down on cruising and other problems, and at times closed parking lots to prevent them from becoming hangouts for troublemakers. The landscaping at the park also suffered for many years, with nearby residents sometimes referring to the park as forgotten. Still, the park has remained a popular gathering place in North Denver and has been the site of races, Denver Municipal Band Concerts, and

A model boat regatta for students from nearby Lake Junior High School at Sloan's Lake in the 1930s or 1940s. *Source:* The Denver Public Library, Western History Collection, X-27730.

since 2001, the Colorado Dragon Boat Festival, among many other events.[7]

For years the park was known as Sloan's Lake Park, but in 1993 controversy erupted when the city of Denver erected new signs at the park identifying it as Sloan Lake Park. Longtime residents and local historians loudly let the city know that the name was Sloan's Lake, that it had always been Sloan's Lake, and that it would always be Sloan's Lake. For several years people demanded that the city change the signs. In 2002 Roger Oram, who lived north of the lake, finally presented enough evidence to convince the city to change the name back to Sloan's Lake, although at the time city workers simply repainted the existing signs instead of installing new ones.[8]

In 1953, with Manhattan Beach a long-distant memory for most people, Dr. LeRoy R. Hafen of the State Historical Society of Colorado, Lawrence W. Marshall of the American Pioneer Trails Association, and the city of Denver joined forces to install a plaque on the west side of the boathouse noting that the area had once been the site of the amusement park. On the afternoon of May 17, 1953, thousands of North Denver residents, some in 1890s costumes, turned out to watch the unveiling of the plaque. Donna Calabrese, head girl at North High School, unveiled it while David M. Abbott, assistant manager for parks and improvements for the city of Denver, accepted it. The sign noted that after the 1908 fire that destroyed the theater "some amusement features continued until 1914," largely ignoring the park's reinvention as Luna Park and the many attractions it offered. After the unveiling, the group went to the former home of Roger Woodbury (who had been involved with Manhattan Beach in the early days) at 25th and Alcott for a skit on his life presented by elementary school students, and then a bus tour of North Denver landmarks. By the time of the ceremony, the men who had devoted so much of themselves to Manhattan Beach were all long gone.[9]

The plaque on the boathouse at Sloan's Lake stating that the area was once home to Manhattan Beach. *Source:* Photo by the author.

After leaving his position as treasurer of Manhattan Beach in 1893, Adam Graff opened a bar on Downing Street in Denver and also served as alderman for the Ninth Ward. His wife Julia died in 1896, and in 1904 he moved to a small ranch outside of Kremmling, Colorado, to be near his daughter Magdalen. There, he continually searched for a large deposit of paraffin that he believed was on his ranch (shortly after his death it was found on a neighboring ranch). He fell ill during the summer of 1922 and was brought to Denver, where he died at St. Luke's Hospital on July 12. In announcing his death, the *Routt County Sentinel* said "he was a pioneer in Denver, where he was long in the ice business, and later he was a proprietor of Manhattan beach, which proved to be an unfortunate investment."[10]

In 1919, eight years after being forced out at Luna Park, Albert Lewin spent $156,000 to build the Central Public Market, a large indoor marketplace, at 14th and Champa Streets in Denver. In 1921, Lewin spent $50,000 to convert the building into the Winter Garden dance hall. The interior walls were painted a "soft pink and purple," fifty hanging lamps and a special colored lighting effect provided illumination inside, and the curtains over the windows were decorated with images of palm trees. The "meet me corners" in the building were designed to "enable handling the 500 couples" who could be on the dance floor at one time and were named after cities and schools in the area. Joining Lewin in the new venture was his son Melvin. Albert Lewin died in Denver on November 5, 1924. His family eventually sold Winter Garden to new owners, who renamed it the Bon Ton Dance Palace and operated it for several more years.[11]

Dr. John Foster, the man who more than anyone else kept Manhattan Beach going, died at his Denver home on March 24, 1945, at age 84. He continued practicing medicine until shortly before his death. In addition to his work at Manhattan Beach, Foster had also worked to build up state and national medical associations and was a founding member of the "National Optomological [sic] Society," according to the *Denver Post*. Writing of Foster's decision to move to Denver in 1891, the *Post* said "Here he lived; here he worked; here he made himself a high position among those who serve humanity thru science." Nowhere in his obituary did the newspaper mention his involvement with Manhattan Beach.[12]

One enduring myth about Manhattan Beach, repeated in numerous histories of amusement parks and Denver, is that it was the first amusement park built west of the Mississippi River. Several amusement resorts in the west predate the opening of Manhattan Beach, including Lagoon Park in Utah (1886), Chutes Amusement Park (1887) and Lincoln Park/Eastlake Park (1881) in Los Angeles, and White City (1888) in Seattle. Manhattan Beach was, however, Denver's first true amusement park, adding a merry-go-round, roller coaster, and other attractions well before Elitch Gardens or Arlington Park began their conversions to amusement parks, and long before Tuileries or Lakeside Amusement Park were built. Whether it was the White City by the Lake, the Coney Island of the West, or the Cut Rate Amusement Park, it set the stage for the Denver parks that followed.[13]

The other enduring myth is that Roger the elephant was killed after his July 5, 1891, rampage and buried in a swamp near the park that later became the parking lot for a grocery store or the Edgewater City Hall. Roger became such an integral part of Denver and Edgewater's history that for many years a mural depicting him surrounded by adoring children at Manhattan Beach was on the side of the Joyride Brewing Company building at 25th Avenue and Sheridan in Edgewater. (The mural was later destroyed when the building was remodeled.) Roger was clearly not killed after causing George Eaton's death in 1891 and remained at Manhattan Beach through the 1892 season. What became of him after that remains a mystery. One intriguing possibility is that Frank C. Bostock, who bought Manhattan Beach's monkeys in 1895, may have also purchased Roger after the 1892 season. For several years Bostock had an elephant named Roger that he exhibited throughout the country, including at the zoo in Indianapolis, Indiana, in 1900 and 1901, at Dreamland on Coney Island in 1904 and 1905, and in Atlanta, Georgia, in

1907. He also had an elephant known as Little Roger, and his brother, Edward Bostock, had an elephant named Sir Roger in Scotland. (Sir Roger, definitely not the Roger from Manhattan Beach, was put to death in 1900 and has been on display in the Kelvingrove Museum in Glasgow ever since.) While a definitive answer on Roger's fate may never be possible, he most definitely did not die at Manhattan Beach in 1891.[14]

Of the almost 5,000 amusement parks built in the United States between 1895 and 1920, most lasted a few seasons at best before disappearing. Some, like Manhattan Beach, managed to last for a couple of decades or more before fading away. Less than one percent of those parks managed to survive for 100 years or more. Amazingly, the two surviving Denver parks, Elitch

The northwest corner of Sloan's Lake Park, the site of Manhattan Beach. The theater would have been on the right behind the parking lot and the boathouse would have been to the left of the lot. The zoo building would have been near the current boathouse, which is just visible on the right side of the photo. *Source:* Photo by the author.

Gardens and Lakeside Amusement Park, both made it into the one percent. Denver mayor Federico Peña visited Elitch's on June 2, 1990, to help celebrate its centennial, while workers at the park were busy readying its new Sidewinder looping roller coaster. At the time, the park was busy preparing to move to a new location in Denver's Central Platte Valley, which would finally happen in time for the 1995 season. Lakeside's centennial celebration in 2008 included a special dinner and tour and an appearance by Denver city auditor Dennis Gallagher playing the part of mayor Robert Speer. To have its two surviving amusement parks reach that milestone was certainly beneficial as Denver seemingly still works to shed its cow town image.[15]

As significant as the centennials were for Elitch's and Lakeside, neither park might have reached them if not for Manhattan Beach. The long-gone park was home to Denver's first merry-go-round and roller coaster, and proved that an amusement park could work in Denver. Manhattan Beach may not have been the first or the largest amusement park west of the Mississippi, but it certainly was important for Denver. Much as Frank W. White described the sudden appearance of the *Frolic* during the Banda Mexicana concert in 1911, Manhattan Beach was a "giant of gold" that briefly appeared on the shores of Sloan's Lake, bringing laughter and fun to tens of thousands of Denverites.[16]

# NOTES

## ABBREVIATIONS:

DP—*Denver Post*
DR—*Denver Republican*
DT—*Denver Times*
FF—File Folder
RMN—*Rocky Mountain News*

## INTRODUCTION

1. Gene Lowall, "Famous Resort at Sloan's Lake Leveled by Fire," *RMN* (February 18, 1940): sec. 2, 10; Deed between Manhattan Beach Company and Roger W. Woodbury, April 24, 1891, Box 1 FF 23, Pinckney C. and William D. Bethell Papers, Stephen H. Hart Library, History Colorado.

2. William F. Mangels, *The Outdoor Amusement Industry: From Earliest Times to the Present* (New York: Vantage, 1952), 3–13.

3. Mangels, *The Outdoor Amusement Industry*, 17–24.

4. Mangels, *The Outdoor Amusement Industry*, 38; John F. Kasson, *Amusing the Million: Coney Island at the Turn of the Century* (New York: Hill and Wang, 1978): 19, 23–26; LeRoy Ashby, *With Amusement for All: A History of American Popular Culture Since 1830* (Lexington: University Press of Kentucky, 2006), 140–41.

5. Nell Irvin Painter, *Standing at Armageddon: The United States, 1877–1919* (New York: W. W. Norton, 1987), 385; David Nasaw, *Going Out: The Rise and Fall of Public Amusements* (Cambridge: Harvard University Press, 1993), 85.

6. William B. Vickers, *History of the City of Denver, Arapahoe County, Colorado: Containing a History of the State of Colorado . . . A Condensed Sketch of Arapahoe County . . . A History of the City of Denver . . . Biographical Sketches . . .* (Chicago: O. L. Baskin, 1880) 291; Stephen J. Leonard and Thomas J. Noel, *Denver: Mining Camp to Metropolis* (Niwot: University Press of Colorado, 1991), 141; "Cemetery Beauty Marred by Weeds on Many Graves," *DP* (August 5, 1906): sec. 3, 4 (weed quote).

7. "The Baron's Bower," *RMN* (June 30, 1882): 3 (quotes 1–3); Frances Melrose, "The Baron's Bower: Von Richtofen's Dream Park," *RMN* (August 15, 1993): 8M; Don Robertson, Morris Cafky, and E. J. Haley, *Denver's Street Railways, Volume 1, 1871–1900: Not an Automobile in Sight* (Denver: Sundance, 1999), 49 (quote 4); Listing for San Souci Park, *Denver City Directory for 1894* (Denver: Corbett and Ballenger, 1894), 871. The spelling of San Souci varies between Sans and San.

8. Jim Prochaska, "The Bottoms Tour Notes," copy provided to the author, 2008; "Denver Drippings," *Colorado Daily Chieftain* (July 10, 1887): 8; "Gala Day for Colored People," *Leadville Daily/Evening Chronicle* (September 21, 1888): 1; Dennis Gallagher, "The Man Who Founded Berkeley Was the Visionary Behind Our Mountain Parks," *Denver North Star* (February 14, 2020), available from https://www.denvernorthstar.com/the-man-who-founded-berkeley-was-the-visionary-behind-our-mountain-parks/, last accessed May 6, 2022.

9. "Recalls Stirring Times of Pioneer Days," *Colorado Transcript* (April 29, 1909): 1; Phil Goodstein, *North Side Story: Denver's Most Intriguing Neighborhood* (Denver: New Social, 2011), 337–38; "Sloan's Lake Neighborhood History," available from https://history.denverlibrary.org/sloans-lake-neighborhood-history, last accessed May 6, 2022. No one is sure who Cooper Lake was named after, but possibilities include Gov. Job Cooper and Kemp Cooper.

10. Family tree for Thomas Morford Sloan, available from https://www.ancestry.com/family-tree/person/tree/3927480/person/140079017321/facts, last accessed May 31, 2022; "Sloan House," *RMN* (January 2, 1866): 3 (quote); The land was listed for sale in *RMN* from April 21, 1872 (p. 1) to April 26, 1872 (p. 3); Goodstein, *North Side Story*, 338; Certificate of Navigation, Boulevard and Sloan Lake Steam Navigation Company, Colorado State Archives, Denver, CO.

11. "On the Ice," *Rocky Mountain Sunday School Casket* (January 1, 1868): 5; Goodstein, *North Side Story*, 338; Alice M. Coleman, *Historical Narrative of the First Sixty Years: Edgewater's Sixtieth Anniversary of Incorporation 1901–1961* (Edgewater, CO, 1961), 7.

12. "Local News," *Denver Daily Times* (June 11, 1872): 1; "Advertisement for Dolly Varden boat trips," *Denver Daily Times* (June 26, 1872; July 6, 1872; July 8, 1872): all page 2; Dexter obit., 1891.

13. "Novel Enterprise," *Denver Daily Times* (February 12, 1874): 4.

14. "City Improvements," *RMN* (January 7, 1874): 3; "Hotel at Cheltenham Heights," *RMN* (June 6, 1873): 4; Goodstein, *North Side Story*, 339–40.

15. Goodstein, *North Side Story*, 339–40; Untitled article, *Denver Daily Times* (March 23, 1874): 4; Certificate of Navigation, Boulevard and Sloan Lake Steam Navigation Company; "The Boulevard Canal," *Denver Daily Times* (March 21, 1874); 3.

16. Coleman, *Historical Narrative*, 7; "The Boulevard Canal"; Untitled article, *Denver Daily Times* (March 26, 1874): 4.

17. "The Ship Canal," *RMN* (April 11, 1874): 4; "The Ship Canal," *RMN* (May 5, 1874): 3.

18. "Brevities," *RMN* (April 25, 1874): 4 (quote); Goodstein, *North Side Story*, 338–39; "Our Steamboat," *Denver Daily Times* (May 16, 1874): 4.

19. "Local Brevities," *RMN* (May 10, 1874): 8; "City Paragraphs," *RMN* (May 11, 1874): 3; "City Paragraphs," *Denver Daily Times* (May 19, 1874): 3.

20. Untitled Article, *Denver Daily Times* (May 23, 1874): 4; "The Steamboat," *RMN* (May 24, 1874): 4; "The Ship Canal," *Denver Daily Times* (May 27, 1874): 4 (quotes 1 and 2); "Highland Park," *RMN* (May 28, 1874): 4 (quote 3).

21. "Statistics of Streetcar Travel," *RMN* (October 11, 1874): 4 (quotes); Goodstein, *North Side Story*, 338–39; "The Ship Canal," *Denver Daily Times* (May 27, 1874): 4; "Highland Park," *RMN* (May 28, 1874): 4; "Territorial Items," *Colorado Daily Chieftain* (May 30, 1874): 3.

22. "Central, Gilpin County," *Denver Mirror* (May 24, 1874): 2; Alan Granruth, *Pennyweights: Bits and Pieces of Gilpin County History* (Central City, CO: Gilpin Historical Society, 2004), 86–88.

23. "Grand Opening of the Elysium Hall," *RMN* (August 8, 1874): 4 (quote 1); Ad for J. M. Johnson, *RMN* (February 28, 1873): 4; "City and Vicinity," *RMN* (December 23, 1873): 4; "Moonlight Excursions," *Denver Daily Times* (June 22, 1874): 4.

24. Regular Trip Ad, *RMN* (September 3, 1874): 4; "Territorial Items," *Colorado Weekly Chieftain* (September 24, 1874): 1; "Territorial Items," *Colorado Daily Chieftain* (September 20, 1874): 3; "City and Vicinity," *RMN* (September 18, 1874): 4; "Territorial Items," *Colorado Daily Chieftain* (September 23, 1874); 2; Untitled article, *Denver Daily Times* (November 6, 1874): 4; "Topics of To-Day," *Golden Weekly Globe* (November 7, 1874): 3; "Editorial Correspondence," *RMN* (November 26, 1874): 2.

25. Rebecca Hunt, "Healers on the Hill: St. Luke's and Presbyterian Hospitals of Denver," *Colorado Heritage* (Summer 2005): 3–6; "Boat Race," *Denver Daily Times* (September 12, 1874): 4; "Boat Race," *Denver Daily Times* (September 19, 1874): 4; "The Colorado Industrial Association," *Denver Daily Times* (March 17, 1875): 4.

26. "State News," *Fort Collins Courier* (October 20, 1881): 2; "Colorado Condensed," *Silver Standard* (June 9, 1888): 1; "Territorial," *Colorado Daily Chieftain* (May 14, 1874): 2.

27. Jerome Smiley, *History of Denver: With Outlines of the Earlier History of the Rocky Mountain Country* (Evansville, IN: Unigraphic, 1971 [1901]), 645.

28. "An Inquiry," *Denver Daily Times* (April 26, 1877): 1.

29. Lowall, "Famous Resort at Sloan's Lake Leveled by Fire"; Listing for Adam Graff, *Corbett, Hoye and Co.'s Eighth Annual City Directory* (Denver: Rocky Mountain News Printing Company, 1880), 249; Listing for Adam Graff, *Corbett and Ballenger's Ninth Annual Denver City Directory* (Unknown printing, available from the Denver Public Library Western History and Genealogy Department,

1881), 179; Listing for Adam Graff, *Corbett and Ballenger's Tenth Annual Denver City Directory* (Denver: Corbett and Ballenger, 1882), 258; Listing for Adam Graff, *Corbett and Ballenger's Eleventh Annual Denver City Directory* (Denver: Corbett and Ballenger, 1883), 296; Listing for Adam Graff, *Corbett and Ballenger's Twelfth Annual Denver City Directory* (Denver: Corbett and Ballenger, 1884), 302; "A Fish Supply," *White Pine Cone* (November 6, 1885): 3.

30. Incorporation Records, Sloan Lake and Park Company, March 5, 1889, Colorado State Archives; "A Destructive Fire," *Denver Republican* (April 17, 1891): 2.

31. Lowall, "Famous Resort at Sloan's Lake Leveled by Fire"; Coleman, *Historical Narrative*, 13.

32. "Sloan's Park," *Svensk-Amerikanska Western* (July 3, 1890): 4; "The New Sloan's Park," *RMN* (June 28, 1890): 3.

33. "The New Sloan's Park" (June 28, 1890); "Sloan's Park" (July 3, 1890); Lowall, "Famous Resort at Sloan's Lake Leveled by Fire"; Robertson, Cafky, and Haley, *Denver's Street Railways, Volume 1*, 203.

34. Untitled article, *Colorado Daily Chieftain* (October 28, 1890): 2.

35. Betty Lynne Hull, *Denver's Elitch Gardens: Spinning a Century of Dreams* (Boulder, CO: Johnson Books, 2003), 7; "Opened to the Public," *DR* (May 2, 1890): 3.

36. "John Elitch, Jr.," *Colorado Exchange Journal* (October 1889): 97; Robertson, Cafky, and Haley, *Denver's Street Railways, Volume 1*, 150, 146; "State News," *Queen Bee* (December, 16, 1889): 2; "A Man and Woman Drowned," *Colorado Daily Chieftain* (July 17, 1890): 4.

37. "A Destructive Fire" (April 17, 1891); Capital Stock Statement of the Manhattan Beach Company, April 30, 1891, Colorado State Archives, Denver, CO.

## CHAPTER 1

1. "Catch the Quarters," *DT* (April 8, 1891): 8.
2. "Catch the Quarters."
3. "Catch the Quarters"; "A City's Beauty Spot," *DT* (May 13, 1891): 6.
4. "Catch the Quarters"; "A City's Beauty Spot."
5. "Catch the Quarters"; Deed between Manhattan Beach Company and Roger W. Woodbury, April 24, 1891, Bethell Papers.
6. "Catch the Quarters."
7. "Catch the Quarters."
8. "A City's Beauty Spot."
9. "A City's Beauty Spot."
10. "A City's Beauty Spot."
11. Untitled article, *DT* (June 24, 1891): 4; "The Elephant Smiled," *DR* (June 27, 1891): 6; "Verify: Is an Elephant Buried Under a Colorado Supermarket?," 9 News television report, available from https://www.9news.com/article/news

/local/verify/verify-is-an-elephant-buried-under-a-colorado-supermarket/73-548063816, last accessed May 30, 2022.

12. "The Elephant Smiled."

13. "The Elephant Smiled"; "Manhattan Beach," *RMN* (June 28, 1891): 3.

14. "Twas a Model Day," *RMN* (June 29, 1891): 3; Ad for Manhattan Beach, *DT* (June 29, 1891): 2.

15. "Twas a Model Day"; Ad for Manhattan Beach (June 29, 1891).

16. "At the Resorts," *DR* (July 5, 1891): 5; Jack Stokes Ballard, *Colorado's Daring Ivy Baldwin: Aviator, Aerialist & Aeronaut* (Charleston, SC: History, 2020), 12–14.

17. "At the Resorts."

18. "At the Resorts."

19. "Terrorized," *RMN* (July 6, 1891): 1.

20. "Terrorized"; "A Frenzied Elephant," *DT* (July 6, 1891): 1.

21. "Terrorized"; "A Frenzied Elephant ."

22. "Terrorized"; "A Frenzied Elephant"; "Trampled by an Elephant," *Morning News* (July 7, 1891): 1; "While Riding an Elephant," *Omaha Daily Bee* (July 6, 1891): 1; "Trampled to Death," *Saint Paul Globe* (July 6, 1891): 1; "His Life Crushed Out," *San Francisco Examiner* (July 6, 1891): 2; Untitled article, *Vernon County Censor* (July 15, 1891): 4; "Dodad af en elefant," *Korrespondenten* (July 15, 1891): 5.

23. "Terrorized."

24. "Terrorized"; Grave of George Eaton, Riverside Cemetery, Denver, CO; George Eaton, Death Record, July 5, 1891, from the 1891 Death Book, Colorado State Archives; "Over a Bluff to His Death," *Northern Idaho News* (March 18, 1904): 2.

25. "Terrorized"; "Trampled by an Elephant."

26. "Death of the Ostriches," *RMN* (February 23, 1892): 8; "Verify: Is an Elephant Buried Under a Colorado Supermarket?"

27. "He Lost His Balloons," *DR* (July 27, 1891): 5.

28. "He Lost His Balloons."

29. "Fell Eight Thousand Feet," *Aspen Times Weekly* (August 22, 1891): 3; "Fell a Mile," *Boston Globe* (August 17, 1891): 8.

30. Deed between Manhattan Beach Company and Roger W. Woodbury, April 24, 1891, Bethell Papers; Untitled article, *Ice and Refrigeration* (September 1891): 138.

31. "Grim War in Denver," *DT* (September 11, 1891): 6; "The Animals Still There," *DR* (September 12, 1891): 5; "Manhattan Beach Trouble," *DR* (September 12, 1891): 5.

32. "Grim War in Denver"; "The Animals Still There"; "Manhattan Beach Trouble."

33. "Grim War in Denver"; "The Animals Still There"; "Manhattan Beach Trouble."

34. "Grim War in Denver"; "The Animals Still There"; "Manhattan Beach Trouble."

35. "Manhattan Beach Trouble"; "Manhattan Is O.K.," *DT* (September 12, 1891): 1.

## CHAPTER 2

1. Ad for Manhattan Beach, *RMN* (January 22, 1892): 8.

2. "Death of the Ostriches"; Deed of Trust Between William Todd and George Darrow, August 31, 1891, Colorado State Archives.

3. "Highlands," *RMN* (February 13, 1892): 6; "Manhattan Beach," *DR* (May 15, 1892): 2 (quote).

4. "Manhattan Beach," *DR* (May 15, 1892).

5. "Manhattan Beach."

6. "A Day at the Beach," *RMN* (May 16, 1892): 8; "Manhattan Beach"; "Manhattan Beach," *RMN* (May 29, 1892): 13.

7. "A Day at the Beach" (all quotes); Ad for Manhattan Beach, *RMN* (May 22, 1892): 13.

8. "Manhattan Beach"; "A Day at the Beach" (quote); Ad for Manhattan Beach, *RMN* (June 11, 1892): 3; "Manhattan Beach," *RMN* (June 19, 1892): 22; Ad for Manhattan Beach, *RMN* (July 1, 1892): 8; Ad for Manhattan Beach, *RMN* (July 4, 1892): 8; Ad for Manhattan Beach, *RMN* (July 5, 1892): 8.

9. Ad for Manhattan Beach, *RMN* (May 6, 1892): 13; Ad for Manhattan Beach, *RMN* (July 5, 1892); Ad for Manhattan Beach, *RMN* (June 11, 1892): 3; "Manhattan Beach," *RMN* (June 19, 1892).

10. Ad for Manhattan Beach, *RMN* (July 1, 1892): 8; "Summer Resorts," *RMN* (July 3, 1892): 11; Ad for Manhattan Beach, *RMN* (July 4, 1892): 8; Ad for Manhattan Beach, *RMN* (July 23, 1892): 3 and 9.

11. "Amusements," *RMN* (July 23, 1892): 9 (quote 1); Ad for Manhattan Beach *RMN* (July 11, 1892): 8; Ad for Manhattan Beach, *RMN* (July 5, 1892): 8; "The May Picnic," *RMN* (July 12, 1892): 2.

12. Ad for Manhattan Beach, *RMN* (August 12, 1892): 8; Ad for Manhattan Beach, *RMN* (August 27, 1892): 8; "Amusements," *RMN* (August 27, 1892): 8; "Manhattan Beach," *RMN* (September 7, 1892): 8; "Highlands," *RMN* (November 16, 1892): 3.

13. Finding Aid Introduction to Bethell Papers.

14. "Manhattan Bonds," *RMN* (February 25, 1892): 8; "Beach Reorganized," *RMN* (March 5, 1892): 10.

15. Exhibits A and B, *Theodore Schrott and Ernst Steinke v. W. D. Bethell, John M. Foster, Roger W. Woodbury, and the Manhattan Beach Company, a Corporation,* Arapahoe County, Colorado District Court, July 19, 1892, Colorado State Archives, Denver, CO; Certificate of Incorporation, Southern Investment Company, June 25, 1892, Colorado State Archives.

16. "Manhattan Bonds," *RMN* (September 18, 1892): 14; Statement of F. E. Wilcox, in *Schrott and Steinke v. Bethell et al. and the Manhattan Beach Company*; "Beach Reorganized"; William Todd to W. D. Bethell, April 5, 1892, Bethell Papers.

17. Statement of John C. Houber and Statement of F. E. Wilcox, both in *Schrott and Steinke v. Bethell et al. and the Manhattan Beach Company*; and Motion to Dismiss the Above Entitled Action as to John M. Foster and the Southern Investment Company, *Schrott and Steinke v. Bethell et al. and the Manhattan Beach Company*, June 21, 1914; Lowall, "Famous Resort at Sloan's Lake Leveled by Fire."

18. "Will Unite Forces," *RMN* (July 23, 1892): 8; "Uniform Prices," *RMN* (July 24, 1892): 8; "Elitch and Manhattan," *DR* (July 24, 1892): 11.

19. David Forsyth, "A Splendid Place: Denver's Arlington Park," *Colorado Heritage* (May/June 2015): 22–31.

20. Coleman, *Historical Narrative*, 13–15.

21. "Highlands," *RMN* (June 14, 1892): 5; "After the Saloons," *RMN* (July 6, 1892): 8.

22. "Changes at Manhattan," *RMN* (October 14, 1892): 2.

23. "An Heiress," *RMN* (December 20, 1892): 1; "After Sloan's Lake," *RMN* (January 10, 1893): 1.

24. "An Heiress"; "A Child of Fortune," *Quad-City Times* (December 27, 1892): 1; *Amanda S. Lockwood, etc. v. James M. Strickler, etc.*, Case Number 1216, Supreme Court of Colorado, Colorado State Archives, Denver, CO.

25. *Lockwood v. Strickler*.

## CHAPTER 3

1. "In Focus," *Boulder Daily Camera* (January 19, 1893): 4; "Got Back His Green," *RMN* (January 28, 1893): 8; "Hibernating in Captivity," *Grand Valley Star* (February 4, 1893): 6.

2. Untitled, *West Side Citizen* (February 10, 1893): 3; "Highlands," *RMN* (November 16, 1892).

3. "Manhattan Opening," *RMN* (May 21, 1893): 8; "Manhattan Beach," *West Side Citizen* (May 26, 1893): 3.

4. "Manhattan Opening," *RMN* (May 21, 1893): 8; "Manhattan Beach," *West Side Citizen* (May 26, 1893): 3.

5. "Amusements," *RMN* (May 29, 1893): 8; "Amusements," *RMN* (June 10, 1893): 5.

6. "Amusements," *RMN* (June 17, 1893): 8; "Amusements," *RMN* (June 22, 1893): 8; "Amusements," *RMN* (June 26, 1893): 8; "Amusements," *RMN* (July 2, 1893): 14 (quote); Hull, *Denver's Elitch Gardens*, 32.

7. "Amusements," *RMN* (June 10, 1893); "Amusements," *RMN* (June 17, 1893); "Ladies of Skydiving: Early History," available from ladiesofskydiving.com/early-history/, last accessed May 9, 2022.

8. "The Roller Coaster Again," *RMN* (March 27, 1893): 2; "Amusements," *RMN* (June 22, 1893); Mangels, *The Outdoor Amusement Industry*, 81–89; "Amusements," *RMN* (July 2, 1893); "Amusements," *RMN* (August 2, 1893): 2; "Amusements," *RMN* (August 4, 1893): 3; Ad for Manhattan Beach, *RMN* (August 14, 1893): 8; "Amusements," *RMN* (August 14, 1893): 8 (last quote); "Amusements," *RMN* (August 18, 1893): 5; Hull, *Denver's Elitch Gardens*, 38.

9. "Amusements," *RMN* (June 26, 1893); "Amusements," *RMN* (July 14, 1893): 8; "Amusements," *RMN* (July 2, 1893); "Denver," *Colorado Farmer* (July 20, 1893): 11.

10. Leonard and Noel, *Denver*, 102–3.

11. "Amusements," *RMN* (August 4, 1893); Ad for Manhattan Beach, *RMN* (August 23, 1893): 8; "Amusements," *RMN* (August 27, 1893): 5 (quote); "This Is Labor Day," *RMN* (September 4, 1893): 5.

12. Untitled, *West Side Citizen* (August 4, 1893): 3; Untitled, *West Side Citizen* (August 18, 1893): 3; Untitled, *West Side Citizen* (June 1, 1894): 3; "Amusements," *RMN* (July 2, 1893): 14 (last three quotes).

13. "Fire Destroys Many Buildings," *Colorado Evening Sun* (September 8, 1893): 1; "Incendiary Fire," *Aspen Times Weekly* (September 9, 1893): 1; "Fury of Flames," *Herald Democrat* (September 9, 1893): 1.

14. "The Summer Resorts," *RMN* (April 22, 1894): 3; "Manhattan Beach Opening," *RMN* (April 29, 1894): 6; "Manhattan Beach," *RMN* (May 27, 1894): 3.

15. "Amusements," *RMN* (June 4, 1894): 4; "Society," *RMN* (June 10, 1894): 5; "Amusements," *RMN* (June 12, 1894): 8; "People Enjoyed It," *RMN* (June 18, 1894): 5; "Amusements," *RMN* (June 24, 1894): 14.

16. "Amusements," *RMN* (June 21, 1894): 2; "Amusements" (June 24, 1894).

17. "Amusements," *RMN* (July 9, 1894): 8; "Green Room Gossip," *RMN* (July 15, 1894): 5 (quotes 1 and 2); "At the Play," *RMN* (July 1, 1894): 7.

18. "Thousands Enjoyed the Day," *RMN* (July 23, 1894): 8; "At the Play," *RMN* (July 1, 1894); "Society," *RMN* (August 19, 1894): 13.

19. "Churches," *RMN* (July 22, 1894): 16 (quote); "Homeopathic Institute Visit to Denver," *RMN* (June 17, 1894): 6.

20. Untitled, *RMN* (June 23, 1894): 4.

21. "Amusements," *RMN* (June 30, 1894): 4; "Amusements," *RMN* (July 27, 1894): 3; "Fiftieth Performance," *RMN* (July 7, 1894): 8; "Amusements," *RMN* (July 28, 1894): 4; "Amusements," *RMN* (August 30, 1894): 2; "Labor Won Laurels," *RMN* (September 4, 1894): 6; "Amusements," *RMN* (September 5, 1894): 8.

22. "Despite Clouded Skies," *RMN* (August 6, 1894): 5; "Labor Won Laurels," *RMN* (September 4, 1894): 6; "Labor Day in Denver," *Avalanche Echo* (September 7, 1894): 1.

23. "Lyceum Theater," *Woman Voter* (September 20, 1894): 6; "A Good Appointment," *DP* (April 19, 1895): 8.

24. "Highland Notes," *DP* (January 7, 1895): 3; "No Man's Land Again," *DP* (January 21, 1895): 8; "A Good Appointment."

25. "Manhattan Beach," *DP* (May 25, 1895): 8; "Manhattan Beach," *RMN* (May 26, 1895): 6; Hull, *Denver's Elitch Gardens*, 23.

26. "Manhattan Beach," *DP* (June 1, 1895): 6 (quotes); "With the Players," *DP* (June 1, 1895): 8; "Manhattan Beach," *DP* (June 10, 1895): 4; "Manhattan Beach," *DP* (May 25, 1895): 8; "Manhattan Beach," *DP* (June 5, 1895): 4; "Amusements," *RMN* (June 3, 1895): 4.

27. "Amusements," *RMN* (June 11, 1895): 4; "Amusements," *RMN* (June 21, 1895): 3; Ad for Manhattan Beach, *RMN* (June 25, 1895): 2; "Amusements," *DP* (July 2, 1895): 4; "Twas a Great Day," *DP* (July 5, 1895): 8; "Where the People Went," *RMN* (July 5, 1895): 8 (quote).

28. "Amusements," *RMN* (July 17, 1895): 4; "Amusements," *RMN* (July 21, 1895): 13; Payments to LeVan, Manhattan Beach Petty Cash Ledger, pp. 42, 48, FF 38, Bethell Papers.

29. "Amusements," *DP* (August 2, 1895): 4; "Amusements," *RMN* (August 9, 1895): 4; "The Merry Stroller," *RMN* (September 1, 1895): 11; "For the Play Goers," *DP* (August 31, 1895): 6 (quote 1); "Amusement Column," *DP* (September 14, 1895): 3 (quote 2); Payment to Ivy Baldwin, Manhattan Beach Ledger, p. 59, FF 38, Bethell Papers; "Amusements," *DP* (September 19, 1895): 4.

30. "Visitors from Arkansas," *DP* (May 21, 1895): 8; "Literary Club Meeting," *DP* (June 14, 1895): 8; "A Pleasant Affair," *DP* (June 26, 1895): 8; "A Birthday Party," *DP* (August 9, 1895): 8; "The Religious News," *DP* (August 24, 1895): 8.

31. "The Y.W.C.A.," *DP* (August 8, 1895): 5; "Society," *RMN* (June 16, 1895): 14; "The Y.W.C.A. Picnic," *DP* (June 21, 1895): 8; "The Y.W.C.A. Picnic," *DP* (June 22, 1895): 4; "The Y.W.C.A. Picnic," *DP* (June 24, 1895): 8.

32. "The Merry Stroller"; Ad for Manhattan Beach, *RMN* (September 16, 1895): 2; "Amusements," *DP* (September 11, 1895): 4; "Amusements," *DP* (September 19, 1895): 4; "Amusement Column," *DP* (September 14, 1895): 3; "Populists to Ratify," *DP* (September 20, 1895): 7; "Amusements," *DP* (September 23, 1895): 4.

## CHAPTER 4

1. "Coney Island History: The Story of Captain Paul Boyton and Sea Lion Park," available from https://www.heartofconeyisland.com/sea-lion-park-coney-island.html, last accessed May 13, 2022; Kasson, *Amusing the Million*, 57–58; Ashby, *With Amusement for All*, 136–37.

2. Hull, *Denver's Elitch Gardens*, 22, 30–31, 37, 38; Forsyth, "A Splendid Place," 25–27; Mangels, *The Outdoor Amusement Industry*, 90.

3. "Theatrical World," *RMN* (May 24, 1896): 11; Ad for Manhattan Beach, *RMN* (May 30, 1896): 2; "Amusements," *RMN* (July 4, 1896): 8.

4. "Amusements," *RMN* (June 8, 1896): 8; "Amusements," *RMN* (June 16, 1896): 6; "Amusements," *RMN* (June 24, 1896): 4; "This Week's Amusements,"

*RMN* (June 28, 1896): 11; Payments to Darling, Manhattan Beach Ledger, pp. 93, 100, 114, FF 38, Bethell Papers.

5. "Amusements," *DP* (July 3, 1896): 4 (quote 1); "Amusements," *RMN* (July 4, 1896): 8 (quote 2); "Plays and Actors," *RMN* (July 5, 1896): 11; "Amusement," *RMN* (July 6, 1896): 8; Roberta Estes, "When Redmen Aren't Red Men," posted September 16, 2014, available from https://nativeheritageproject.com/2014/09/16/when-redmen-arent-red-men/, last accessed January 30, 2023.

6. Alan Griffin, "Sam Lockhart: Elephant Trainer Extraordinaire," available from https://leamingtonhistory.co.uk/sam-lockhart-elephant-trainer-extraordinaire/, last accessed May 30, 2022.

7. "Music and Drama," *RMN* (July 26, 1896): 11; "Amusements," *RMN* (July 29, 1896): 4 (quote 1); "Amusements," *RMN* (August 10, 1896): 4 (quote 2); "Had Their Toes Trimmed," *RMN* (August 7, 1896): 8; "Amusements," *RMN* (August 12, 1896): 8; Payments to Professor Lockhart, Manhattan Beach Ledger, pp. 104, 106, 109, FF 38, Bethell Papers.

8. "Amusements," *RMN* (August 10, 1896): 4; "Amusements," *RMN* (August 17, 1896): 4; "Music and Drama," *RMN* (August 30, 1896): 11 (quote 2); "Theatrical Talk," *DP* (September 12, 1896): 3 (quote 1); "Amusements," *RMN* (August 12, 1896): 8 (quote 3); "Amusements," *RMN* (August 17, 1896): 4; Costs for Phantoscope from Manhattan Beach Ledger, pp. 112, 114, FF 38, Bethell Papers.

9. Edrington to Foster, February 10, 1897, FF 12, Bethell Papers; "Bikes and Bikers," *RMN* (August 10, 1896): 8; "Theatrical Gossip," *RMN* (May 30, 1897): 12.

10. "Among the Theaters," *RMN* (May 16, 1897): 17 (quote); Ad for Manhattan Beach, *DP* (May 27, 1897): 5; "Amusements," *RMN* (May 31, 1897): 5; "Amusements," *RMN* (June 15, 1897): 5; Ad for Manhattan Beach, *RMN* (July 4, 1897): 4; Ad for Manhattan Beach, *RMN* (July 20, 1897): 5; "Amusements," *DP* (August 20, 1897): 8.

11. "At the Theaters," *RMN* (June 13, 1897): 11 (quote); "Old Time Circus Man to Be Buried in East," *Los Angeles Evening Express* (August 15, 1919): 7; "Man Who First Did Triple Jump Over Elephant Dies in L.A.," *The Bulletin* (August 16, 1919): 1; "State Medical Society," *Herald Democrat* (June 17, 1897): 2; "Editors," *DP* (June 25, 1897): 10; Ad for Manhattan Beach, *RMN* (July 4, 1897); "Amusements," *DP* (July 6, 1897): 5; "Flag Festival at Manhattan Beach," *DP* (September 3, 1897): 8.

12. "Ticks by Telegraph," *Craig Courier* (July 24, 1897): 1; "Games Are Barred," *RMN* (July 25, 1897): 16 (quotes); "Plenty of Liquor Sold," *DP* (August 2, 1897): 3; "Accidents," *DP* (July 6, 1897): 8.

13. "Teapot Tempest," *DP* (June 15, 1897): 8 (quote); "Won the Fight," *DP* (July 29, 1897): 7.

14. Edrington to Foster, February 18, 1898, FF 13, Bethell Papers; Edrington to Foster, March 12, 1898, FF 13, Bethell Papers; "Manhattan's Players," *RMN*

(June 2, 1898): 9 (Giffen quote); Payment on mortgage on animals, Manhattan Beach Ledger, p. 166, FF 38, Bethell Papers; Bostock to Foster, April 23, 1895, FF 15, Bethell Papers; Sale of monkeys to Bostock, Manhattan Beach Ledger, p. 168, FF 38, Bethell Papers.

15. "Manhattan Beach," *DP* (March 15, 1898): 6; "Manhattan's Players," *RMN* (June 2, 1898): 9; "Stars of the Stage," *RMN* (June 5, 1898): 14; "Coming Attractions," *DP* (June 11, 1898): 5; "Gossip About Plays and Players," *DP* (May 21, 1898): 5 (war quote); "Amusements," *RMN* (June 21, 1898): 8; "Amusements," *RMN* (June 24, 1898): 7; "Amusements," *RMN* (July 4, 1898): 3; Ad for Manhattan Beach, *DP* (July 21, 1898): 5; Ad for Manhattan Beach, *RMN* (August 19, 1898): 5; "Amusements," *RMN* (September 5, 1898): 3; "Manhattan Beach," *DP* (June 10, 1898): 5 (excellent quote); "Amusements," *RMN* (June 18, 1898): 8; "Amusements," *RMN* (June 21, 1898): 8; "Amusements," *RMN* (August 9, 1898): 8.

16. "A Thief at Manhattan Beach," *DP* (July 21, 1898): 5; "A Sneak Thief at the Beach," *DP* (July 15, 1898): 7; "Chance for the Phonograph," *DT* (July 1, 1898): 13.

17. "Two More Saloons Gone," *DP* (April 8, 1899): 5; "Fish Killed by Dynamite," *RMN* (March 25, 1899): 10; "Volunteer Fire Companies," *RMN* (April 26, 1899): 8.

18. "Beauty Spots of Denver," *RMN* (March 26, 1899): 8; "Attractions for the Week," *DT* (June 11, 1899): 16; "Midsummer Church Festival," *RMN* (June 4, 1899): 20.

19. "What Is Done and Said About Theatricals," *RMN* (June 11, 1899): 16 (quote 1); "Amusements," *DP* (June 12, 1899): 5 (quote 2); Ad for Manhattan Beach, *RMN* (June 4, 1899): 10; Ad for Manhattan Beach, *RMN* (June 18, 1899): 10; Ad for Manhattan Beach, *DP* (June 29, 1899): 5; "Amusements," *RMN* (July 12, 1899): 10; Ad for Manhattan Beach, *DP* (July 25, 1899): 5; Ad for Manhattan Beach, *RMN* (August 15, 1899): 5; "Amusements," *RMN* (August 21, 1899): 8; "Summer Shows," *RMN* (August 27, 1899): 13 (quote 3).

20. "Oculists and Aurists Have a Day with the Doctors," *RMN* (June 21, 1899): 2; "Society," *DP* (September 2, 1899): 8 (quote); "Help the Fund," *RMN* (August 6, 1899): 1.

21. "Capt. W. D. Bethell Sells Leavenworth Holdings," *RMN* (July 3, 1899): 8; "Control of Manhattan Beach," *RMN* (September 23, 1899): 10 (quote).

22. "A Talk About Plays and Players Generally," *DP* (January 28, 1900): 15.

23. "The Manhattan Season," *DT* (May 27, 1900): 24; "Cumberland '61," *DT* (June 3, 1900): 24.

24. "Theatrical," *DT* (June 5, 1900): 4 (quote 1); "Amusements," *RMN* (June 14, 1900): 8; "'The Misses' and 'Incog,'" *DT* (June 17, 1900): 24 (quote 2); "This Week's Attractions and Chit-Chat About Players," *DP* (June 24, 1900): 17.

25. "Manhattan Beach Fireworks," *DP* (July 2, 1900): 10; "A Terrific Naval Battle," *DP* (July 3, 1900): 12; "Amusements," *RMN* (July 5, 1900): 10.

26. "Manhattan Beach," *DP* (July 5, 1900): 5; Ad for Manhattan Beach, *DP* (July 19, 1900): 5; Frank W. White, "Midsummer Amusements," *DP* (August 5, 1900): 15 (quote 1); "Coming Attractions," *DP* (August 5, 1900): 15 (quote 2); Caroline Lawrence Dier, *The Lady of the Gardens: Mary Elitch Long* (Hollywood: Hollycrafters, 1932), 61; "Amusements," *RMN* (August 10, 1900): 7; "Amusements," *RMN* (August 20, 1900): 10.

27. Dier, *The Lady of the Gardens*, 64; "Buster in Amusements," *DT* (March 15, 1901): 8.

28. "Happy Thousands," *DT* (May 18, 1901): 2 (quote); "Manhattan Opens Season," *RMN* (May 19, 1901): 12; "Thousands Participated in the Times May Festivities," *DT* (May 19, 1901): 1, 5.

29. "Amusements," *RMN* (June 20, 1901): 6; Ad for Manhattan Beach, *DP* (June 29, 1901): 7; "The Wizard at the Beach," *DP* (June 30, 1901): 20; "Fourth's Program," *DP* (July 3, 1901): 6.

30. Ad for Manhattan Beach, *DP* (July 7, 1901): 14; "Amusements," *RMN* (July 13, 1901): 6; "Amusements," *RMN* (July 22, 1901): 5; "Melodrama at Gardens, Songs at Beach," *RMN* (July 7, 1901): 10 (quote 1); "The Climax of Excellent Summer Entertainments," *DP* (August 11, 1901): 16 (quote 2).

31. Smiley, *History of Denver*, 908–10.

32. "The Real Worth," *RMN* (October 13, 1901): 4; "After Manhattan Beach," *RMN* (August 5, 1901): 6; "Manhattan Beach Changes Hands—Joseph Hellbrun Has Option," *DT* (August 10, 1901): 7; "Manhattan Leased," *DT* (August 28, 1901): 2.

33. "Summer Amusement," *DP* (February 8, 1902): 2; "Renovation Commences at Manhattan Beach," *DP* (March 4, 1902): 8; "Improvements at the Beach," *RMN* (March 5, 1902): 8; "Making Ready for Summer Joys at Outdoor Resorts," *DP* (May 18, 1902): 19 (quote 1); "Topics of the Wings," *RMN* (May 18, 1902): Magazine Section, 5 (quote 2).

34. "Improvements at the Beach"; "Making Ready for Summer Joys at Outdoor Resorts"; "Music and Drama," *DT* (May 26, 1902): 5; "Amusements," *DR* (May 26, 1902): 8; Dawn Raffel, *The Strange Case of Dr. Couney: How a Mysterious European Showman Saved Thousands of American Babies* (New York: Blue Rider, 2018), 223; "Stage and Foyer," *RMN* (May 25, 1902): Magazine Section, 3 (quote 1); "Buffalo Fountain for Denver," *DP* (March 5, 1902): 2; "Opening of Cool Resorts," *DP* (March 11, 1902): 18; "Opening of Manhattan Means Summer Here," *DP* (March 26, 1902): 5; "Topics of the Wings" (quote 2).

35. "Topics of the Wings."

36. "Making Ready for Summer Joys at Outdoor Resorts"; "Topics of the Wings"; Ad for Manhattan Beach, *RMN* (May 18, 1902): 14; "Lives by His Great Daring," *RMN* (May 17, 1902): 5.

37. "Beach Company Here," *DP* (May 16, 1902): 2; "Making Ready for Summer Joys at Outdoor Resorts"; "Stage and Foyer"; "Topics of the Wings."

38. "Opening of Manhattan Means Summer Here."

39. "Opening of Manhattan Means Summer Here"; "Amusements," *DR* (May 26, 1902): 8; "Music and Drama"; "Amusements," *RMN* (June 2, 1902): 6.

40. Certificate for Transportation of Corpse for Benjamin Bowen, Colorado State Board of Health, June 1, 1902; "Rash Aeronaut Loses His Life in the Lake," *DP* (May 27, 1902): 1; "Drops to Death," *RMN* (May 27, 1902): 8.

41. "Drops to Death"; "Aeronaut Drowns in Denver Lake," *Daily Journal* (May 28, 1902): 1; "Bowen's Body Found," *DT* (June 1, 1902): 26; "Ivy Baldwin Will Not Abandon Balloons," *DP* (May 30, 1902): 14 (quote).

42. "Music and Drama," *DT* (June 7, 1902): 6; "Music and Drama," *DT* (June 6, 1902): 7; "'The Little Trooper' at Manhattan," *DT* (June 8, 1902): 24 (quote 1); "Amusements," *DT* (June 13, 1902): 6 (quote 2); Ad for Manhattan Beach, *DP* (June 29, 1902): 2 (quote 3).

43. "Trainmen's Day Off at Manhattan Beach," *DP* (June 16, 1902): 10; "Amusements," *RMN* (June 26, 1902): 6; "Amusements," *RMN* (July 5, 1902): 7; "Gathering of Hibernians," *DP* (July 6, 1902): 6; "Pythians Make Merry at Manhattan Beach," *RMN* (August 3, 1902): sec. 1, 4; "Wins Fine Vase," *RMN* (August 15, 1902): 14; "This Is 'Debs Day,'" *DP* (August 24, 1902): 9; "Debs' Theories," *RMN* (August 25, 1902): 2.

44. "'The Little Trooper at Manhattan'"; "Amusements," *DT* (June 13, 1902): 6; "Stageland," *RMN* (June 15, 1902): Magazine Section, 3; "Bills of the Play," *RMN* (June 22, 1902): Magazine Section, 3 (quote 1); "The Gig for Summer Amusements in Denver Has Been Fixed," *DP* (June 15, 1902): 9 (quote 2); "Stop Beef Killing Contest," *DP* (August 1, 1902): 16; "Novel Contests of the Butchers at a Picnic," *DP* (August 18, 1902): 3; "Butchers' Big Barbecue," *Longmont Ledger* (September 19, 1902): 1.

45. "'The Little Trooper,'" *DP* (June 9, 1902): 7 (quote 1); "Amusements," *RMN* (June 20, 1902): 9 (quote 2); "Manhattan Beach Company Seen to Great Advantage," *DP* (June 24, 1902): 8; "Amusements," *DP* (July 10, 1902): 5 (quote 3); "Amusements," *RMN* (June 12, 1902): 7.

46. "Amusements," *DP* (August 12, 1902): 5; "What Theaters Offer This Week and Next," *DP* (August 17, 1902): 28; "Amusements," *RMN* (August 20, 1902): 6; "'Said Pasha' Closes Manhattan Beach Season," *DP* (August 24, 1902): 5; "Amusements," *RMN* (August 29, 1902): 5; "To Help Stranded 'Merry Merry' to New York," *DT* (August 28, 1902): 3; "Stranded Chorus Gets $250," *DT* (August 30, 1902): 5; "More Manhattan Suits," *DP* (September 24, 1902): 10.

47. "Many New Features to Be Seen at Manhattan Beach," *RMN* (May 25, 1903): 13; "Opening of Manhattan," *DP* (May 27, 1903): 8; "Amusements," *RMN* (June 8, 1903): 2; Ad for Manhattan Beach, *RMN* (June 14, 1903): 8.

48. Ad for Manhattan Beach, *RMN* (June 14, 1903); "Two Fires Visit Theater at Manhattan Beach," *RMN* (June 18, 1903): 2; "Summer Theatricals in Full Swing at All the Playhouses," *DP* (June 14, 1903): 21; "Thousands Crowding All the Gardens and Summer Theaters of Denver," *DP* (July 12, 1903): 7 (polite

quote); "Amusements," *RMN* (June 23, 1903): 5; "Summer Theatricals in Full Blast at All Denver Garden Resorts," *DP* (June 28, 1903): 7; "Fair Giantess Finds the Man She Can Love," *DP* (August 4, 1903): 10; "Ella Ewing," available from https://historicmissourians.shsmo.org/ella-ewing, last accessed May 16, 2022; "Manhattan's Stock Company the Hit of the Beach's Season So Far," *DP* (June 27, 1903): 6.

49. Ad for Manhattan Beach, *RMN* (June 14, 1903); "Amusements," *RMN* (June 23, 1903): 5; "Woman the Best in the World with Broadsword," *DP* (July 28, 1903): 8; "Amusements," *RMN* (August 20, 1903): 9.

50. "Turners Hold Monster Picnic at Manhattan Beach," *RMN* (June 29, 1903): 12; "Athletic Carnival of Turners Held Yesterday at Manhattan Beach," *RMN* (September 7, 1903): 10.

51. "Amusements," *DP* (July 3, 1903): 5; "Manhattan Naval Battle," *DP* (July 5, 1903): 6 (quotes 1 and 2); "Outdoor Sports and Games Closed Labor Day Exercises," *RMN* (September 8, 1903): 11 (quote 3); "Union Men Deported Themselves at Manhattan," *DP* (September 8, 1903): 6.

## CHAPTER 5

1. "Manhattan Beach Opens Next Saturday in Brightest Array," *DR* (June 12, 1904): 11; "New Corporations," *Detroit Free Press* (May 17, 1904): 7; "Giffen to Manage Manhattan Beach," *RMN* (May 23, 1906): 4.

2. "Manhattan Beach Opens Next Saturday in Brightest Array" (quotes 1, 4); "Manhattan Beach Is a Fair Bower," *RMN* (June 19, 1904); 12 (quotes 2, 3).

3. "Manhattan Beach Opens Next Saturday in Brightest Array"; "Manhattan Beach Is a Fair Bower" (quote); "Opening of Manhattan," *DP* (June 19, 1904): 2; "Manhattan Beach, Elitch's, Broadway," *DP* (June 19, 1904): 8.

4. "Opening of Manhattan"; "Manhattan Beach, Elitch's, Broadway"; "The Woman in the Proscenium Box," *RMN* (June 12, 1904): Magazine Section, 7 (quote).

5. "Manhattan Beach Is a Fair Bower" (quote 1); "Concerning the Dear Delight of Homicide," *RMN* (June 19, 1904): Magazine Section, 5; "Manhattan Beach Was Threatened by Fire," *RMN* (June 19, 1904): sec. 1, 10; "Opening of Manhattan" (quote 2).

6. "Amusements," *DP* (June 20, 1904): 5.

7. "Circus and Drama Will Amuse," *DP* (June 26, 1904): 8, 9; "Amusements," *RMN* (June 29, 1904): 7; Valerie Wingfield, "The General Slocum Disaster of June 15, 1904," available from https://www.nypl.org/blog/2011/06/13/great-slocum-disaster-june-15-1904, last accessed May 16, 2022.

8. "Storming of Port Arthur at Manhattan Beach," *DP* (July 3, 1904): 8 (quote); "Amusements," *RMN* (July 4, 1904): 7.

9. "Amusements," *DP* (July 4, 1904): 7; "Amusements," *RMN* (July 4, 1904): 7; "Amusements," *DP* (July 5, 1904): 5; "Amusements," *DP* (July 7, 1904): 8; Ad for Manhattan Beach, *DP* (July 10, 1904): 8.

10. "Children Romp at Manhattan Beach," *DP* (July 12, 1904): 6 (quote); "Coming Events," *DP* (July 10, 1904): 11; "Women's Relief Corps Give Benefit Picnic," *DP* (July 14, 1904): 12; "Amusements," *DP* (July 22, 1904): 9.

11. "Broncho Busting and Vaudeville at Manhattan," *DP* (July 17, 1904): 5 (quotes 1, 2); "Broncho Busters, Trick Riders and Ropers at Manhattan Beach," *RMN* (July 17, 1904): sec. 2, 8; "'Bucking Rastus' Causes Much Amusement at Manhattan Beach," *RMN* (July 21, 1904): 14 (quote 3); "Amusements," *DP* (July 18, 1904): 2 (quote 4).

12. "The Plays This Week," *DP* (July 24, 1904): 8; "Davies Bitten Again by One of His Pet Snakes," *RMN* (July 27, 1904): 7; "Amusements," *DP* (August 1, 1904): 10; "Vaudeville at Manhattan Beach All the Week," *DP* (August 14, 1904): 9; "Amusements," *DP* (August 22, 1904): 2; "Amusements," *DP* (August 18, 1904): 5 (quote).

13. "Amusements," *DP* (July 29, 1904): 3 (quotes); "Amusements," *DP* (July 23, 1904): 5; "Amusements," *DP* (July 27, 1904): 7; "Where the Cherry Greets the Platte," *DP* (July 17, 1904): 5; *Catalogue of Copyright Entries, Part 3: Musical Compositions Index, Nos. 31–34 August 1909* (Washington, DC: Government Printing Office, 1909), 188898; "Miscellaneous Briefs," *Colorado School Journal* (1922–1923): 38–40.

14. "Thousands Throng Manhattan Beach at Banner Picnic for St. Vincent's," *RMN* (August 7, 1904): sec. 1, 8 (quote); "Society Girls Will Aid Benefit Picnic," *DP* (July 28, 1904): 12; "Picnic Netted $2,642 for St. Vincent's," *DP* (October 11, 1904): 7.

15. "Amusements," *DP* (August 29, 1904): 9 (quote 1); "Eventful Closing at Manhattan Beach," *DP* (September 4, 1904): 7; "Coming Attractions," *RMN* (September 4, 1904): Magazine Section, 6; "Amusements," *RMN* (September 6, 1904): 5 (quote 2); Untitled, *RMN* (September 11, 1904): Magazine Section, 6; "Picnic at Manhattan to Open the Campaign," *RMN* (August 30, 1904): 7; "Democrats to Give a Picnic," *DP* (September 9, 1904): 16.

16. "Roller Skating Rink for Manhattan Beach," *DP* (April 28, 1905): 9; "Realty Notes and Gossip," *RMN* (April 30, 1905): Small ad section, 1; "A Hippodrome Track and Skating Pavilion for Manhattan Beach," *RMN* (May 7, 1905): 12; "Manhattan Beach to Open Shortly," *DP* (May 15, 1905): 9; "Great Roller Rink at Manhattan Beach," *DP* (May 21, 1905): 9; "Summer Garden Season Opens with Many Delightful Diversions," *DP* (May 28, 1905): 8; "Manhattan Beach, with Waving of Flags, Tooting of Whistles and Music, Opened to Public," *RMN* (May 28, 1905): sec. 2, 8.

17. "Manhattan Beach, with Waving of Flags, Tooting of Whistles and Music, Opened to Public" (quotes 1, 3, 5); "Great Preparations are Being Made for Opening of Popular Manhattan Beach," *RMN* (May 21, 1905): Magazine Section, 4 (quote 2); "Boating to Be a Feature at Manhattan Beach This Summer," *DR* (May 26, 1905): 4; "Amusements," *DP* (June 9, 1905): 2; "Amusements," *RMN* (June 2, 1905): 6 (quote 4).

18. "Manhattan Beach, with Waving of Flags, Tooting of Whistles and Music, Opened to Public" (quote); "Summer Garden Season Opens with Many Delightful Diversions."

19. "Amusements," *RMN* (May 29, 1905): 6; "Amusements," *RMN* (June 3, 1905): 8 (quote 1); "Amusements," *DP* (June 5, 1905): 2 (quotes 2, 3).

20. "Manhattan Beach, with Waving of Flags, Tooting of Whistles and Music, Opened to Public"; "Attractions This Week at the Broadway, Elitch's and Manhattan," *RMN* (June 4, 1905): Magazine Section, 7; "Amusements," *RMN* (June 6, 1905): 7; "Children Won't Pay," *DP* (June 15, 1905): 6; "Amusements," *RMN* (June 22, 1905): 7; "Where Denver Whiles Away Leisure Hours," *RMN* (June 25, 1905): Magazine Section, 6; "Amusements," *DP* (July 6, 1905): 2; Frank W. White, "At the Summer Resorts," *DP* (July 2, 1905): 13.

21. "Attractions This Week at the Broadway, Elitch's and Manhattan."

22. "Amusements," *DP* (July 15, 1905): 2; "Amusements," *RMN* (July 10, 1905): 2; "Amusements," *RMN* (July 24, 1905): 3; Ad for Manhattan Beach, *DP* (August 10, 1905): 5; "Bills at the Playhouses," *DP* (September 3, 1905): 9.

23. "Monster Pyrotechnic Display at Manhattan Beach for the Fourth," *RMN* (July 2, 1905): sec. 2, 2; "Great Fireworks for the Fourth," *RMN* (July 2, 1905): 14; "Lake of Fire at Manhattan," *DP* (July 2, 1905): 3; "Fourth a Day of Patriotism," *DP* (July 5, 1905): 3; "Manhattan Beach Resembled 'Gay Coney Island'—Fireworks at Night," *DP* (July 5, 1905): 2 (quote).

24. "Picnic Brings Tidy Amount," *DP* (July 2, 1905): 3; "Private Parties at Beach Resort," *RMN* (July 23, 1905): Magazine Section, 6; "Daily Picnics at Manhattan Beach," *RMN* (July 30, 1905): Magazine Section, 7; "St. Vincent's Picnic This Year Will Eclipse All Predecessors," *RMN* (July 16, 1905): sec. 1, 2; "Balloon Goes Up for the Orphans," *RMN* (August 5, 1905): 6; "Ten Thousand Friends of the Orphans Made Manhattan Beach a Veritable Treasure Trove for St. Vincent's," *DP* (August 6, 1905): 3; "Democrats Having Fun at Manhattan Beach," *DP* (August 12, 1905): 6 (quote).

25. "Amusements," *RMN* (August 23, 1905): 10; "Bronco Busting on Theater Stage," *RMN* (August 27, 1905): Magazine Section, 6; "Bucking Broncos at Manhattan This Week," *DP* (August 27, 1905): 9; "Cook Drum Corps and Ladies' Drill Team Hold Picnic at Manhattan Beach," *DP* (August 30, 1905): 5.

26. "Good Attractions at the Theaters," *DP* (September 10, 1905): 9 (quote); "Good Crowds Visit Manhattan," *DP* (September 17, 1905): 20; Ad for Manhattan Beach, *DP* (September 17, 1905): 20.

27. "The Tuileries," *DR* (July 29, 1906): 15; "The Tuileries," *RMN* (June 23, 1907): sec. 2, 8; Jack Foster, "What Became of Tuileries?" *RMN* (August 9, 1959): 21A.

28. Hull, *Denver's Elitch Gardens*, 30–31, 37–38.

29. "Popular Resort About to Open," *RMN* (May 19, 1906): 16; "New Amusements Secured for Season at Manhattan Beach," *DP* (May 20, 1906): sec. 3, 3; Caitlyn Pascal, "Arcade Origins in the Japanese Rolling Ball: How Tamakorogashi

Shaped the World of Modern Gaming," *Nikkei Voice*, available from http://
nikkeivoice.ca/arcade-origins-in-the-japanese-rolling-ball-how-tamakorogashi
-shaped-the-world-of-modern-gaming, last accessed March 30, 2022; "Manhattan Beach to Be Opened for Season Tomorrow," *DP* (May 25, 1906): 12.

30. "Giffen to Manage Manhattan Beach" (quote 1); "F. W. W. Has Recollec-
tions," *DP* (May 27, 1906): sec. 2, unknown page (quote 2); Dier, *The Lady of the
Gardens*, 103 (quote 3); "Manhattan Beach Has Opened Wide Her Gates and
the Pleasure Lovers Are Flocking There," *DP* (May 27, 1906): sec. 1, 5 (quote 4).

31. "Attractions for Week in Urban and Suburban Theaters," *RMN* (June 3,
1906): unknown page number but 54th page in issue (quote); Frank W. White,
"Denver Summer Amusement Season," *DP* (June 17, 1906): sec. 2, 1; "Amusements," *RMN* (June 12, 1906): 5; Frank W. White, "An Intermediate Theatrical Season," *DP* (July 3, 1906): 7; Ad for Manhattan Beach, *DP* (August 5,
1906): sec. 3, 4.

32. "Denver Assault," *Park County Bulletin* (August 3, 1906): 3; "Mullen
Brings Suit Against Tyson Dines," *Durango Semi-Weekly Herald* (August 6,
1906): 3; "D-M Affair in Topical Song at Local Resort Brings Request to Have
It Quashed," *RMN* (August 9, 1906): 5 (quote); "Tyson Dines Makes Apology,"
*Daily Sentinel (Grand Junction)* (December 22, 1901): 6.

33. "Two More Actors Stricken," *DP* (July 20, 1906): 1; "Accused of Malpractice," *Aspen Times Weekly* (July 22, 1906): 1; "Dr. Brandt Coming Here," *Daily
Sentinel* (June 3, 1907): 4.

34. "Attractions Especially Arranged to Amuse the Elks," *RMN* (July 15,
1906): unknown page number but 52nd page in issue; "The Fourth Spent by
Denverites in the Most Idyllic Manner," *DP* (July 5, 1906): 9; "Thousands
Celebrated the Day at Manhattan Beach," *DP* (July 5, 1906): 13; "Midsummer
Amusements at the Resorts," *DP* (July 8, 1906): 7 (quote); "Democrats Steer
Crowds Against Games," *DP* (August 26, 1906): sec. 2, 3; "Two More Actors
Stricken"; Mangels, *The Outdoor Amusement Industry*, 164–65.

35. "Manhattan Beach Will Entertain St. Vincent's Orphans," *DP* (July 25,
1906): 6; "Owned Manhattan One Whole Day," *DP* (July 30, 1906): 2 (quote);
"Democrats Steer Crowds Against Games."

36. "Boating Party Goes to Death in Squall," *Denver Times* (June 23, 1906): 1;
"Times Clinches Record as Most Fearless Faker," *DP* (June 24, 1906): 8.

37. "Young Woman Garbed as Man Makes Love to Aged Widow," *RMN*
(August 14, 1906): 1, 6; "Man Loves Man and Woman Woman in Two Queer
Cases," *DP* (August 14, 1906): 1, 7.

38. "Capt. Bethell Succumbs to Long Illness," *DR* (August 20, 1906): 1;
"Manhattan Beach," *RMN* (September 9, 1906): sec. 3, 4; "Manhattan Beach,"
*DT* (September 2, 1906): sec. 1, 11; "Manhattan Beach," *RMN* (September 2,
1906): sec. 3, 4; "Manhattan Beach," *RMN* (May 26, 1907): sec. 2, 8; "Manhattan
Beach," *DR* (July 28, 1907): sec. 2, 15 (for lights); "Manhattan Beach," *DR* (May
26, 1907): sec. 2, 19.

39. "Manhattan Beach," *RMN* (May 26, 1907): sec. 2, 8; "Manhattan Beach," *DR* (May 26, 1907): sec. 2, 19; "Manhattan Beach," *DR* (June 2, 1907): sec. 2, 19; "Manhattan Beach," *RMN* (June 9, 1907): sec. 2, 8; "Manhattan Beach," *RMN* (June 16, 1907): sec. 2, 8; "Manhattan Beach," *RMN* (June 23, 1907): sec. 2, 8; "Manhattan Beach," *DR* (June 30, 1907): sec. 2, 15; "Press Agents' Promises for Manhattan Beach, Tuileries, and the Elitch Gardens," *RMN* (June 7, 1907): sec. 3, 3; Manhattan Beach," *DR* (July 14, 1907): sec. 2, 15; "Manhattan Beach," *DR* (July 21, 1907): sec. 2, 15; "Manhattan Beach," *RMN* (July 28, 1907): Society, 3; "Boodle for Finding at Broadway, 'The Mocking Bird' Will Warble at Tabor—Something Doing Elsewhere," *RMN* (August 4, 1907): Society, 3; "Good Season at Denver Resorts," *RMN* (August 11, 1907): Society, 3 (quote).

40. Stephen R. Wilk, *Lost Wonderland: The Brief and Brilliant Life of Boston's Million Dollar Amusement Park* (Amherst and Boston: Bright Leaf, 2020), 52–53.

41. "Manhattan Beach," *DR* (June 2, 1907): sec. 2, 19; "Manhattan Beach," *RMN* (June 9, 1907): sec. 2, 8; "Manhattan Beach," *DR* (June 16, 1907): sec. 3, 32; "Woman's Wit Won Her Damage Suit," *DP* (January 5, 1908): sec. 1, 4; "Manhattan Beach," *RMN* (June 23, 1907): sec. 2, 8; "Manhattan Beach," RMN (June 30, 1907): sec. 2, 8; "Press Agents' Promises for Manhattan Beach, Tuileries, and the Elitch Gardens"; "Manhattan Beach," *RMN* (July 14, 1907): Society, 3; "Manhattan Beach," *DR* (July 21, 1907): sec. 2, 15; "Good Season at Denver Resorts"; "Manhattan Beach," *DR* (August 25, 1907): sec. 2, 15.

42. "Manhattan Beach," *DR* (June 2, 1907): sec. 2, 19; "Boodle for Finding at Broadway, 'The Mocking Bird' Will Warble at Tabor—Something Doing Elsewhere"; Ad for Manhattan Beach, *DR* (August 18, 1907): 2; Manhattan Beach program, July 22, 1907, Manhattan Beach Clipping File, Western History and Genealogy Department, Denver Public Library.

43. David Forsyth, *Denver's Lakeside Amusement Park: From the White City Beautiful to a Century of Fun* (Boulder: University Press of Colorado, 2016), 24–28.

44. Forsyth, *Denver's Lakeside Amusement Park*, 35–38.

45. "Funeral of Lewin to Be Conducted Sunday Afternoon," *DP* (November 6, 1924): 30; Mildred Sweet, Oral History Interview, July 16, 1981, Rocky Mountain Jewish Historical Society Oral History Collection, University of Denver Archives.

46. "Manhattan Beach," *RMN* (May 24, 1908): sec. 3, 5.

47. "Manhattan Beach," *RMN* (May 24, 1908): sec. 3, 5 (quote 1); "Manhattan Beach," *RMN* (May 31, 1908): sec. 3, 3; "Varied Amusements for the Play Goer," *DP* (June 14, 1908): Magazine Section, 6 (quote 2); "Manhattan Beach," *RMN* (June 14, 1908): sec. 3, 3.

48. "Raising Money to Entertain the Big Convention," *DP* (June 4, 1908): sec. 3, 3; "At the Theaters," *DP* (July 8, 1908): 10; "Democratic Club

Picnic on Saturday," *DP* (August 11, 1908): 3; "B. R. T. Picnic at Manhattan Beach," *DP* (August 21, 1908): 9.

49. "Raising Money to Entertain the Big Convention"; "Hugo Clark Winner of Broncho Busting Contest," *DP* (July 13, 1908): 6; "Manhattan Beach," *RMN* (June 21, 1908): sec. 3, 3; "Manhattan Beach," *RMN* (June 28, 1908): sec. 3, 3; "Manhattan Beach," *RMN* (July 5, 1908): sec. 3, 3; "Manhattan Beach," *RMN* (July 12, 1908): sec. 3, 3; "Manhattan on the Lake," *Jewish Outlook* (July 31, 1908): 8.

50. "Manhattan Beach," *RMN* (August 2, 1908): sec. 3, 3 (quote); "Manhattan Beach," *RMN* (August 16, 1908): sec. 3, 3; Winifred Black, "This Little Girl's Very Naughty; She Must Be, She Says, Because Nobody in the World Loves Her," *DP* (August 19, 1908): 1; Winifred Black, "Buy Those Tickets If You Want to Help a Poor Little Crippled Girl," *DP* (August 23, 1908): 1; Winifred Black, "Little Anita to Have Her Wheel Chair and a First-Class Physician—Hurrah!," *DP* (August 26, 1908): 1; "Manhattan Beach," *RMN* (August 23, 1908): sec. 3, 3.

51. "Historic Manhattan Beach Theater Burns with Loss of $50,000," *DP* (December 27, 1908): 1, 2.

52. "Historic Manhattan Beach Theater Burns with Loss of $50,000."

53. "Historic Manhattan Beach Theater Burns with Loss of $50,000"; "Manhattan May Be New Suburb," *DP* (January 17, 1909): sec. 3, 9.

54. "Manhattan Beach Owners Are Sued," *DP* (February 1, 1909): 7; "City in Brief," *Detroit Free Press* (November 25, 1909): 5.

55. "At Manhattan Beach," *DP* (July 4, 1909): sec. 1, 5; "Manhattan Beach Opens Today; New Management," *RMN* (July 4, 1909): sec. 1, 4 (quotes).

56. Ad for Manhattan Beach, *DP* (August 22, 1909): sec. 3, 2; "Woman Champion Buster Will Ride Noted Outlaw," *RMN* (July 18, 1909): sec. 2, 2; Wanted Ad for Manhattan Beach, *DP* (July 31, 1909): 9.

57. Forsyth, *Denver's Lakeside Amusement Park*, 44; Mildred Sweet Oral History; "Lewin Leases Manhattan Beach for Fifteen Years," *DP* (September 13, 1909): 8.

## CHAPTER 6

1. "Lewin Leases Manhattan Beach for Fifteen Years"; "Company to Boom Manhattan Beach Incorporates; $100,000," *RMN* (October 30, 1909): 7; "Ohio River Steamboat Is to Be Operated on Sloan's Lake, Denver," *RMN* (October 31, 1909): sec. 2, 10.

2. "Ohio River Steamboat Is to Be Operated on Sloan's Lake, Denver"; "Denver Soon to Have Its First Steamboat," *DP* (November 11, 1909): 4; "Rival Liquor Men in Contest Over Rent of 'Famous,'" *DP* (December 12, 1909): sec. 3, 4.

3. "Rival Liquor Men in Contest Over Rent of 'Famous'"; Listing for The Famous, *Corbett and Ballenger's 39th Annual Denver City Directory* (Denver: Corbett and Ballenger, 1911), 502.

4. "Battle of Monitor and Merrimac to Be Reproduced at Gardens," *DP* (February 20, 1910): sec. 1, 4; "Launching of Steamboat on the Lake at New Luna Park," *DR* (April 17, 1910): 9; "14,000 See Cordelia Hamlin Name the 'Frolic,'" *RMN* (April 18, 1910): 3; "Luna Park, Denver, Offers Concessions," *Billboard* (April 16, 1910): 59; "Denver Park News," *Billboard* (May 21, 1910): 28; "Luna Park, Denver's Prettiest Resort, Offers Many Alluring New Attractions," *DP* (June 14, 1910): 8.

5. "14,000 See Cordelia Hamlin Name the 'Frolic'"; "Fourteen Thousand See Winner of News-Times Contest Christen the City's First Steamboat," *DT* (April 18, 1910): 2; "Thousands Witness Launching of Steamboat in New Luna Lake," *DR* (April 18, 1910): 7; "Summer Opens Its Season of Beautiful Days," *DR* (April 18, 1910): 5.

6. "Fourteen Thousand See Winner of News-Times Contest Christen the City's First Steamboat"; "Steamboat Popular Attraction Among Amusements at Luna Park," *DR* (May 29, 1910): sec. 2, 6; "Launching of Steamboat on the Lake at New Luna Park."

7. "Fine Little Theater for the New Amusement Resort at the Beach," *DR* (May 1, 1910): 7.

8. "Fine Little Theater for the New Amusement Resort at the Beach"; "Steamboat Popular Attraction Among Amusements at Luna Park" (quote); "Luna Park, Denver's Prettiest Resort, Offers Many Alluring New Attractions."

9. "Luna Park," *DR* (June 5, 1910): sec. 3, 4 (quote 1); "First Esquimau Baby Born in Colorado," *DP* (June 10, 1910): 9; Ad for Luna Park, *DR* (June 12, 1910): 4; "Luna Park," *DR* (June 19, 1910): sec. 2, 7; "Steamboat Popular Attraction Among Amusements at Luna Park" (quote 2).

10. "Denver's Summer Resorts Entertain Home People and Bring Tourists," *Denver Municipal Facts* (July 30, 1910): 3, 4.

11. "Gay Crowds Dance on Deck of First Denver Steamboat," *DP* (May 30, 1910): 5; "Steamboat Popular Attraction Among Amusements at Luna Park"; "Monday," *Telluride Journal* (June 2, 1910): 5; "Luna Park, Denver's Prettiest Resort, Offers Many Alluring New Attractions."

12. "Biggest Steamboat Proves the Attraction at Opening," *DR* (May 29, 1910): 3 (quote); Ad for Luna Park, *DR* (May 29, 1910): 4.

13. "Biggest Steamboat Proves the Attraction at Opening"; Ad for Luna Park, *DR* (May 29, 1910): 4; Ad for Luna Park, *DR* (June 12, 1910): 4; "Walton and Gehring Meet at Luna Tonight," *DP* (June 24, 1910): 14; "Gehring Defeats Walton in Two Straight Falls," *DP* (June 25, 1910): 6; "Luna Park," *DR* (June 19, 1910): sec. 2, 7; "Promise Made by the Press Agents," *DR* (June 26, 1910): sec. 2, 6.

14. "Promises Made by the Press Agents"; Ad for Luna Park, *DR* (June 26, 1910): 12; "Luna Park," *DR* (July 3, 1910): sec. 2, 3; "Boat Parties See Peril of Deep," *DP* (July 5, 1910): 5.

15. "Luna Park," *DR* (July 10, 1910): sec. 2, 6; Ad for Manhattan Beach, *DR* (July 10, 1910): 4; "Labor Notes," *United Labor Bulletin* (July 21, 1910): 2; "An Interesting Labor Meeting," *United Labor Bulletin* (May 12, 1910): 1.

16. "Luna Park," *DR* (July 31, 1910): sec. 2, 6; "Amusements," *DR* (August 13, 1910): 12; "Luna Park," *DR* (August 14, 1910): sec. 2, 6; "Battle of Manila Is Fought Again in Mimic Engagement," *DP* (August 14, 1910): sec. 1, 11.

17. "Luna Park," *DR* (July 17, 1910): sec. 2, 6; "Luna Park," *DR* (July 24, 1910): sec. 2, 6; "Luna Park," *DR* (July 31, 1910): sec. 2, 6.

18. "Hundreds of Sunday School Children Compete in Athletics at Luna Park," *DR* (July 31, 1910): 10; "Salvation Army Picnic for Poor on August 4," *DP* (July 30, 1910): 8.

19. "Luna Park," *DR* (July 31, 1910): sec. 2, 6; "Luna Park," *DR* (August 7, 1910): sec. 2, 6 (quote); "Luna Park," *DR* (August 14, 1910): sec. 2, 6; "Luna Park," *DR* (August 28, 1910): sec. 2, 6.

20. "Luna Park," *DR* (August 14, 1910): sec. 2, 6; "Luna Park," *DR* (August 21, 1910): sec. 2, 6; "Chariots and Floats for Moose Circus Gorgeously Decorated," *DP* (August 9, 1910): 11; "Luna Park," *DR* (August 28, 1910): sec. 2, 6; "Gay Crowds Fill Summer Gardens During Labor Day," *DP* (September 6, 1910): 7.

21. "A Call to the Patriotic," *The Statesman* (July 30, 1910): 5; "Emancipation Celebration," *The Statesman* (September 17, 1910): 1; "City News," *The Statesman* (June 25, 1910): 4; "Denver News," *The Statesman* (July 30, 1910): 9; "Denver Parks Are Not for Colored," *The Statesman* (May 14, 1910): 8.

22. "Denver Locals," *The Statesman* (September 26, 1908): 12; "Emancipation Celebration"; "The R.M.A.C. Quartette," *The Statesman* (June 18, 1910): 12; "Denver Personals," *The Statesman* (September 24, 1910): 13.

23. "Colorado News," *Durango Semi-Weekly Herald* (November 7, 1910): 1; "Work Has Begun on Park Bathing Beach," *DP* (January 22, 1911): sec. 1, 9; "To Have Many Attractions," *United Labor Bulletin* (January 19, 1911): 3; Certificate of Incorporation, Colorado Amusement Company, Colorado State Archives.

24. "'The Follies' at the Broadway, Biggest Show of Its Kind," *DP* (May 21, 1911): sec. 2, 8; Finding Aid, J. E. Roach Banda Mexicana Music Collection, Michelle Smith Performing Arts Library, University of Maryland; "The Band's All Here," *DP* (May 28, 1911): sec. 2, 8.

25. "The Band's All Here"; Niheer Dasandi, "Battle of Ciudad Juárez," *Encyclopedia Britannica*, available from https://www.britannica.com/event/Battle-of -Ciudad-Juarez, last accessed May 20, 2022.

26. "Opening of Luna Park Today Promises Well," *RMN* (May 21, 1911): sec. 3, 3; Ad for Luna Park, *RMN* (May 21, 1911): sec. 3, 3; "Luna Park," *DR* (June 2, 1911): 12; "Bathing Beach at Luna Open; New Features Are Various," *RMN* (June 11, 1911): sec. 3, 4 (quote); "Luna Park," *DR* (June 16, 1911): 12 (quote); "Theaters and Gardens," *RMN* (May 28, 1911): sec. 3, 1, 7; "Luna Park Presents Beautiful Appearance at the Opening," *RMN* (June 4, 1911): sec. 3, 3.

27. "Bathing Beach at Luna Open; New Features Are Various"; Frank W. White, "Banda Mexicana Ought to Play Dreamier Music," *DP* (June 4, 1911): sec. 1, 10.

28. "Assembly Declares Luna Park Unfair," *United Labor Bulletin* (May 18, 1911): 1; "Mexican Peons to Displace Americans," *United Labor Bulletin* (June 1, 1911): 1 (quotes); "Luna Park Openly Defies the Public," *United Labor Bulletin* (June 8, 1911): 1; "Lakeside and Luna Park Features Fail," *DP* (June 18, 1911): sec. 2, 8; "Three Banda Mexicana Concerts Canceled," *DP* (June 25, 1911); sec. 1, 1; Finding Aid, J. E. Roach Banda Mexicana Music Collection.

29. "Luna Park," *DR* (June 2, 1911): sec. 2, 2; "Wild West Show Is Feature of Luna Park," *DT* (July 2, 1911): sec. 3, 8.

30. "Luna Park Amusements," *United Labor Bulletin* (July 20, 1911): 3; "Luna Park to Have Bronco Busting Contests Today," *RMN* (July 9, 1911): sec. 3, 3; "Barbecue Broil, German Style, Today's Luna Park Feature," *RMN* (July 16, 1911): sec. 3, 3; "Feast at Luna Park," *DP* (July 16, 1911): sec. 2, 8; "Doings and Dancing at Luna," *DP* (July 23, 1911): sec. 2, 8; "Free Watermelon Feast at Luna Park Today," *RMN* (July 30, 1911): sec. 3, 4; "Meet in Broadsword Combat at Luna Park Today," *DT* (August 6, 1911): sec. 3, 4; "At Luna Park," *DR* (August 6, 1911): sec. 2, 2.

31. "Doings and Dancing at Luna"; "Luna Park," *DR* (July 23, 1911): sec. 2, 4; "Dancing Pavilion at Luna Draws Great Throngs," *RMN* (July 23, 1911): sec. 3, 3.

32. "Dancing Pavilion at Luna Draws Great Throngs"; "Promises Made by the Press Agents," *DR* (August 13, 1911): sec. 2, 2; "Luna Ideal for Outings; Bathing Is Feature," *DT* (August 13, 1911): sec. 3, 6 (quote 1); "Free Watermelon Feast at Luna Park Today" (quote 2).

33. "Management of Luna Park Is Changed," *DP* (August 19, 1911): 9.

34. "Every Luna Park Patron Gets Free Lunch Today," *RMN* (August 27, 1911): sec. 3, 6; "Luna Park," *DR* (August 27, 1911): sec. 2, 2; Ad for Manhattan Beach, *RMN* (September 1, 1911): sec. 5, 2; "Luna Park Plans Novel Labor Day Stunts," *RMN* (September 3, 1911): sec. 3, 6; "Luna Park," *DR* (September 3, 1911): sec. 2, 2.

35. All from *The Statesman*: Ad for Emancipation Day Celebration (August 26, 1911): 5; Ad for Roller Skating at Luna Park (October 7, 1911): 5; "Denver News" (October 21, 1911): 4; "Pryor's Dope on Sports and Stage" (December 9, 1911): 8; "Pryor's Dope on Sports and Stage" (December 16, 1911): 8; Ad for Skating Rink at Luna Park (November 11, 1911): 2; Ad for Masquerade Roller Skating Carnival at Luna Park (March 9, 1912): 8; "Denver Personal" (April 6, 1912): 4.

36. Certificate of Incorporation, Luna Park Company, September 23, 1911, Colorado State Archives, Denver, CO; "Rejuvenated Manhattan Beach Will Be Reopened Next Saturday," *DP* (June 2, 1912): sec. 2, 11 (quotes); Ad for Manhattan Beach, *RMN* (June 2, 1912): sec. 5, 2.

37. Incorporation Records, Manhattan Beach Amusement Company, January 20, 1912, Colorado State Archives, Denver, CO; Ad for Manhattan Beach, *RMN* (June 2, 1912): sec. 5, 2; "Summer Resorts Open for Season with New Glories," *DP* (May 31, 1912): 13 (quote 1); "The Attractions at Manhattan," *DP* (June 16, 1912): sec. 2, 8 (quote 2); "Rejuvenated Manhattan Beach Will Be Reopened Next Saturday."

38. Ad for Manhattan Beach, *RMN* (June 2, 1912): sec. 5, 2; Ad for Manhattan Beach, *DP* (June 9, 1912): sec. 2, 6.

39. "The Attractions at Manhattan," *DP* (June 16, 1912): sec. 2, 8; "Colorado Society Starts Its Annual Exodus to Resorts," *DP* (June 23, 1912): sec. 2, 2; "Look Here Kiddies! 20,000 of You Are to Celebrate," *DP* (June 17, 1912): 9; "The Post's Young Guests Have Day of Rare Fun at Manhattan," *DP* (June 20, 1912): 9; "Free Vaudeville at Manhattan," *DP* (June 23, 1912): sec. 2, 8.

40. "The Attractions at Manhattan"; "Free Vaudeville at Manhattan"; Frank W. White, "F. W. W. Protests Against 'Sinking of Titanic' Exhibit," *DP* (June 16, 1912): sec. 2, 8.

41. "Free Vaudeville in the Open Air," *DR* (June 16, 1912): sec. 2, 2; Ad for Manhattan Beach, *DP* (June 20, 1912): 7; "Naval Fight to Be Feature of Fourth at Manhattan," *RMN* (June 30, 1912): sec. 5, 2; "Free Farce Comedy at Manhattan," *DP* (July 7, 1912): sec. 2, 6; Hull, *Denver's Elitch Gardens*, 30–31.

42. "Day at Manhattan to Be Lively One," *DP* (July 3, 1912): 6; Ad for Manhattan Beach, *DP* (July 3, 1912): 7; "Manhattan Thrills for the Fourth of July," *DR* (June 30, 1912): sec. 2, 2; "Florence Sale [sic] Company Stays Season at Manhattan Beach," *RMN* (July 7, 1912): sec. 5, 2.

43. "Free Vaudeville at Manhattan"; "Manhattan Beach Has 12,000 Visitors," *DP* (June 25, 1912): 7; "Manhattan Beach," *DT* (June 12, 1912): sec. 5, 2.

44. Ad for Manhattan Beach, *DP* (July 27, 1912): 8; "Labor Denounces Sentence on F. G. Bonfils as Outrage," *DP* (July 28, 1912): sec. 1, 1; "Judge's Bible Joke Was Sacrilege, Says Socialist Leader," *DP* (July 28, 1912): sec. 1, 3; "Socialist Picnic a Success," *United Labor Bulletin* (August 1, 1912): 1.

45. Ad for Manhattan Beach, *DP* (August 4, 1912): sec. 2, 12; Ad for Manhattan Beach, *DP* (August 18, 1912): sec. 2, 6; Ad for Manhattan Beach, *DP* (August 25, 1912): sec. 2, 10; "Kids' Judge Will Be Actor Today," *DP* (September 29, 1912): sec. 3, 2.

46. Ad for Third Annual Outing, *The Statesman* (September 17, 1912): 5; "City News," *The Statesman* (September 21, 1912): 5; "City News," *The Statesman* (September 14, 1912): 5; "Bull Moose Skating Rink," *The Statesman* (October 12, 1912): 4; "City News," *Denver Star* (February 1, 1913): 2; "City News," *Denver Star* (May 10, 1913): 8.

47. "Mrs. Dillon Makes Good at Park, Urges Manager's Job for Sex," *RMN* (September 7, 1913): sec. 3, 2; Ad for Manhattan Beach," *RMN* (May 25, 1913): sec. 3, 3; Ad for Manhattan Beach, *RMN* (May 29, 1913): 2; "Black Hawk News," *Gilpin Observer* (May 8, 1913): 4; "'Auto Accident' Is Hair Raiser

Manhattan Beach Opens Today," *RMN* (May 30, 1913): 10; Ad for Manhattan Beach, *RMN* (June 8, 1913): sec. 3, 6.

48. "Birdman Baldwin Gets Ducking at Manhattan Beach," *DP* (May 19, 1913): 5; Ad for Manhattan Beach, *RMN* (July 27, 1913): sec. 3, 6; "Ivy Baldwin Takes Aeroplane Tumble," *RMN* (June 13, 1913): 8; "Tower Grows in Lake; Mermaids to Splash!," *RMN* (July 16, 1913): 7; "Bronco Busting at Manhattan Beach," *RMN* (July 3, 1913): sec. 3, 6; "This Week's Amusement Features," *DP* (June 29, 1913): sec. 2, 8 (quote); "Girl Falls from Roller Coaster," *DP* (July 21, 1913): 1.

49. "Tramway Club to Stage Port Arthur's Fall Again," *RMN* (June 21, 1913): 14; "Eastern Star to Give Dance by Moonlight on Steamship," *DP* (July 13, 1913): sec. 1, 11; "Tower Grows in Lake, Mermaids to Splash!"; "Boat Races Mark Picnic at Manhattan Beach," *RMN* (July 22, 1913): 10; " 'Kiddies' Are to Reign at Manhattan Beach," *RMN* (July 22, 1913): 3; Ella Miriam Sullivan, "Phi Beta Girls and Guests Will Enjoy Moonlight Dance at Castle Rock Tonight," *DP* (July 31, 1913): 5; "Orphanage to Have Benefit Saturday," *DP* (August 15, 1913): 5; "1,500 Happy Kiddies Enjoy News Outing," *RMN* (August 28, 1913): 12.

50. "Variety of Entertainment at Manhattan Beach," *RMN* (August 3, 1913): sec. 3, 6 (quote); Ad for Manhattan Beach, *DP* (August 10, 1913): 3; "Stage Coach Holdup for Manhattan Beach Patrons," *RMN* (August 14, 1913): 14; Ad for Manhattan Beach, *RMN* (August 31, 1913): sec. 3, 6.

51. "Mrs. Dillon Makes Good at Park, Urges Manager's Job for Sex"; "Luna Park Company's Holdings Foreclosed," *DP* (October 1, 1913): 6.

52. Ad for scrap from roulette building at Manhattan Beach, *DP* (October 6, 1913): 14; "Steamer Frolic a Wreck," *RMN* (October 24, 1913): 12; Ad for Denver Wrecking Company Old Yard, *DP* (January 25, 1914): sec. 3, 9.

53. "Denver Plane a Success," *RMN* (February 12, 1914): 3; "Wagner's Airship Flies Over Lake," *DP* (February 12, 1914): 4; "Denver Men Conquer Altitude; Build Passenger Airplane," *DP* (February 15, 1914): sec. 1, 3.

54. Ad for Midsummer Fest, *Denver Star* (July 11, 1914): 5; Ad for concessions to lease, *DP* (May 31, 1914): Want Ads, 10; Ad for sale or lease of rowboats, gasoline launch, and box ball alleys, *DP* (June 7, 1914): Want Ads, 10; "Manhattan Beach," *DP* (June 14, 1914): sec. 2, 6; Ad for Manhattan Beach, *DP* (June 17, 1914): 7; "City News," *Denver Star* (July 25, 1914): 5; "City News," *Denver Star* (August 8, 1914): 5; Ad for Last Midsummer Outing and Dance, *Denver Star* (August 8, 1914): 8; "City News," *Denver Star* (September 12, 1914): 5. George Morrison was Black and at one time had a contract with Columbia Records race records division. He later performed at Lakeside Amusement Park, where his band was renamed the Rigadooners.

55. Ad for Denver Wrecking Company Old Yard, *DP* (August 1, 1915): Want Ads, 10; Ad for tables, chairs, and refreshment equipment for sale, *DP* (August 18, 1915): 16; Ad for Denver Wrecking Company, *DP* (October 15, 1916): Wanted

Section, 11; Ad for Denver Wrecking Company, *DP* (December 17, 1916): Want Ads, 8; "Defunct Corporations," *RMN* (September 1, 1916): 11.

56. "Manhattan Beach Ball Park to Be Completely Remodeled This Season," *DP* (April 14, 1918): 11; "Edgewater Club Wins Eleven-Inning Contest," *RMN* (May 13, 1918): 8; Ad for Annual Campmeeting of the Colorado Conference of Seventh-Day Adventists, *DP* (June 16, 1928): 8.

## CONCLUSION

1. Thomas J. Schlereth, *Victorian America: Transformations in Everyday Life, 1876–1915* (New York: HarperPerennial, 1992), 238–39.

2. Leonard and Noel, *Denver*, 156–57, 144–45; Thomas J. Noel and Barbara S. Norgren, *Denver: The City Beautiful and Its Architects, 1893–1941* (Denver: Historic Denver, 1987), 10; "Albert Lewin," *Intermountain Jewish News* (November 6, 1924): 4.

3. Leonard and Noel, *Denver*, 145–46.

4. "City May Buy Land Near Sloan's Lake," *DP* (September 3, 1936): 23.

5. Goodstein, *North Side Story*, 343–44; "Manhattan Beach," *RMN* (June 29, 1922): 6; "Sloan's Lake Neighborhood History."

6. "Rocky Mountain Aquabats," *Rocky Mountain Life* (July 1947): 35–39.

7. Goodstein, *North Side Story*, 344–46.

8. "Sloan's Lake Neighborhood History"; Goodstein, *North Side Story*, 346–47; "Metro Digest," *DP* (July 10, 2002): B-02.

9. "Marker Slated for Site of Manhattan Beach," *RMN* (May 16, 1953): 26; "Manhattan Beach Plaque Unveiled," *DP* (May 19, 1953): 13; "Editorial Notes," *Colorado Magazine* (July 1953): 237.

10. "Adam Graff, Pioneer and Former Denver Alderman, Is Dead," *DP* (July 13, 1922): 17; "To Mine Natural Paraffin," *Routt County Sentinel* (September 29, 1922): 4; "Among Our Neighbors," *Routt County Sentinel* (July 21, 1922): 4.

11. "Albert Lewin"; Mildred Sweet Oral History; "Denver's New Public Market Has a Few Choice Spaces Left," *Fort Collins Courier* (July 31, 1919): 7; "Big New Dance Palace Is Open," *Denver Jewish News* (October 12, 1921): 3; Ad for Grand Opening of the Bon Ton Dance Palace, *Denver Clarion* (December 18, 1924): 7.

12. "John Foster, Noted Denver Doctor, Dies," *DP* (March 24, 1945): 3.

13. Catherine Armstrong, "The Oldest Amusement Park In the West Is Right Here In Utah and It's Amazing," available from https://www.onlyinyourstate.com/utah/oldest-amusement-park-ut/, last accessed July 6, 2022; "Early Southern California Amusement Parks," available from https://waterandpower.org/museum/Early_ Southern_ California_ Amusement_ Parks.html, last accessed July 6, 2022.

14. While there is no guarantee that they refer to Roger the elephant from Manhattan Beach, these articles are about the elephant that Frank Bostock exhibited around the United States in the early 1900s. "A Census of the Zoo,"

*Indianapolis News* (November 17, 1900): 20; "Deaths in the Zoo," *Indianapolis News* (November 19, 1900): 2; "The Zoo," *Indianapolis News* (March 26, 1901): 12; "Elephants Fight in Dreamland," *New York Tribune* (September 7, 1904): 14; "Bostock Elephant Nearly Saves a Life," *Brooklyn Times Union* (June 20, 1905): 4; "Roger Mourns for Comrade," *Atlanta Journal-Constitution* (December 6, 1907): 4; Kirsty McKenzie, "Glasgow History: The True Story Behind the Famous Stuffed Elephant Which Has Been on Display in Kelvingrove for 120 Years," *Glasgow Live* (August 28, 2021), available from https://www.glasgowlive.co.uk/whats-on/whats-on-news/glasgow-history-true-story-behind-21425109, last accessed July 6, 2022.

15. Paul Hutchinson, "Elitch's Marks Start of Second Century," *DP* (June 30, 1990): 5C; Forsyth, *Denver's Lakeside Amusement Park*, 3–4.

16. White, "Banda Mexicana Ought to Play Dreamier Music."

# Bibliography

## Primary Sources

### Manuscript Collections

Bethell, Pinckney C. and William D. Papers. Stephen H. Hart Research Center. History Colorado.

J. E. Roach Banda Mexicana Music Collection. Finding Aid. Michelle Smith Performing Arts Library. University of Maryland.

### Government Documents

Boulevard and Sloan Lake Steam Navigation Company. Certificate of Navigation. March 21, 1874. Colorado State Archives, Denver, CO.

*Catalogue of Copyright Entries, Part 3: Musical Compositions Index, Nos. 31–34 August 1909*. Washington, DC: Government Printing Office, 1909.

Certificate for Transportation of Corpse for Benjamin Bowen. June 1, 1902. Colorado State Board of Health.

Colorado Amusement Company. Certificate of Incorporation. December 16, 1910. Colorado State Archives, Denver, CO.

Eaton, George. July 5, 1891. 1891 Death Book. Colorado State Archives, Denver, CO.

Luna Park Company. Certificate of Incorporation. September 23, 1911. Colorado State Archives, Denver, CO.

Manhattan Beach Amusement Company. Incorporation Records. January 20, 1912. Colorado State Archives, Denver, CO.

Manhattan Beach Company. Capital Stock Statement. April 30, 1891. Colorado State Archives, Denver, CO.

———. Indenture. August 31, 1891. Colorado State Archives, Denver, CO.

Sloan Lake and Park Company. Incorporation Records. March 5, 1889. Colorado State Archives, Denver, CO.

Southern Investment Company. Incorporation Records. June 25, 1892. Colorado State Archives, Denver, CO.

## Books

Dier, Caroline Lawrence. *The Lady of the Gardens: Mary Elitch Long*. Hollywood: Hollycrafters, 1932.

Smiley, Jerome C. *History of Denver: With Outlines of the Earlier History of the Rocky Mountain Country*. Evansville, IN: Unigraphic, 1971 (reprint of 1901 edition).

Vickers, William B. *History of the City of Denver, Arapahoe County, and Colorado: Containing a History of the State of Colorado . . . A Condensed Sketch of Arapahoe County . . . A History of the City of Denver . . . Biographical Sketches . . .* Chicago: O. L. Baskin, 1880.

## Newspapers

*Aspen (Colorado) Times Weekly*
*Atlanta Journal-Constitution*
*Avalanche Echo (Glenwood Springs, Colorado)*
*Boston Globe*
*Boulder (Colorado) Daily Camera*
*Brooklyn Times Union*
*Bulletin, The (Pomona, California)*
*Colorado Daily Chieftain*
*Colorado Evening Sun*
*Colorado Farmer*
*Colorado Transcript* aka *Golden Transcript*
*Craig (Colorado) Courier*
*Daily Central City Register*
*Daily Journal (Telluride, Colorado)*
*Daily Sentinel (Grand Junction, Colorado)*
*Denver Clarion*
*Denver Daily Times*
*Denver Jewish News*
*Denver Mirror*
*Denver Post*
*Denver Republican*
*Denver Star*
*Denver Times*
*Detroit Free Press*
*Durango (Colorado) Semi-Weekly Herald*
*Fort Collins (Colorado) Courier*
*Gilpin (County, Colorado) Observer*
*Golden (Colorado) Weekly Globe*
*Grand Valley Star (Grand Junction, Colorado)*
*Herald Democrat (Leadville, Colorado)*
*Indianapolis News*

*Intermountain Jewish News (Colorado)*
*Jewish Outlook (Denver, Colorado)*
*Korrespondenten (Salt Lake City, Utah)*
*Leadville (Colorado) Daily/Evening Chronicle*
*Longmont (Colorado) Ledger*
*Los Angeles Evening Express*
*Morning News (Wilmington, Delaware)*
*New York Tribune*
*Northern Idaho News*
*Omaha Daily Bee*
*Park County (Colorado) Bulletin*
*Quad-City Times (Davenport, Iowa)*
*Queen Bee (Denver, Colorado)*
*Rocky Mountain News (Denver, Colorado)*
*Rocky Mountain Sunday School Casket (Black Hawk, Colorado)*
*Routt County (Colorado) Sentinel*
*Saint Paul (Minnesota) Globe*
*San Francisco Examiner*
*Silver Standard (Silver Plume, Colorado)*
*Statesman, The (Denver, Colorado)*
*Svensk-Amerikanska Western (Denver, Colorado)*
*Telluride (Colorado) Journal*
*United Labor Bulletin (Denver, Colorado)*
*Vernon County (Wisconsin) Censor*
*West Side Citizen (Denver, Colorado)*
*White Pine Cone (Gunnison County, Colorado)*
*Woman Voter (Denver, Colorado)*

## *Periodicals*
*Billboard*
*Colorado Exchange Journal*
*Denver Municipal Facts*
*Ice and Refrigeration*

## *Court Cases*
*Amanda S. Lockwood, etc. v. James M. Strickler, etc.* Case Number 1216. Supreme Court of Colorado. Colorado State Archives, Denver, CO.
*Theodore Schrott and Ernst Steinke v. W. D. Bethell, John M. Foster, Roger W. Woodbury, and the Manhattan Beach Company, a Corporation.* Arapahoe County, Colorado District Court. July 19, 1892. Colorado State Archives, Denver, CO.

## City Directories

Corbett, Hoye and Co.'s Eighth Annual City Directory. Denver: Rocky Mountain News Printing Company, 1880.

Corbett and Ballenger's Ninth Annual Denver City Directory. Unknown printing, available from the Denver Public Library Western History and Genealogy Department, 1881.

Corbett and Ballenger's Tenth Annual Denver City Directory. Denver: Corbett and Ballenger, 1882.

Corbett and Ballenger's Eleventh Annual Denver City Directory. Denver: Corbett and Ballenger, 1883.

Corbett and Ballenger's Twelfth Annual Denver City Directory. Denver: Corbett and Ballenger, 1884.

Corbett and Ballenger's 39th Annual Denver City Directory. Denver: Corbett and Ballenger, 1911.


## Other

Eaton, George. Grave. Riverside Cemetery, Denver, CO.

"Editorial Notes." Colorado Magazine (July 1953): 237.

"Miscellaneous Briefs." Colorado School Journal (1922–1923): 38–40.

"Rocky Mountain Aquabats." Rocky Mountain Life (July 1947): 35–39.

Sweet, Mildred. Oral History Interview. July 16, 1981. Rocky Mountain Jewish Historical Society Oral History Collection. University of Denver Archives.


## SECONDARY SOURCES

Armstrong, Catherine. "The Oldest Amusement Park in the West Is Right Here in Utah and It's Amazing." Only In Your State (January 10, 2017). Available from https://www.onlyinyourstate.com/utah/oldest-amusement-park -ut/, last accessed July 6, 2022.

Ashby, LeRoy. With Amusement for All: A History of American Popular Culture Since 1830. Lexington: University Press of Kentucky, 2006.

Ballard, Jack Stokes. Colorado's Daring Ivy Baldwin: Aviator, Aerialist & Aeronaut. Charleston, SC: History, 2020.

Coleman, Alice M. Historical Narrative of the First Sixty Years: Edgewater's Sixtieth Anniversary of Incorporation 1901–1961. Edgewater, CO, 1961.

"Coney Island History: The Story of Captain Paul Boyton and Sea Lion Park." Luna Park: Heart of Coney Island. Available from https://www .heartofconeyisland.com/sea-lion-park-coney-island.html, last accessed May 13, 2022.

Dasandi, Niheer. "Battle of Ciudad Juárez." Encyclopedia Britannica. Available from https://www.britannica.com/event/Battle-of-Ciudad-Juarez, last accessed May 20, 2022.

"Early Southern California Amusement Parks." Water and Power Associates. Available from https://waterandpower.org/museum/Early_Southern _California_Amusement_Parks.html, last accessed July 6, 2022.

"Ella Ewing." Historic Missourians. State Historical Society of Missouri. Available from https://historicmissourians.shsmo.org/ella-ewing, last accessed May 16, 2022.

Estes, Roberta. "When Redmen Aren't Red Men." Native Heritage Project. Posted September 16, 2014. Available from https://nativeheritageproject .com/2014/09/16/when-redmen-arent-red-men/, last accessed January 30, 2023.

Forsyth, David. "A Splendid Place: Denver's Arlington Park." *Colorado Heritage* (May/June 2015): 22–31.

———. *Denver's Lakeside Amusement Park: From the White City Beautiful to a Century of Fun.* Boulder: University Press of Colorado, 2016.

Gallagher, Dennis. "The Man Who Founded Berkeley Was the Visionary Behind Our Mountain Parks." *Denver North Star* (February 14, 2020). Available from https://www.denvernorthstar.com/the-man-who-founded -berkeley-was-the-visionary-behind-our-mountain-parks/, last accessed May 6, 2022.

Goodstein, Phil H. *North Side Story: Denver's Most Intriguing Neighborhood.* Denver: New Social, 2011.

Granruth, Alan. *Pennyweights: Bits and Pieces of Gilpin County History.* Central City, CO: Gilpin Historical Society, 2004.

Griffin, Alan. "Sam Lockhart: Elephant Trainer Extraordinaire." Leamington History Group (August 2, 2014). Available from https://leamingtonhistory .co.uk/sam-lockhart-elephant-trainer-extraordinaire/, last accessed May 30, 2022.

Hull, Betty Lynne. *Denver's Elitch Gardens: Spinning a Century of Dreams.* Boulder: Johnson Books, 2003.

Hunt, Rebecca. "Healers on the Hill: St. Luke's and Presbyterian Hospitals of Denver." *Colorado Heritage* (Summer 2005): 2–17.

Kasson, John F. *Amusing the Million: Coney Island at the Turn of the Century.* New York: Hill and Wang, 1978.

"Ladies of Skydiving: Early History." Available from ladiesofskydiving.com/early-ly-history/, last accessed May 9, 2022.

Leonard, Stephen J., and Thomas J. Noel. *Denver: Mining Camp to Metropolis.* Niwot: University Press of Colorado, 1991.

Mangels, William F. *The Outdoor Amusement Industry: From Earliest Times to the Present.* New York: Vantage, 1952.

McKenzie, Kirsty. "Glasgow History: The True Story Behind the Famous Stuffed Elephant Which has Been on Display in Kelvingrove for 120 Years." *Glasgow Live* (August 28, 2021). Available from https://www

.glasgowlive.co.uk/whats-on/whats-on-news/glasgow-history-true-story
-behind-21425109, last accessed July 6, 2022.

Nasaw, David. *Going Out: The Rise and Fall of Public Amusements*. Cambridge: Harvard University Press, 1993.

9 News Television Report. "Verify: Is an Elephant Buried Under a Colorado Supermarket?" Article by Brandon Rittiman and Anna Staver
(May 4, 2018). Available from https://www.9news.com/article/news/local
/verify/verify-is-an-elephant-buried-under-a-colorado-supermarket/73
-548063816, last accessed May 30, 2022.

Noel, Thomas J., and Barbara S. Norgren. *Denver: The City Beautiful and Its
Architects, 1893–1941*. Denver: Historic Denver, 1987.

Painter, Nell Irvin. *Standing at Armageddon: The United States, 1877–1919*. New
York: W. W. Norton, 1987.

Pascal, Caitlyn. "Arcade Origins in the Japanese Rolling Ball: How Tamakorogashi Shaped the World of Modern Gaming." *Nikkei Voice* (January
18, 2022). Available from http://nikkeivoice.ca/arcade-origins-in-the
-japanese-rolling-ball-how-tamakorogashi-shaped-the-world-of-modern
-gaming, last accessed March 30, 2022.

Prochaska, Jim. "The Bottoms Tour Notes." Copy provided to the author, 2008.

Raffel, Dawn. *The Strange Case of Dr. Couney: How a Mysterious European Showman Saved Thousands of American Babies*. New York: Blue Rider, 2018.

Robertson, Don, Morris Cafky, and E. J. Haley. *Denver's Street Railways, Volume
1, 1870–1900: Not an Automobile in Sight*. Denver: Sundance, 1999.

Schlereth, Thomas J. *Victorian America: Transformations in Everyday Life, 1876–
1915*. New York: HarperPerennial, 1992.

"Sloan's Lake Neighborhood History." Denver Public Library. Genealogy,
African American & Western History Resources. Available from https://
history.denverlibrary.org/sloans-lake-neighborhood-history, last accessed
May 6, 2022.

Wilk, Stephen R. *Lost Wonderland: The Brief and Brilliant Life of Boston's Million
Dollar Amusement Park*. Amherst and Boston: Bright Leaf, 2020.

Wingfield, Valerie. "The General Slocum Disaster of June 15, 1904" (blog: June
13, 2011). New York Public Library. Available from https://www.nypl.org
/blog/2011/06/13/great-slocum-disaster-june-15-1904, last accessed May
16, 2022.